DINGHY AND
SMALL CRAFT
REVIEW
09/10

IN ASSOCIATION WITH SHANICK

ADLARD COLES NAUTICAL
LONDON

Published by Adlard Coles Nautical
an imprint of A & C Black Publishers Ltd
36 Soho Square, London W1D 3QY
www.adlardcoles.com

First edition published 2010

ISBN 978-1-4081-2270-9

A CIP catalogue record for this book is available from the British Library.

This book is produced using paper that is made from wood grown in managed, sustainable forests. It is natural, renewable and recyclable. The logging and manufacturing processes conform to the environmental regulations of the country of origin.

Typeset in Arial 10pt
Printed and bound in Spain by GraphyCems

Note: while all reasonable care has been taken in the publication of this book, the publisher takes no responsibility for the use of the methods or products described in the book.

Introduction

Welcome to the 2009 – 2010 edition of the *Dinghy and Small Craft Review*.

We trust that you will find the information contained within the book helpful. Over one hundred and twenty dinghy, multihull and small keelboat classes are featured, together with a wealth of information. Each class has a full page "directory" entry and photograph, to give a good idea of the boat's qualities, in addition to reports on the major events for most of the featured designs, which give a good idea of the extent of their racing, and the types of places you could be visiting with your boat!

With so many classes available, choosing a new boat is always likely to be tricky, so the easy reference within this book is aimed at making it a simpler task for the would-be dinghy owner. However it is also interesting to have a single reference to the year's events, so that you can see which sailors are competing in more than one class (and in some cases, wonder how they organise so much holiday).

With this in mind, we have introduced a competition this year to win a £100 gift voucher from Rooster Sailing. To enter, simply nominate your dinghy sailor of the year and forward it to info@dinghyreview.co.uk

This book is now being published and distributed by Adlard Coles (which is the nautical imprint of A&C Black Publishers), one of the oldest and most respected of all nautical publishers. I would like to take this opportunity to thank Janet Murphy, the Director in charge of Adlard Coles, and her team, who have been extremely helpful (and tolerant!).

Whilst the information in this book is obviously important, it would not be possible without the assistance and co-operation of a large number of photographers from around the world. My thanks to all of them, and also to the advertisers who have joined us this year, who have helped make this project viable.

If I have missed any classes, or if you feel that there are improvements and developments that can be made for next year's edition, please don't hesitate to contact me.

Good sailing

Mike Porter
Emsworth Media Ltd
info@dinghyreview.co.uk

Contents

If you have flown on one of these...

you've already tried our work!

...own engineering requirements.

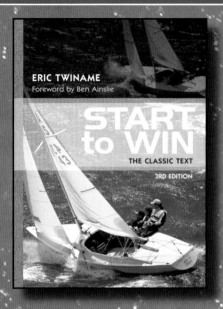

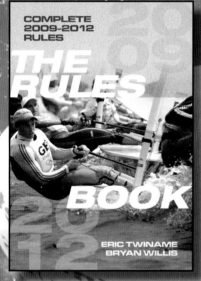
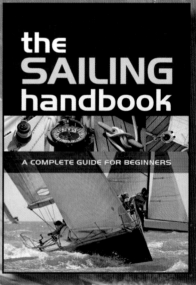

Crewed Classes

Albacore

Type	Dinghy	Weight	109 kg
Crew	2; Sit out	Sail area M&J	11.65 sq m
PN	1066	Spi type	None
Length	4.57 m	Designer	Uffa Fox
Beam	1.53 m		www.albacore.org.uk

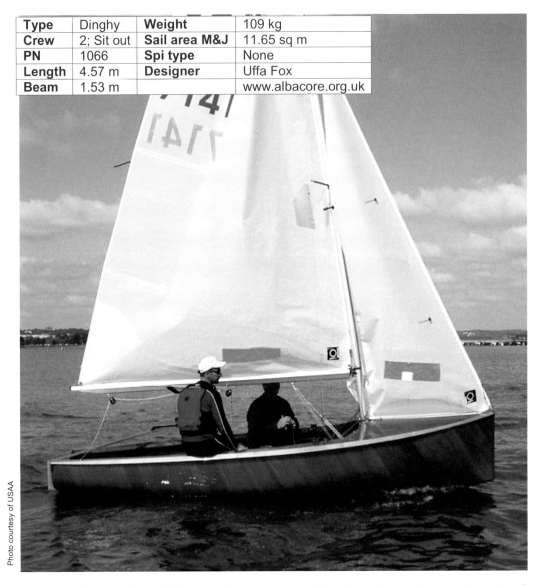

Photo courtesy of USAA

The Uffa Fox-designed Albacore is a two man sit-out design, with no spinnaker. It is a restricted class, allowing some development in deck layout, and is available in either wood or GRP. It is spacious inside, and therefore has become popular as a cruising boat, but its large sail area and round bilged construction make it an exciting racing boat in a breeze. It is a boat that rewards the novice and expert alike, and has a full racing programme, that includes International meetings. The Albacore is raced at more than 30 clubs within the UK.

Albacore International Championships

Largs Sailing Club   18 - 24 July 2009

With a container of Albacores from Canada, and entries from the USA, interest in the 2009 Albacore Nationals and International Championships was quite intense. The bi-annual "International" aspect of the event was to dominate the latter half of the sailing programme, with the Nationals as a "tune-up" event.

Fifty two boats came to the line as the event opened in a lively 15 – 18 knot breeze. First race honours were taken by Will Gulliver and Steve Graham from Northampton, ahead of Americans Barney Harris and David Byron, making a strong defence of their title with Chris Turner and Simon Maguire in third whilst fourth place was claimed by Judy and Paul Armstrong.

Three races were held on Day Two of the event, with a variety of conditions from calm up to 15 knots. Harris and Byron began to make their intentions clear, with two race wins and a third position in the lightest race, to lead from Will Gulliver and Steve Graham, whilst Chris Turner and Simon Maguire were in third overall. After discard, just one point separated Gulliver from Harris in the National Championships, which had one more day to run, before the event continued to the end of the Internationals.

Despite leading by a single point into the final day of the National title fight, Barney Harris and David Byron were unable to make the most of their position, allowing Brits Will Gulliver and Steve Graham to take the title. With a brisk breeze, the pair of competitors fought their way to the front of the fleet in each of the races, with Harris/Byron taking the first victory. In the second race it was Gulliver who took a comfortable win, leaving the final race of the day to decide the result. Gulliver and Graham established a lead in the fresh conditions which he held to the finish, with Harris in second, leaving them on equal points, but Gulliver's four wins gave him the result on tie-break for his first National Albacore title, having previously been a Phantom National winner. Third position overall in the Nationals went to Chris Turner and Simon Maguire, with the evergreen Judy and Paul Armstrong in fourth overall and the first husband and wife crew.

P	Helm	Crew	Club	Pts	R1	R2	R3	R4	R5	R6	R7
1	Will Gulliver	Steve Graham	NSC	9	1	1	5	3	2	1	1
2	Barney Harris	David Byron	PRSA	9	2	3	1	1	1	2	2
3	Chris Turner	Simon Maguire	TSC	24	3	10	3	2	11	3	3
4	Judy Armstrong	Paul Armstrong	SDSC	31	4	5	8	5	4	7	6
5	Nigel Potter	Mark Fowler	NCSC	32	8	2	9	4	7	4	7
6	Jerry Rook	James Wallace	LR SC	36	9	7	2	11	8	6	4

The fourth day of racing produced strong, gusty conditions, with two races sailed, the first in predominantly light conditions! Despite the efforts of the breeze, Judy and Paul Armstrong took the lead in this heat, and held it to the finish ahead of Canadians Warner and Andrew Monteiro, with Robert Lyne and Peter Grey in third. As the fleet awaited the second start, the conditions increased once again, with twenty five knots of wind and a shortened course, with only half the fleet gaining a result. This race saw the two series-front runners back to form, with Gulliver and Graham taking the winning gun ahead of Harris and Byron. With a lay-day beckoning for the Wednesday, the fleet returned to shore looking forward to a more restful day, before the culmination of the week's sailing. Thursday saw medium strength winds from the south which opened up the results slightly. The first race of the day was won by Jerry Rook and James Wallace ahead of John and Janet Woffinden with Gulliver and Graham reinforcing their position with a third. The second race of the day saw Turner and Maguire dominate ahead of the Canadian team of Allan Measor and Richard Piercey with the Armstrong's building on their position with a third. However, it wasn't possible to hold back the series leaders for the whole day, and for the final race, Gulliver and Barney Harris showed their mettle, with Harris, and crewman David Byron taking the win to lead the championship into the final day by just one point with two races still to go. The race for third overall is also quite tight, with Rook and Wallace leading Turner and Maguire by just one point, with the Armstrong's three points further back.

With the deciding races being held in a Force three, conditions suited Turner and Maguire well, and they clocked up two excellent race wins to cement their position in third place overall. The two protagonists kept a somewhat distant eye on one another, and a poor race for Gulliver and Graham on the first heat of the day left them with an significant gap to make up which they were unable to do. Thus Harris and Byron took their third International Trophy in the fourteen years that they have been sailing together, whilst Gulliver and Graham rounded off a good week that saw them take the National Championships for the first time. Turner and Maguire's form at the end of the week ensured that they took third spot ahead of Rook and Wallace, whilst fifth position went to the consistent Armstrongs.

P	Helm	Crew	Pts	R1	R2	R3	R4	R5	R6	R7	R8	R9	R10	R11	R12	R13	R14
1	B Harris	D Byron	24	2	3	1	1	1	2	2	8	2	4	6	1	3	2
2	W Gulliver	S Graham	33	1	1	5	3	2	1	1	10	1	3	7	2	13	6
3	C Turner	S Maguire	46	3	10	3	2	11	3	3	7	4	8	1	17	1	1
4	J Rook	J Wallace	49	9	7	2	11	8	6	4	4	3	1	5	3	2	4
5	J Armstrong	P Armstrong	60	4	5	8	5	4	7	6	1	6	13	3	6	5	10
6	N Potter	M Fowler	88	8	2	9	4	7	4	7	ocs	5	18	23	5	7	12
7	N Herbert	M Booth	93	5	6	ocs	8	15	5	14	15	8	9	8	4	8	3
8	A Measor	R Piercey	103	6	4	6	6	19	10	5	25	14	15	2	12	15	8

B14

Type	Dinghy	Sail area M&J	17 sq m
Crew	2; On racks	Spi type	Asymmetric
PN	865	Spi area	29 sq m
Length	4.25 m	Designer	Julian Bethwaite,1989
Beam	2.9 m in wings		www.B14.org
Weight	64 kg		

A scaled-down 18-foot Skiff, the B14 delivers exhilarating sailing, high quality international racing, and as much fun as you can handle. It is the fastest two-person "body-swung" sailing boat in the world. Hiking from the wide wings, blasting at 20-plus knots with over 50 sq m of downwind sail area is like nothing else in the world. It is a drug that attracts a growing number of addicts around the world, offering World and National Championships in both the northern and southern hemispheres!

B14 World Championships

Royal Yacht Club of Tasmania, Australia   5 – 10 January 2009

Following a successful pre-Worlds series with forty seven entries, which was won by the UK team of Mark Barnes and Pete Nicholson, with UK National Champion Nick Craig sailing with Matt Johnson in third behind local favourites Guy Bancroft and Nick Barlow, a fleet of fifty boats competed in the World Championships. With eleven who had travelled from the UK to make the most of the Australian sunshine, the week's racing was held on the ideal sailing waters of Hobart's Derwent River.

Whilst the first day's racing at the World Championships was lost due to strong winds, the efficient race organisation were able make up the lost time, and a ten race series finally saw Australians Guy Bancroft and Nick Barlow from McRae Yacht Club on Victoria's Port Phillip take the title with a margin of eleven points from Mark Barnes and Pete Nicholson who had managed to get the better of Bancroft in the pre-Worlds regatta. Third position went to Nick Richardson and Alan Nicholas from Tasmania, ahead of Bancroft's clubmate, Dave Lorimer with Raf Heale in fourth, and then a clutch of British crews in the next three places; Chris Bines and Dave Gibbons in fifth, Nick Craig with Matt Johnson in sixth and Mark Watts and George Morris in seventh.

Bancroft's son, Rhys, rounded off a great week for the family, finishing in eighth overall with crew Joey Randall, and winning the Under 25 award!

Photo courtesy of Fred Koolhof

2009 B14 World Champions Guy Bancroft and Nick Barlow.

Bancroft's previous two attempts at the title had both resulted in top three finishes, and the fifty one year old's experience obviously paid dividends as he finally finished the event with a score-card boasting top four results in all of his 'counting' races.

Photo courtesy of Fred Koolhof

Second overall Mark Barnes and Pete Nicholson.

P	Nat	Helm	Crew	R1	R2	R3	R4	R5	R6	R7	R8	R9	R10	Pts
1	AUS	G Bancroft	N Darlow	1	4	3	25	4	2	4	11	4	2	24
2	GBR	M Barnes	P Nicholson	5	1	12.5	8	1	5	8	5	2	17	35
3	AUS	N Richardson	A Nicholas	6	2	16	1	3	3	11	7	5	8	35
4	AUS	D Lorimer	R Heale	8	5	5	9	6	7	5	14	3	1	40
5	GBR	C Bines	D Gibbons	33	12	1	11	2	10	2	9	7	6	48
6	GBR	N Craig	M Johnson	3	7	12.5	10	51	11	6	2	14	3	54.5
7	GBR	M Watts	G Morris	7	9	11	4	10	12	1	8	15	51	62
8	AUS	R Bancroft	J Randell	9	3	4	7	51	17	9	12	6	12	62
9	AUS	C Bibby	S Cunningham	16	18	2	3	11	20	14	16	1	5	68
10	AUS	R Reynolds	L McMillan	15	10	17	6	5	15	3	1	51	51	72
11	GBR	D Hayes	S Dwyer	17	17	6	18	51	1	10	4	16	11	82
14	GBR	T Harrison	J Ratcliffe	25	13	7	5	51	4	22	17	12	20	100
16	GBR	A Davis	T Barsley-Dale	2	16	24	17	9	19	12	23	22	9	106
18	GBR	S Hadley	N Webster	12	26	21	14	8	23	21	13	18	51	130
20	GBR	C Turner	P Eltringham	28	21	15	13	51	27	33	24	9	7	144
26	GBR	G Brown	L Fermor	24	29	20	34	51	9	24	20	31	19	176
45	GBR	T Harris	L Walter	51	42	42	51	29	40	43	42	51	51	340

B14 European Championships

Carnac, France   28 - 31 August 2009

The B14 European Championships got off to something of a faltering start. With the forecast of fifteen knot winds, the fleet launched full of optimism, but the wind quickly exceeded that and the race officer suggested a return to shore!

Day Two was more successful with the wind building to twelve knots. Race winners for the day were Dave Hayes and Richie Bell, Mark Barnes and Pete Nicholson and Nick Craig with Toby Lewis after some close racing and Hayes and Bell went into the evening at the top of the leader board with the consistent Mark Emmett and Allan Stuart in second ahead of Tim Harrison and Jonny Radcliffe - each separated by just one point!

Day Three saw lighter winds and Mark Barnes and Pete Nicholson took the first race whilst Tim Harrison and Jonny Radcliffe took the second and third heats, but as they entered the final day, any one of five boats was still in contention for the overall title.

The final day's conditions were challenging with a force two and a tricky chop. Hayes and Bell started strongly with two wins in the first two races which gave them a two point lead over Harrison and Ratcliffe at the start of the final race. Hayes and Bell worked through the fleet to second in the final race, which was just enough to give them the title at the last gasp. The battle for third was also a tight run thing, with Nick Craig and Toby Lewis gaining the necessary position at the last with fourth going to Mark Emmett and Allan Stuart.

P	Helm	Crew	Nat	R1	R2	R3	R4	R5	R6	R7	R8	R9	R10	Pts
1	D Hayes	R Bell	GBR	2	3	6	2	12	2	2	1	1	2	15
2	T Harrison	K Ratcliffe	GBR	4	1	3	7	7	1	1	2	3	1	16
3	N Craig	T Lewis	GBR	5	22	1	9	10	4	10	4	2	4	31
4	M Emmett	A Stuart	GBR	7	4	2	1	6	10	8	5	4	3	32
5	M Barnes	P Nicholson	GBR	3	DSQ	9	3	1	9	5	3	11	6	39
6	A Davis	T Barsley Dale	GBR	1	9	5	5	2	14	6	12	7	12	47
7	M Watts	G Morris	GRB	11	5	8	4	3	16	15	7	9	7	54
8	W McGrath	M McGrath	GRB	8	7	15	8	15	5	11	10	14	9	72
9	S Hollingsworth	C Murphy	GRB	9	12	10	14	4	18	9	11	8	13	76
10	A Cadre	F Cadre	FRA	6	17	12	15	14	12	14	6	6	10	80

B14 Nationals

Mayflower Sailing Club   23 - 25 May 2009

Twenty seven entrants travelled down to Plymouth over the late May bank holiday weekend to compete in the National Championships; the same number as in 2008, showing that the B14s are riding out the economic storm as well as any!

With the first day's races struggling with incredibly light breezes, it was the two Team Dynamic Sails boats who led at the close of play, with Dave Dobrijevic and Phil Eltringham counting a first and two third places, ahead of Tim Fells, returning to the fleet after a couple of years off, and now sailing with James Stewart; this pairing posted a solid four, five, two. Racing on the second day was delayed awaiting a sea breeze that failed to arrive. In light conditions two races were held, and Dobrijevic and Eltringham gained two more third places to retain the overall lead going into the final day. Both of the day's races were won by 2008 National Champions Nick Craig and Toby Lewis which pulled them up to third overall.

As the final day dawned, it was obviously going to be another test of patience and guesswork, with Race Six getting underway in a light northerly. In the leading group throughout, the race was won by Tim Harrison and Jonny Ratcliffe, with Dave Dobrijivec and Phil Eltringham in second and Mark Barnes with Tom Pygall showing back at the front of the fleet. Initially race seven was started and then subsequently was abandoned as the wind shut down completely. It looked as though that would conclude the event, but a bit of a resurgence in the breeze did give hope and race seven was reset, with Nick Craig and Toby Lewis taking the race ahead of Harrison and Ratcliffe and Barnes and Pygall, with Dobrijivec and Eltringham dropping back to sixth. A slight increase to five to ten knots for the final race again Craig and Lewis in strong form, taking the win in a last leap at the Championships, but they were just too far back to defeat eventual winners Tim Harrison and Jonny Ratcliffe, whilst Dave Dobrijivec and Phil Eltringham, who had led from the outset, had to be happy in third position after a trying final day!

P	Boat	Helm	Crew	Pts
1	Anthill Mob	Tim Harrison	Jonny Ratcliffe	18
2	Team Gill	Nick Craig	Toby Lewis	21
3	Dynamic Sails	Dave Dobrijevec	Phil Eltringham	21
4	Sketch/North	Dave Hayes	Richie Bell	30
5	Dynamic Sails 2	Tim Fells	James Stewart	42
6	Seavolution	Mark Barnes	Tom Pygall	42
7	Simmons&Simmons/Hyde Sails	Mark Watts	George Morris	45
8	Winged Monkey	Mark Elkington	Charlie Game	60
9	9th Acxiom	Mark Emmett	Allen Stuart	61
10	Hyde Sails	Alan Davis	T Barnsley-Dale	67

Buzz

Type	Dinghy
Crew	2; 1 on trapeze
PN	747
Length	4.2 m
Beam	1.92 m
Weight	90 kg
Sail area M&J	12.85 sq m
Spi type	Asymmetric
Spi area	17.4 sq m
Designer	Ian Howlett
	www.bu22.co.uk

Photo courtesy of Mark Bloomfield

America's Cup designer Ian Howlett worked with former Fireball World Champion John Caig to design the Buzz, a two-man racing dinghy that has also proven popular as a training boat with its kindly handling and controllable rig. Featuring a trapeze for the crew, and a manageable asymmetric spinnaker, the boat has proven popular with young sailors and husband-and-wife teams, and is raced competitively to championship level.

Buzz National Championships

Lee-on-the-Solent Sailing Club   5 - 6 September 2009

Fourteen boats attended the Buzz National Championships, held in conjunction with the ISO Nationals at Lee-on-the-Solent Sailing Club in early September, in often varied and exciting conditions.

Three races were scheduled for the first day, in winds gusting up to thirty knots, and with breaking waves on the beach making launching a nightmare! However, with the beach team's assistance, everyone made it afloat and the racing got underway.

Masters of the conditions were certainly Simon Cory and Clare Hansell; they won the first race from Jon and Ethna Haines, and then took the second race from Ed and Sarah Styles. To round off their day, in worsening conditions, they also took the third win of the day from Andy Holmes and Janet Shaw to put themselves in a strong position for the second day.

With lighter conditions on Sunday, there was something of an adjustment in the results with the first race of the day going to Stuart Bailey and Zoe Noble, with Jon and Ethna Haines in second. However, Cory and Hansell then found their form again, and took the final two races of the day and, with it, the National Championships. In the first of these two victories they were followed home by Stuart Bailey and Zoe Noble, whilst Ed and Sarah Styles followed them in the final race.

This left Cory and Hansell with a perfect score of five wins for the title, but whilst they dominated the event, the positions behind were very tightly contested, with Stuart Bailey and Zoe Noble pipping Ed and Sarah Styles for second overall on tie-break.

P	SN	Helm	Crew	Club	R1	R2	R3	R4	R5	R5	Pts
1	1201	Simon Cory	Clare Hansell	DSC	1	1	1	4	1	1	5
2	0	Stuart Bailey	Zoe Noble	MYC	4	4	3	1	2	4	14
3	969	Ed Styles	Sarah Styles	DSC	3	2	4	3	4	2	14
4	971	Jon Haines	Ethna Haines	LSC	2	11	6	2	6	3	19
5	1100	John Cass	Julia Blackman	DSC	5	3	8	5	3	8	24
6	1061	Chris Dutton	Martin Wyman	DSC	7	6	5	7	7	5	30
7	1027	Jane Noble	Mark Wilson	LSC	9	10	10	6	5	6	36
8	987	Roger Eyre	Penny Eyre	RSC	8	5	7	8	9	10	37
9	919	Ian Staples	Jess Staples	SSC	10	8	DNF	9	8	7	42
10	763	Mark Turner	Tris Turner	WSC	12	9	9	11	10	9	48

Cherub

Type	Dinghy
Crew	2; on trapeze
PN	1050
Length	3.7 m
Beam	1.8 m
Weight	50 kg
Sail area M&J	15.5 sq m
Spi type	Asymmetric
Spi area	21 sq m
Designer	Various
	www.sailingsource.com/cherub

Photo courtesy of Annie Porter

Originating in the early 1950s in New Zealand, the Cherub remains one of the fastest 12ft dinghies available. As a development class, the Cherub has continued to embrace new developments as they come along, and the current-day version sees both crew members on trapeze, and a large asymmetric spinnaker enhancing the boat's downwind performance. This is not a beginner's boat and is best sailed by light, but experienced, hands!

Cherub National Championship

Babbacombe Corinthian Sailing Club   12 - 15 August 2009

In sunny weather with a pleasant seven to twelve knot breeze, reigning champions Pete Barton and Roz Allen made the most of the conditions in the first race and took the victory ahead of William and Lucy Lee. This was the start of something of a trend, as the leading pair actually went on to win all but one of the fourteen heats raced, and made up their tally with a disappointing second position in the twelfth! This was a race that was won by the series runners-up, William and Lucy Lee who also were equally dominant in second position, following Barton and Allen over the line eleven times in the course of the event!

The second day saw similar fickle breezes, in the five to ten knot range, whilst on the third day the medium wind came through in hefty gusts to make the whole thing more entertaining, and the final day's fifteen to twenty knot winds at last gave the heavy weather exponents something to grin about. Regardless of all of this variation in wind however, there was nothing to undermine the prowess of either Barton and Allen, or the Lees, who continued with their relentless quest! Third position overall went to Paul Croote and Chris Crabb who swapped places with class newcomers Andrew and Jill Peters in their new boat, whilst fifth went to Graham and Eddie Bridle.

P	Helm	Crew	Club	R1	R2	R3	R4	R5	R6	R7	R8	R9	R10	R11	R12	R13	R14	Pts
1	Peter Barton	Roz Allen	RLYC	1	1	1	1	1	1	1	1	1	1	1	2	1	1	11
2	William Lee	Lucy Lee	WYC	2	2	2	2	3	2	5	2	2	2	2	1	2	2	21
3	Paul Croote	Chris Crabb	CVSC	4	4	3	3	7	4	12	5	3	3	3	3	4	4	38
4	Andrew Peters	Jill Peters	QMSC	3	3	5	4	2	3	2	3	4	18	6	10	8	7	42
5	Graham Bridle	Eddie Bridle	BSC	5	6	4	7	4	5	4	7	5	4	4	7	7	5	53
6	Jack Mills	Ewan Harris	BSC	6	7	7	5	18	18	18	4	8	5	7	4	3	3	59
7	Dean Ralph	Simon Jones	WYC	10	5	6	6	6	6	3	8	6	6	5	5	5	18	59
8	Alex Adams	Adem Ikibiroglu	WYC	7	9	10	12	9	10	7	9	9	7	8	6	6	6	83
9	Alex Cramp	Tim Noyce	MMA	11	8	9	9	8	8	9	6	11	8	10	8	9	8	90
10	Roland Trim	Hayley Trim	WSC	13	18	13	18	18	11	6	11	7	9	9	9	10	18	116

Comet Duo

Type	Dinghy	Weight	88 kg
Crew	2; Sit out	Sail area M&J	9 sq m
PN	1179	Spi type	None
Length	3.7 m	Designer	Andrew Simmons, 1990
Beam	1.52 m		www.cometduo.co.uk

Photo courtesy of Comet Duo Assoc

Designed by boat-builder Andrew Simmonds, the Comet Duo is a natural extension to the single handed Comet, offering simple yet rewarding sailing for beginners and families alike, but without the complication of spinnakers and the associated ropework! The Duo is an ideal boat to start sailing with, or to gravitate into racing. It is manoeuvrable and easy to handle, and the enthusiastic class association will do their utmost to point new owners in the right direction.

Comet Trio

Type	Dinghy	Weight	134 kg
Crew	2; Sit out	Sail area M&J	12.53 sq m
PN	1086	Spi type	Asymmetric
Length	4.6 m	Spi area	9.28 sq m
Beam	1.83 m	Designer	Phil Morrison
			www.comettrio.org.uk

The Trio is a beamy family dinghy which is equally at home being raced or cruised. Fitted with an optional genniker to improve performance, the Trio can be fitted with aft tank storage, and an outboard motor bracket to enhance the day-sailing experience. Whilst it is raced with a crew of two, the Trio can be sailed comfortably with three or four on board; she really is a modern day all-rounder for the whole family!

Comet Trio National Championships

Hamble River Sailing Club   14 - 17 August 2009

A fleet of twenty eight Comet Trios competed in their National Championships held over three days at Exe SC, in conditions which varied from light, shifty breezes to fresh Force four winds.

Unusually, the event attracted all of the class's past champions, but they were all beaten by a new face, eighteen year old Iain Horlock crewed by Debbie Woodcock from the host club. In the course of the six race event, Iain won four of the races and discarded a third position.

Horlock's only real competition during the weekend came from fellow club member Les Arscott, sailing with Andy Williams. They scored two wins in their tally, leaving them well clear of the battle for third place which has between two past champions, Peter and Marjorie Scott from Shustoke SC, and Andrew and Caroline McAusland, who were the previous year's champions. With only one point separating them at the end of the regatta, third position went to the Scotts.

P	Helm	Crew	R1	R2	R3	R4	R5	R6	Pts
1	I Horlock	D Woodcock	1	1	3	2	1	1	3
2	L Arscott	A Williams	15	3	1	1	2	DNC	6.5
3	P Scott	M Scott	4	4	2	7	3	12	13
4	A McAusland	C McAusland	9	DNF	4	3	4	3	14
5	G Farrant	M Booker	2	9	8	4	9	4	18
6	S Garrett	N Groucutt	12	2	7	6	5	11	20
7	B Horlock	C Horlock	8	5	14	5	7	7	24
8	T Brewster	T Elliot	5	6	12	8	10	14	29
9	M Sydenham	C Broady	11	11	10	10	8	2	30
10	M Davies	J Davies	7	8	5	11	DNF	DNC	31

Comet Zero

Photo courtesy of Fotoboat

Type	Dinghy	Weight	70 kg
Crew	1 - 2; Sit out	Sail area M&J	6.42 sq m
PN	1250	Spi type	Asymmetric
Length	3.45 m	Spi area	4.65 sq m
Beam	1.42 m	Designer	Andrew Simmons

The Zero is a great boat for beginners to sailing; neat in size and light in weight, she can be enjoyed by anyone, yet the cockpit is spacious enough to give you room to stretch your legs! There are plenty of bench seats to accommodate your friends, and the rig is simple and easy to use, so there is nothing to stop you getting afloat! In addition to the basic set up, the Zero is also available with an asymmetric spinnaker, and then makes a great fun youth racer.

Devon Yawl

Type	Dinghy; ballasted	Weight	435.84 kg
Crew	2 or more	Sail area M&J	15.5 sq m
Length	4.88 + 0.69 m (bowsprit)	Spi type	None
Beam	1.88 m	Designer	Devon Craft
			www.devonyawl.org

The Devon Yawl is a boat that is fun to own and fun to sail. As an all-weather racer, the boat is fast and responsive, satisfying for both the novice and the expert. The Devon Yawl can be sailed easily single-handed and yet has room for the family to enjoy. The weight of the centre-plate and ballast contribute a great deal to her inherent stability coupled with a hull shape that gives the excellent performance that one would expect from a boat with such a long history of working at sea as well as racing. She is truly a performance day-sailor.

Devon Yawl National Championships

6 - 7 June 2009

Thirteen Devon Yawls visited the next Olympic sailing venue this summer to try out the equipment, and to make use of the best of sailing know-how and organisation that is available within the UK.

2009 National Champions are Andrew Hattersley and William Hamilton of Topsham Sailing Club who finished with an impressive four wins, discarding one fourth position. Tim Pettitt and Tony Callcut from Yealm Yacht Club, who were last year's champions, were demoted to second position this year, but they did manage to fend off Dittisham SC's Mike and Simon Bennett by one point, whilst last year's runner up, Ed Williams-Hawkes, finished in fourth position overall.

P	Helm	Crew	Club	R1	R2	R3	R4	R5	Pt	Nett
1	Andrew Hattersley	William Hamilton	TSC	1	1	4	1	1	8	4
2	Tim Pettitt	Tony Callcut	YYC	4	3	1	3	4	15	11
3	Mike Bennett	Simon Bennett	DSC	5	5	3	2	2	17	12
4	Ed Williams -Hawkes	T Coombe	TSC	3	4	2	5	9	23	14
5	Adrian Bull	David Bull, RichBaker		2	2	9	10	10	33	23
6	Michael Roberts	James Roberts	TCYC	6	7	7	4	6	30	23

18ft Skiff

Type	Dinghy
Crew	3; All on trapeze
PN	675
Length	5.48 m
Beam	4.25 m
Weight	82.5 kg
Sail area M&J	Unlimited
Spi type	Asymmetric
Spi area	Unlimited
Designer	Various
	www.uk18footer.org

Photo courtesy of Chris Rea (www.crayivp.com)

Originally raced in Sydney Harbour, and sailed by a crew of up to 14, the 18ft Skiff has come a long way to become the ultimate sailing machine. With huge sails, a selection of rigs, and three men trapezing from massive racks, this is an extremely fast machine. The 18ft Skiff is raced on a growing circuit with Europe and the USA as centres, in addition to Australia.

18ft Skiff JJ Giltinan International Championships

Sydney Harbour   13 – 22 February 2009

Thirty two 18ft Skiffs competed for the 2009 J J Giltinan International Championships, which is the equivalent of the class World Championships. Whilst the majority of the fleet were made up of boats from the host country, there were also competitors from New Zealand, USA, Canada, and one from the UK, in the form of Andy Budgen, crewed by Matt McGovern and James Barker.

With a seven race series to complete, the front runners after the first five races were Euan McNicol, Aaron Links and Trent Barnabos sailing *Southern Cross Constructions*, but a gaggle of four other boats were all within striking distance, including last year's Champions, *Gotta Love It 7*, sailed by Seve Jarvin, Sam Newton and Tom Clout. Following the conclusion of the penultimate race, things were no clearer! With just one race to go, there were still five boats within five points, with *Southern Cross Constructions* still holding the advantage, whilst *Gotta Love It 7* was just one point back. The UK team, sailing *Project Racing,* were in sixth overall, struggling slightly after a first race disaster when they rounded a mark in the wrong direction whilst battling for the lead, and having to retire as a result.

The final showdown race saw the result of the event in abeyance until the very end. *Southern Cross Constructions* eventually crossed the line in fourth position, enough to take the title by one point from *Active Air-2UE,* sailed by Matthew Searle, Archie Massey and Dan Wilsdon. However, in the course of the race the title could have gone in any number of directions! *Gotta Love It 7* led the race, and therefore the Championships, until the wind had a change of heart, and dumped them back in the pack, to finally finish in eighth position for third overall. This wind change was enough to give McNicol and his team a second chance, having been over four minutes behind the leaders at the first mark. It dragged them back into contention, and their fourth place finish was just enough to take the title as *Active Air-2UE* dropped a place to Jonathan Whitty, Dan Higlett and Tom Anderson in *Panasonic* towards the end of the race. Final race winner was John Winning, sailing with Andy Haye and Dave Gibson in *Yandoo,* lifting them to sixth overall ahead of Andy Budgen's *Project Racing*.

P	Name	Helm and Crew	R1	R2	R3	R4	R5	R6	R7	Pts
1	*SouthernCrossConstructions*	E McNicol/A Links/T Barnabos	2	4	6	1	3	4	4	18
2	*Active Air-2UE*	M Searle/A Massey/D Wilsdon	3	1	4	4	4	16	3	19
3	*Gotta Love It 7*	S Jarvin /S Newton /T Clout	7	2	1	5	5	2	8	22
4	*appliancesonline.com.au*	J Winning Jr/D Ewings/T Austin	6	7	7	2	1	1	7	24
5	*Rag and Famish Hotel*	J Harris/P Harris/S Babbage	5	3	2	3	6	12	6	25
6	*Yandoo*	J Winning/A Hay/D Gibson	12	10	9	21	7	3	1	42
7	*Project Racing*	A Budgen/M McGovern/J Barker	33	9	3	10	2	9	14	47
8	*Smeg*	H Stodart/D Phillips/J Beck	1	6	11	18	10	15	5	48
9	*SLAM*	G Rollerson/A Young/F Warren	9	12	22	9	11	6	11	58
10	*Pure Blond*	J Francis/R Bell /B Phillips	14	13	10	6	15	8	17	66

Gotta Love It 7, third at the 2009 J J Giltinan International Championships

18ft Skiff Nationals

Hayling Island Sailing Club   23 - 25 May 2009

A disappointing fleet of just six boats turned up at Hayling Island for the National Championships over the late-May bank holiday weekend. Despite the lack of entries, however, the competition was of an excellent standard, with Dave Hall leading his team of Paul Constable and Alec Mackinlay on board *Ronstan*, whilst multi-champion, Andy Richards, sailing with Andrew Fairley and Will Penfold on *Pindar*, and Ed Browne, Mark Tait and Jack Christophers on *Gill* all finishing the first day within one point of each other, with *Ronstan* just in the driving seat, by dint of taking two race wins.

The second day's racing saw four further races completed, and again the *Ronstan* boys excelled, with three wins and a fifth position, to open up a gap of four points to *Pindar* who had a first, second, third and sixth on the second day, to lead *Gill* by a further three points with the final day still to go.

With the prospect of a further three races due for the final day, everything was still to play for. However, in the event it was not possible to hold any more racing on the Monday, and therefore the overall results stayed as they were over-night with Dave Hall, Paul Constable and Alec Mackinlay winning the UK National Championship title.

P	Name	Helm/Crew	Club	R1	R2	R3	R4	R5	R6	R7	Tot	Nett
1	*Ronstan*	Dave Hall Paul Constable Alec Mackinlay	TBSC	4	1	1	1	1	5	1	14	9
2	*Pindar*	Andy Richards Andrew Fairley Will Penfold	DSC	1	4	2	2	6	1	3	19	13
3	*Gill*	Ed Browne Mark Tait Jack Christophers	BSC	2	2	3	5	3	4	2	21	16
4	*Pica*	Jamie Mears Matt Gill Stewart Mears	RCYC	3	3	4	4	2	2	4	22	18

Enterprise

Type	Dinghy	Weight	124 kg
Crew	2; Sit out	Sail Area M&J	10.7 sq m
PN	1116	Spi Type	None
Length	4.04 m	Designer	Jack Holt, 1956
Beam	1.62 m		www.sailenterprise.org.uk

Photo courtesy of Fotoboat

When Jack Holt drew the Enterprise in 1956, he could not have imagined its success. With some 23,000-odd boats having been produced, and an extremely competitive international race circuit, the racing section of the class continues to flourish. In addition, the boat is also extensively used as a family sailing boat, and the traditional pale blue sails can be seen just about anywhere around our coastline. Through the years, the boat has been produced in plywood and GRP, but it is only in the last few years that the glass boats have become equally competitive with the plywood versions, and this has done much to ensure that the racing fleet continues to grow.

Enterprise National Championships

Brixham Yacht Club   1 – 7 August 2009

As soon as the Lark class vacated Brixham at the end of their Nationals, fifty four Enterprises turned up to experience the waters of Torbay at the end of a couple of busy weeks for the Devon venue, which had also seen the Laser Nationals at the end of July. The first race saw the familiar name of Nick Craig, crewed by Sheena Craig, take the winning gun ahead of Russell Short and Katy Fry, with Gareth Shaw and Verity Pope in third.

With a steady Force four on the second day, Torbay produced very exciting conditions and the opportunity for an additional two races. The winning gun in the first race of the day was taken by Alan and Matt Johnson ahead of Nick and Sheena Craig, with 2008 National Champion Tim Sadler adding to his sixth place from the first race. In the second heat of the day, the top two positions were reversed, with the Craigs taking their second winning gun of the week, with the Johnsons in second position, ahead of Jeremy Stephens, crewed by Will Searle who finished third this time was.

Race Officer, Robin Meads reported that in Race Four there was very little wind, but managed to complete one round before the fleet ran out of wind altogether. A forecast sea breeze did not materialize and it was then necessary to relay an Olympic course for Race Five in the direction of Paignton to make the most of a South Westerly breeze. The race was shortened.

There was no racing due to poor visibility and torrential rain on Day Three, but whilst it was fluky on Day Four, it was a beautiful day. The race was won by Nick and Sheena Craig, ahead of Pete Lawson and son Jack, with Paul and Tracy Hobson. Race Five was again won by Alan and Matt Johnson; their second victory of the week, but again it was the Craigs who came in second and underlined their position as likely Champions.

With two races scheduled for Thursday, a lot of the competitors and race team would have been pleased to see a good solid breeze; however, they actually found a fickle three and a half knot wind that disappeared and filled in from another direction. In the sixth race, the win was taken by Ann Jackson and Alan Skeens, just ahead of the ever-present Nick and Sheena Craig, with Aly Morrish and Charles Bowyer in third position. The next race was held in similarly tricky conditions, and this time the Craigs took the winning gun, ahead of Mike and Verity Birch, and Tim and Hannah Sadler.

The final day of the Championships was glorious for spectators but not so good for the fleet that were looking forward to a good sail. Despite starting in a ten to twelve knot breeze, a sunny three knots soon became the actual conditions and the first race was finished after one lap. The second race was an Olympic triangle and was set off in a sea breeze, with the 180 degree wind shift from the first race. This Olympic course started in ten knots which dropped to five knots. At least it meant that the final two races were concluded and a satisfactory end point reached. With no need to sail in the last race, the Craigs regained the National title counting just first and second place results, from Alan and Matt Johnson who took second position on tiebreak from Jeremy Stephens and Will Searle, with the defending Champions, Tim and Hannah Sadler, in fourth position.

P	Helm	Crew	R1	R2	R3	R4	R5	R6	R7	R8	R9	Pts
1	N Craig	S Craig	1	2	1	1	2	2	1	2	55	12
2	A Johnson	M Johnson	10	1	2	12	1	22	5	5	1	37
3	J Stephens	W Searle	8	5	3	5	6	23	4	4	2	37
4	TSadler	H Sadler	6	3	7	9	8	15	3	3	4	43
5	A Fry	C Wheatley	5	4	4	20	32	19	10	1	10	73
6	P Hobson	T Hobson	33	18	24	3	7	17	6	16	3	94
7	J Scutt	N Scutt	31	8	16	11	3	13	16	10	18	95
8	B Moss	J Moore	7	44	8	10	4	6	8	26	26	95
9	R Short	K Fry	2	21	10	26	13	25	12	7	6	96
10	A Jackson	A Skeens	14	14	18	19	10	1	15	21	13	104

505

Type	Dinghy
Crew	2; 1 on trapeze
PN	902
Length	5.05 m
Beam	1.88 m
Weight	45.37 kg
Sail area M&J	12.3 sq m
Spi type	Symmetric
Spi area	23.25 sq m
Designer	John Westell
	www.sail505.org

In a breeze, there are few boats as great to sail, or as enjoyable to watch, as the John Westell-designed 505, now beyond its fifty-fifth year! The addition of a larger spinnaker a few years ago has pepped up the performance, and this thoroughbred racer continues to attract many of the top sailors for an international circuit that includes annual World and National Championship. This is certainly a boat for the experienced sailor rather than the newcomer to sailing.

505 World Championships

San Francisco, USA   15 - 29 August 2009

After a World Championships warm-up event, racing for the North American Championships, ninety eight international competitors appeared on the start line for the 505 World Championships, hosted by St Francis Yacht Club, on San Francisco Bay, for the start of the nine race event.

The event opened with a twenty five knot blast through the Golden Gate Bridge, and there was a degree of carnage as competitors became accustomed to the harsh sailing conditions, with over a dozen boats being towed in. At the end of the first day, with two races completed, the overall lead was held by Mike Holt (an ex-pat Brit now based in the US) and Carl Smit with a first and a second to their credit despite sailing much of the second race with a badly bent mast! Australian legend and three time World Champion Chris Nicholson, sailing with Casey Smith, was next in the pecking order with a third and fourth, and then two USA boats, Nick Adamson and Steve Bourdow, and Howie Hamlin and Ian Mitchell both had two top six results to start their campaign. Hamlin sailed with Mitchell for the North Americans, and for the start of the Worlds, but was scheduled to change crew to America's Cup skipper Paul Cayard for the bulk of the week; thirty years after Cayard had been runner-up as crew at the 505 Worlds in South Africa!

After the second day, when there was just one race, Mike Holt and Carl Smit still held the lead overall following a second place finish behind the Pre-Worlds winners, Mike Martin and Jeff Nelson, who had broken a mast on Day One. Both of the leading boats replaced masts overnight, but this didn't seem to effect their performance, and the introduction of discards brought Martin and Nelson right back to the fore in the overall standings. Australia's Nicholson and Smith stood in a strong third position overall, with Howie Hamblin and Paul Cayard now in fourth after scoring a sixth position in the day (after battling a disqualification with the Committee).

With lighter breezes on the third day, it was expected that Mike Martin and Jeff Nelson would not have things quite so much their own way, but now that the discard had come in, they were sitting at the top of the score sheet counting four first places after they picked up two more race wins in conditions from eight to twenty knots of breeze. They led at every mark in both races, and completed dominated the fleet throughout. Mike Holt and Carl Smit remained in a strong second position having added two more second places, whilst Aussie Chris Nicholson and Casey Smith were third, with two additional third places in their score-line. Gradually dropping out of contention were Hamblin and Cayard, especially as they decided to forfeit the redress that they had been given for a gate-boat incident earlier in the week. Having won the protest, Cayard went home and thought about it, and checked the rules. Whilst they had won the protest, his feeling was that they shouldn't have, and so the pair went back to the Committee to accept the disqualification!

After a lay-day, and with uncharacteristically light winds, racing resumed and the hitherto unbeatable Martin and Nelson showed a chink in their armour. Recording a twelfth and second in their two races, they dropped to second overall behind Mike Holt and Carl Smit, who earned a third and fourth, and took a six point lead into the Friday racing with two races scheduled, and a final heat due on Saturday. The races on Thursday were won by Dalton Bergan and Fritz Lanzinger of the US, and Australia's Malcolm Higgins and Nick Johnston who were something of a surprise, being in thirty second position overall.

On the penultimate day, Holt really just needed to sail Martin into the fleet to take the title overall, and attempted this action from the start. However, the process went wrong went Martin slipped away, leaving Holt in the second rank of starters, and playing catch-up for the rest of the day, gaining from the twenties at one stage to finish in ninth, their worst position of the week. Mike Martin, by contrast, despite sailing in conditions that were lighter than he would have chosen, managed to pull through the fleet to win, and open up a comfortable five point gap on Holt for the final day. Chris Nicholson and Casey Smith from Australia remained in third position, whilst second place in this race left Dalton Bergan and Fritz Lanzinger on level points with Nicholson, battling for the final podium position.

Martin and Nelson were delighted to find an eighteen knot breeze on the final day, and they did the rest of the work to take the World Championship with an excellent forty six second victory. With Mike Holt and Carl Smit, the only real competition for the title at the end of the week, scoring a fourth position, they could do nothing to prevent Martin and Nelson from taking the title that looked likely to go their way throughout the week, although a broken mast (and consequent retirement) added an element of doubt throughout the week. Nicholson and Smith held on to third overall, whilst the UK's defending champions, Ian Pinnell and Carl Gibbon, finished in tenth overall as top British boat.

P	Helm	Crew	Nat	R1	R2	R3	R4	R5	R6	R7	R8	R9	Pts
1	Mike Martin	Jeff Nelson	USA	1	DNF	1	1	1	12	2	1	1	8
2	Mike Holt	Carl Smit	USA	2	1	2	2	2	3	4	9	4	16
3	Chris Nicholson	Casey Smith	AUS	4	3	3	3	3	7	8	8	3	26
4	Jens Findel	Johannes Tellen	GER	72	5	6	15	12	2	3	10	5	36
5	Dalton Bergan	Fritz Lanzinger	USA	8	8	4	10	15	1	5	2	16	38
6	Nick Adamson	Steve Bourdow	USA	9	2	13	4	4	4	17	14	2	38
7	Howie Hamlin	Paul Cayard	USA	5	6	RAF	7	14	5	10	5	6	44
8	Tyler Moore	Geoff Ewenson	USA	11	13	11	15	16	8	6	4	10	63
9	Ryan Cox	Stuart Park	USA	12	11	12	6	8	6	15	22	8	63
10	Ian Pinnell	Carl Gibbon	GBR	7	14	8	13	20	10	11	3	DNF	66

505 European Championship 2009

Kieler Woche   24 - 28 June 2009

One hundred and one of Europe's best 505 sailors joined the annual Kiel Week celebrations to contest their European Championship at the end of June.

After two days' racing, and five heats, the early leader overall was Dr Wolfgang Hunger and Julien Kleiner, who started the regatta with two race wins, and then sailed consistently to end the second day with a five point lead over the legendary Danes, Jorgen and Jacob Boysen-Möller, with another Danish team, Jan Saugmann and Morten Ramsbaek, in third position. Hunger has made something of a habit of winning the Europeans, with eight previous Championships to his credit! With the Boysen-Möller brothers unable to race on the second day, his competition for the title seemed likely to come from further in the pack, but with World Champions Ian Pinnell and Carl Gibbon back in sixth overall on twenty nine points, they needed to start making a move.

In the event, strong winds and big seas caused the cancellation of the next day's racing, which put the Boysen-Möller pairing back in the hunt, with everything still to play for. However, the final three races didn't make much of an impact on the overall placings, with Hunger and Kleiner adding a further three top four results, to take the Championship with a five point margin, with Saugmann and Ramsbaek winning two of the last three to sustain their runners-up position ahead of the Danish Boysen-Möller brothers. Pinnell and Gibbon finished in sixth place overall (one place behind the top girl, German Meike Schomäker), whilst the only other UK entry, of Owen Tudor and Toby Winchester, finished in fifty third position overall.

Hunger is a regular competitor at Kieler Woche, and his victory this year means that he has now won this annual event at Kiel seventeen times, making him the most successful Kieler Woche sailor ever, which of course is quite an achievement in such a major event.

P	Helm	Crew	Nat	R1	R2	R3	R4	R5	R6	R7	R8	Pts
1	Dr Wolfgang Hunger	Julien Kleiner	GER	1	1	3	11	2	3	4	1	11
2	Jan Saugmann	Morten Ramsbæk	DEN	4	7	2	7	3	1	1	5	16
3	Jorgen Boysen-Möller	Jacob Boysen-Möller	DEN	5	4	5	2	1	6	2	2	16
4	Jens Findel	JohannesTellen	GER	8	23	1	1	11	DNF	5	4	30
5	Meike Schomäker	Holger Jess	GER	3	20	9	3	5	7	15	3	30
6	Ian Pinnell	Carl Gibbon	GBR	21	10	7	6	6	2	6	7	34
7	Lutz Stengel	Frank Feller	GER	2	16	18	4	13	10	9	11	49
8	Stefan Köchlin	Andreas Achterberg	GER	22	29	4	9	9	18	3	6	49
9	Philippe Boite	Fabrice Toupet	FRA	7	9	15	5	15	5	14	10	50
10	Martin Görge	Rainer Görge	GER	17	5	6	17	23	4	32	9	58

505 National Championships

Royal Torbay Yacht Club   11 - 14 June 2009

Thirty six entrants travelled to Torbay for the 2009 505 National Championships, held concurrently with the 2009 Flying Dutchman Nationals.

With an unexpectedly breezy first day reigning World Champion Ian Pinnell and Carl Gibbon revelled in the conditions to take the race ahead of Terry Scutcher and Christian Diebitsch whilst, in slightly more friendly conditions, these positions reversed for the second race.

Day Two dawned murky, light and fairly unpleasant! In breezes reminiscent of the 2008 Worlds, Pinnell picked his way around the course in the first race of the day to take a second win. However, the second race of the day (for the extra-long 'Race of the Year') initially saw Pinnell down in the mire. With the additional time at his disposal, he managed to pull himself back into contention in pursuit of early leaders Charlie Walters and Dougal Cram. Walters did manage to hang onto the lead for a win, leaving Pinnell with another second place to consolidate his overall status.

Two wins on the third day of the event was enough to secure Pinnell and Gibbon the National Championship title with two races in hand, although they did attend the first race of the final day. In light and disappointing conditions, they retired to the bar for the final race, and to contemplate a very successful event. Scutcher and Diebitsch continued their form throughout the event to take second position overall, whilst third place went to Alex Barry and Charles Dwyer, ahead of Russell and Andrew Short, with Charlie Walters and Dougal Cram finishing in fifth position.

P	Helm	Crew	R1	R2	R3	R4	R5	R6	R7	R8	Pts
1	Ian Pinnell	Carl Gibbon	1	2	1	2	1	1	5	37	8
2	Terry Scutcher	Christian Diebitsch	2	1	5	6	2	3	3	2	13
3	Alex Barry	Charles Dwyer	6	3	4	4	4	2	7	1	18
4	Russell Short	Andrew Short	4	4	10	3	3	5	1	7	20
5	Charlie Walters	Dougal Cram	9	10	2	1	5	4	11	5	26
6	Stuart Turnbull	Jason Lunn	7	8	6	5	7	7	2	4	31
7	Tim Bird	Richard Nurse	21	12	3	7	6	14	4	3	35
8	Matt Hart	Craig Hurrell	5	7	12	9	17	8	9	6	44
9	Martin Hodgson	Adrian Miles	8	6	8	8	13	10	6	9	45
10	Harry Briddon	Simon Briddon	3	5	16	13	8	6	13	17	48

49er

Type	Dinghy	Weight	94 kg
Crew	2; on trapeze	Sail area M&J	21.2 sq m
PN	747	Spi type	Asymmetric
Length	4.99 m	Spi area	38 sq m
Beam	3 m	Designer	Julian Bethwaite, 1995
			www.49er.org.uk

Photo courtesy of Jean-Marie Liot / DPPI / TTV / SOF 2009

Born from the development of eighteen-foot skiffs in Sydney Harbour, the 49er changed the face of sailboat racing when, in a rare moment of modern thinking, ISAF voted the 49er in to the Olympic sailboat line-up, bringing high-performance skiff sailing to the international community. The standards of international racing are very high; however, the class has a wide appeal and boasts strong national fleets as well as an active club racing scene. It remains one of the ultimate sailing challenges.

49er World Championships

Lake Garda   12 - 19 July 2009

A fleet of eighty seven boats attended the 2009 49er World Championships at Lake Garda, with all but five utilising the new carbon rig which has done much to rebuild interest in this extreme Olympic Class.

For the early party of the week, racing was separated into three flights, and early leaders were Brits Dave Evans sailing with Simon Hiscocks with ex World Champions Stevie Morrison and Ben Rhodes in third and Paul Campbell-James and Mark Asquith in fourth, showing a pretty impressive start to the regatta for the large UK contingent. The second day saw Morrison/Rhodes pull through to the lead ahead of Campbell-James/Asquith whilst some of the class "big-guns" started moving up, with Nico Karth of Austria, Nathan Outteridge of Australia and the Sibello brothers of Italy all moving into the top six.

As the fleet racing changed into the finals, a change of conditions, to more fickle breezes, seemed to suit the Australian Nathan Outteridge with crew Iain Jensen. The reigning World Champions, together with the ever-consistent Sibello brothers of Italy, were able to lay down three consistent results on the first day of the finals, whilst the two British crews of Stevie Morrison and Ben Rhodes, and John Pink and Rick Peacock both took a race win in the course of the day, but still dropped down to fourth and third by the end of the day.

The second day of finals racing, held in eleven knot breezes, saw a further three races of the series completed, with Outteridge and Jensen holding a four point lead over the rapidly improving Nico Karth and Nikolaus Resch, who added an impressive two wins and a second to their overnight score, to move up from fifth. With Morrison and Rhodes fending off the Sibello brothers, Pink and Peacock still in the top five, well clear of sixth, Chris Draper and Peter Greenhaugh and Paul Campbell-James with Mark Asquith also still in the top ten, British interest was assured in the closing stages of the regatta.

With four of the ten boat medal race coming from the UK, there was a great chance of one of the boats bringing home a significant reward, and on this occasion it was the Development pairing of Pink and Peacock. In their first World Championships to-gether, they were rewarded with an excellent second position overall, behind the reigning champion, Nathan Outteridge and Iain Jensen, whilst third place overall went to the extremely consistent Italian brothers, Pietro and Gianfranco Sibello. Stevie Morrison and Ben Rhodes, the 2007 World Champions, finished in fourth position, whilst Chris Draper and Peter Greenhaugh completed the event in sixth and Paul Campbell-James and Mark Asquith rounded off the UK medal race contingent, fin-ishing in ninth.

P	Nat	Helm/Crew	1	2	3	4	5	6	7	8	9	F1	F2	F3	F4	F5	F6	F7	F8	MR	Pts
1	AUS	Nathan Outteridge, Iain Jensen	2	2	10	4	2	1	3	5	8	2	1	4	7	4	6	4	8	4	59
2	GBR	John Pink, Rick Peacock	4	6	2	5	1	2	2	3	2	17	5	1	16	5	9	8	3	6	74
3	ITA	Pietro Sibello, Gianfranco Sibello	7	4	1	2	20	1	4	2	1	8	8	2	6	6	14	1	7	14	74
4	GBR	Stevie Morrison, Ben Rhodes	1	1	7	3	1	3	1	4	8	1	15	20	8	3	3	15	1	10	77
5	AUT	Nico Delle Karth, Nikolaus Leopold Resch	3	1	4	1	6	2	4	4	6	16	12	7	1	2	1	21	4	12	80
6	GBR	Chris Draper, Peter Greenhalgh	2	10	6	6	3	7	1	1	10	4	14	12	2	7	15	2	5	8	90
7	DEN	Peter Hansen, Soren Hansen	3	3	9	5	1	10	4	8	9	11	7	8	9	17	2	12	10	2	103
8	FRA	Manu Dyen, Christidis Stephane	4	7	4	3	17	3	18	3	1	13	2	6	10	1	RDF	7	9	16	103.2
9	GBR	Paul Campbell-James, Mark Asquith	2	5	2	2	3	1	6	6	21	23	4	24	3	9	17	5	12	18	118
10	ESP	Iker Martinez, Xavier Fernandez	15	15	4	1	3	4	3	1	2	7	9	13	RDG	13	8	14	6	20	119

2009 49er World Champions Nathan Outteridge and Iain Jensen

The Dinghy & Smallcraft Review
2009~2010

49er European Championships

Zadar, Croatia   29 August - 5 September 2009

Sixty four crews converged on the beautiful venue of Zadar in Croatia for the 49er European Championships with representatives from nineteen countries, and a strong contingent from the UK.

At the conclusion of the Gold Series qualifying, the French team were in control, with Manu Dyen and Stephane Christidis in the lead, Mogan Lagravviere and Yann Rocherieux in second and Julien d'Ortoli and Noe Delpech in fourth, with the dominance only being broken by the reappearance on the Olympic circuit of Paul Brotherton, sailing once again with Mark Asquith, who had put together the most consistent of all the teams in the qualifying races. Amongst the other Team GB members, John Pink and Rick Peacock, Silver medallists at the World Championships, entered this sector of the racing in sixteenth, with David Evans and Simon Hiscocks in twentieth, whilst the performance of youngsters James Peters and Dicken Maclean (at twenty fifth) was also worthy of note in their first international 49er regatta.

As the Gold Series continued, Italians Pietro and Gianfranco Sibello came to the top of the pack, and led overall going into the final day's sailing. However, they were only one point clear of Brotherton and Asquith who were continuing their good form. They were however looking likely to be the only GB team in the medal race unless John Pink and Rick Peacock could get a good result in the final fleet race; they were in twelfth position going into it. On the final day, the last points race decided the medal race competitors, and a fourth place confirmed Pink and Peacock had a place in the top ten. The final race was held just off the club, with the windward mark some ten metres from the shore, giving the spectators a great chance to see the racing. It was won by Austrians Nico Delle Karth and Kilolaus Resch, with the Sibellos in second position, confirming their title, and Brotherton and Asquith in third, giving them an extremely commendable Silver medal in the Championships to mark their return to 49er sailing.

P	Nat	Helm/Crew	R1	R2	R3	R4	R5	R6	R7	R8	R9	R10	R11	R12	R13	R14	R15	R16	R17	R18	Pts
1	ITA	P Sibello G Sibello	2	8	6	2	23	10	10	2	2	2	2	15	19	9	2	3	7	2	86
2	GBR	P Brotherton M Asquith	4	7	7	3	1	2	4	3	3	20	4	14	2	2	DNF	7	16	3	98
3	AUT	N Delle Karth N Resch	5	3	6	1	3	5	15	9	14	9	14	2	18	7	1	DNF	1	1	100
4	FRA	M Dyen S Christidis	7	1	1	1	6	9	12	1	1	4	22	8	5	15	17	11	5	8	104
5	FIN	L Lehtinen K Bask	3	1	11	11	13	9	7	19	10	1	5	1	8	13	9	1	14	6	115
6	FRA	M Lagravviere Y Rocherieux	7	5	1	3	2	4	3	8	BFD	19	6	6	21	12	13	13	12	5	124
7	DEN	P K Andersen N Thorsell	6	14	2	10	8	13	8	12	20	3	18	17	14	1	8	9	2	4	135
8	FRA	A Silvy U Hoffmann	9	3	3	8	9	8	2	14	10	6	24	9	16	3	14	6	9	OCS	137
9	GBR	J Pink R Peacock	12	6	12	9	14	5	4	11	11	17	10	22	3	18	3	2	4	7	141
10	UKR	R Luka S Patkovski	1	8	8	8	4	6	5	7	13	8	15	7	9	10	10	21	19	OCS	147

49er National Championships

Hayling Island Sailing Club   22 - 24 August 2009

Twenty five 49ers competed in the National Championships at Hayling Island, utilising the pre 2009 rigs in order to open the event to more "local" sailors. This also gave the opportunity for several of the class "stars" to sail with unfamiliar crews, and to spread their knowledge around, which can only be to the benefit of the class in the long run. The event became something of a tussle between two of the more experienced class protagonists, Dave Evans, crewed by Edward Powys, and Olympian Simon Hiscocks, crewed by class coach Harvey Hillary. Evans took the Championships with a near perfect finish to the event, scoring two wins and a second place in the final three races which pulled them through from second position at the end of the penultimate day, albeit by the narrowest deficit of just 0.5pt. Both teams had a BFD to discard when sufficient races had been completed.

Third position overall was taken by Rick Peacock, sailing with Alec Boere who similarly finished strongly, with two third places on the final day, which lifted him clear of the first "guest" in the class, 29er sailor Tom Durham who sailed with George Hand for the event to earn an excellent fourth overall. On the final day, Durham and Hand also took part in the opening of the 29er Nationals, and completed an additional three races (holding the overnight lead in that event too!) Max Richardson, another 29er expert, finished in sixth position overall, sailing with Nick Redding (more normally seen at the front of Bleddyn Mon's 29er); in the course of the weekend they actually won two races and gained a second place, but had to count a DNS in their final scores, which pushed them back overall.

P	Helm	Crew	R1	R2	R3	R4	R5	R6	R7	R8	Tot	Nett
1	Dave Evans	Edward Powys	BFD	3	2	3	5	1	1	2	43	17
2	Simon Hiscocks	Harvey Hillary	3	4	BFD	1	3	3	5	17	62	36
3	Rick Peacock	Alec Boere	9	19	5	6	7	10	3	3	62	43
4	Tom Durham	George Hand	10	11	4	2	13	9	4	11	64	51
5	Daniel Hare	Jamie Hare	7	9	9	4	6	8	13	8	64	51
6	Max Richardson	Nick Redding	4	1	BFD	DNS	1	7	2	14	81	55
7	Alistair Kissane	Ronan Wallace	5	7	8	DNS	8	13	8	9	84	58
8	Jonathan Heathcote	Chopper Eatwell	16	14	BFD	5	9	2	11	5	88	62
9	Simon Marks	Jonny Clegg	2	16	BFD	DNS	2	4	12	1	89	63
10	Chris Gill	Jon Gill	11	6	BFD	DNS	4	6	6	4	89	63

International 470

Type	Dinghy
Crew	2; 1 on trapeze
PN	973
Length	4.7 m
Beam	1.68 m
Weight	120 kg
Sail area M&J	12.7 sq m
Spi type	Symmetric
Spi area	13 sq m
Designer	Andre Cornu
	www.470.org

Designed by Andre Cornu, the 470 is another international success, reinforced by its continued selection as one of the Olympic classes. The boat is raced in more than forty countries, and is most popular with the lighter crews, hence its current use at the Games for both men and women. This two-man dinghy is built only in GRP, and with one crew member supported on trapeze, it offers exciting sailing, and the symmetric spinnaker makes the boat a handful as soon as you turn off-wind.

470 World Championships

Rungsted Harbour, Denmark   23 - 29 August 2009

A fleet of ninety five men's teams, and fifty seven women's, competed for the 470 World Championship, held to the north of Copenhagen, and the event started with an eight knot breeze that built into the mid teens.

After three days of qualifying, the fleet was split into Gold, Silver and Bronze racing for Day Four of the event; the Men's division was led by Sven and Calle Coster and, whilst both counting start line penalties, the two top British teams, reigning champions Nic Asher and Elliott Willis and Nic Rogers and Pom Green were still in the mix, along with Luke Patience and Stuart Bithell. However, as the week progressed, Asher and Elliott, and Rogers and Green both struggled with conditions and fell by the wayside leaving Patience and Bithell as the only UK entrants in the medal race on the final day. By this stage Croatia's Šime Fantela and Igor Marenic had pretty much taken control of the men's fleet, and a second spot in the final heat behind Australians Matt Belcher and Malcolm Page was sufficient to confirm their World Championship title. A solid fourth place lifted the British pairing of Luke Patience and Stuart Bithell to the Silver medal position to continue the excellent record that the Brits have in this class. They knocked the Japanese pairing of Ryunosuke Harada and Yugo Yoshida into third on tie-break, whilst the early pacemakers from Holland, Sven and Kalle Coster, had to be content with fourth overall.

In the women's division, the racing was pretty well dominated by the very consistent Dutch duo of Lisa Westerhof and Lobke Berkhout. Leading for much of the week, they additionally took the medal race victory which confirmed that the title was theirs. Their main opposition, Tara Pacheco and Berta Betanzos from Spain, could do no better than seventh in the final heat, but this was still enough to retain the Silver medal, whilst Bronze was won by Ingrid Petitjean and Nadège Douroux from France. Our own Pippa Wilson and Saskia Clarke finished in seventh overall, an excellent start for a brand new partnership in the class, whilst Penny Clark and Katrina Hughes also enjoyed a great week, finishing in ninth.

P	Nat	Men's 470 World Championships	R1	R2	R3	R4	R5	R6	R7	R8	R9	R10	R11	R12	R13	Pts
1	CRO	Šime Fantela, Igor Marenic	3	2	1	1	6	7	8	8	13	16	4	1	2	58
2	GBR	Luke Patience, Stuart Bithell	12	5	4	4	9	15	1	6	30	7	7	2	4	80
3	JPN	Ryunosuke Harada, Yugo Yoshida	2	5	12	2	6	3	BFD	2	8	9	3	18	5	80
4	NED	Sven Coster, Kalle Coster	1	9	3	1	2	1	22	7	16	11	10	10	7	85
5	AUS	Matthew Belcher, Malcolm Page	7	5	8	3	2	5	14	11	9	14	12	13	1	91
6	AUT	Matthias Schmid, Florian Reichstaedter	14	1	2	3	3	2	17	17	11	1	14	25	3	91
7	FRA	Pierre Leboucher, Vincent Garos	4	11	4	4	1	6	BFD	27	2	10	8	3	6	92
8	ESP	Onan Barreiros, Aaron Sarmiento	10	7	6	11	14	1	2	9	1	DNF	5	16	DSQ	104
9	ARG	Lucas Calabrese, Juan De la Fuente	4	19	5	8	7	7	9	25	12	6	13	4	8	110
10	GRE	Panagiotis Mantis, Pavlos Kagialis	11	8	11	13	1	16	BFD	22	3	2	2	9	OCS	120

P	Nat	Women's 470 World Championships	R1	R2	R3	R4	R5	R6	R7	R8	R9	R10	R11	R12	R13	Pts
1	NED	Lisa Westerhof, Lobke Berkhout	2	2	3	2	1	4	4	6	3	8	6	1	1	36
2	ESP	Tara Pacheco, Berta Betanzos	4	11	4	1	6	5	3	3	8	10	2	2	7	62
3	FRA	Ingrid Petitjean, Nadège Douroux	2	2	19	9	4	2	1	18	4	2	4	6	9	72
4	ITA	Giulia Conti, Giovanna Micol	17	5	1	7	3	1	2	2	7	13	15	5	6	73
5	AUS	Elise Rechichi, Tessa Parkinson	19	6	1	5	2	3	10	16	12	6	9	11	3	87
6	NZL	Jo Aleh, Olivia Powrie	15	1	9	1	5	8	BFD	20	10	4	10	4	2	91
7	GBR	Pippa Wilson, Saskia Clark	8	4	3	2	6	2	11	21	13	14	8	10	5	91
8	JPN	Ai Kondo, Wakako Tabata	6	10	2	5	2	7	17	17	11	11	13	3	4	95
9	GBR	Penny Clark, Katrina Hughes	14	1	5	7	1	15	8	9	16	12	7	7	10	106
10	USA	Erin Maxwell, Kinsolving Farrar Isabelle	5	5	15	6	12	11	18	22	5	9	1	9	8	112

470 European Championship

Lake Traunsee, Austria   5 - 14 June 2009

A fleet of one hundred and twenty one fought out the 470 European Championship in Austria, with eighty two crews in the men's fleet, and thirty nine sailing in the women's. The main contingent was split into two sections for qualifying purposes, whilst the smaller women's fleet competed as a single fleet throughout. The week's sailing was beset with poor winds and testing conditions.

In the men's fleet, much interest was focused on Gold Medal winning crew Malcolm Page, now sailing with long term rival Mathew Belcher following Nathan Wilmot's retirement. They were joined by Nicolas Charbonnier, now sailing with Baptiste Meye-Dieu, and the World number one ranked Coster brothers of the Netherlands. With World number two, Gideon Kliuger and Udi Gal from Israel joined by GBR's Nick Rogers, now sailing with Pom Green, competiton looked as though it would be tight, but conditions were so difficult that many, including Rogers and Green, never really got into the hunt, and finished in a disappointing thirty fifth; second Brit behind Ben Saxton and David Kohler who finished in twenty first overall. Amongst the rest of team GB, Jonny McGovern and Christian Birrell finished in forty third, Matthew Mee and Max Capener were forty ninth, and Luke Patience and Callum McDonald were sixty second, completing a disappointing regatta for the UK competitors.

The regatta was won by Harada Ryunosuke and Yoshida Yugo of Japan, pulling clear with a win in the final race, with Croatia's Šime Fantela and Igor Marenic in runners-up spot, having been in contention throughout the week. Germany's Lucas Zellmer and Heiko Seelig were third.

P	Nat	Helm	Crew	Q1	Q2	Q3	Q4	Q5	Q6	F1	F2	Pt
1	JPN	H Ryunosuke	Y Yugo	8	4	9	1	1	DNC	14	1	38
2	CRO	S Fantela	I Marenic	2	1	5	1	21	21	7	6	43
3	GER	L Zellmer	H Seelig	8	11	17	3	4	5	9	36	57
4	ITA	M Zandona	E Scotti	1	25	9	18	1	6	25	3	62
5	AUS	M Belcher	M Page	7	1	15	17	2	10	11	29	63
6	NED	S Coster	K Coster	10	13	DSQ	8	7	11	1	15	65
7	FRA	N Charbonnier	B Meyer-Dieu	14	7	2	7	14	19	32	4	67
8	GRE	P Mantis	P Kagialis	6	9	10	12	12	3	23	19	71
9	GRE	P Kambouridis	G Orologas	5	25	13	10	14	2	20	10	74
10	ITA	F Zeni	N Pitanti	1	9	7	7	27	15	16	23	78

In the women's fleet the entry was led by reigning champions Sylvia Vogl and Carolina Flatscher, sailing in their home waters, with World number two (Ai Kondo Wakoko Tabata from Japan) and number three (Giulia Conti and Giovanna Micol from Italy) heading the challenge. There were three UK entries in the fleet; Penny Clark and Saskia Clark, continuing their fairly intense programme to get to grips with this new two person challenge, and also Hannah Mills with Katrina Hughes, as well as Kate and Sarah Williams. At the end of a difficult week, it was the two Clarks who finished in top position, in thirteenth position with Mills and Hughes in seventeenth and the Williams in thirty seventh. The winners overall were Conti and Micol of Italy, with Japan's Kondo and Tabata in Silver medal position, and New Zealand's Jo Aleh and Olivia Powrie in third place. Vogl, the reigning champion finished in seventh, whilst Mandy Mulder and Merel Witteveen (who was Silver medalist in the Yngling in Beijing) continued their progress with a ninth place overall (including two top-two finishes in the week.

P	Nat	Helm	Crew	R1	R2	R3	R4	R5	R6	Pt
1	ITA	Conti Giulia	Micol Giovanna	1	6	1	5	6	28	19
2	JPN	Kondo Ai	Tabata Wakako	5	1	2	14	12	2	22
3	NZL	Aleh Jo	Powrie Olivia	12	8	3	6	4	14	33
4	ESP	Pacheco Tara	Betanzos Berta	15	7	7	13	2	6	35
5	GRE	Economou Anthi	Tsigaridi Olga	7	5	5	30	10	11	38
6	NED	Fokkema Margriet	Jongens Marieke	16	12	14	1	RDG	1	38.8
7	AUT	Vogl Sylvia	Flatscher Carolina	17	3	16	4	28	4	44
8	ESP	Gallego Marina	Rita Roman Julia	2	10	19	10	16	8	46
9	NED	Mulder Mandy	Witteveen Merel	RAF	19	8	2	1	19	49
10	DEN	Koch Henriette	Sommer Lene	3	16	20	16	7	7	49

International 420

Crew	2; 1 on trapeze	Sail area M&J	7.98 sq m
PN	1087	Spi type	Symmetric
Length	4.2 m	Spi area	9.02 sq m
Beam	1.71 m	Designer	Christian Maury
Weight	64 kg		www.420sailing.org.uk

Photo courtesy of Dave Kneale/Volvo Ocean Race

The 420 is a straight-forward boat to sail – fast and rewarding, yet equally at home as a training boat; these are some of the reasons that over 50,000 boats have been produced worldwide, and that there is still such an enthusiastic racing circuit with World, European, as well as National Championships. With one crew member on trapeze, and a symmetric spinnaker to power the boat, this is a design that is particularly suited to lighter-weight crews, and has therefore been a huge success as a youth boat over the years.

420 World Championships

Fraglia Vela Riva, Lake Garda   29 July - 5 August 2009

Lake Garda must have had one of its busiest ever summers, with regatta after regatta through the main months of summer. At the beginning of August, the 420s used the beautiful venue as the backdrop for their World Championships, with two hundred and six boats entered from thirty different countries and the fleet divided into one hundred and twenty two boys and eighty four girls. The boys' course was positioned to the right hand side of the lake, close to Limore, whilst the girls were further north towards Torbole. As is the way nowadays, the initial fleet racing was to decide the combatants in the Gold and Silver fleets for the final days of the event, with an aim to have six qualifying races within that period, but with a minimum of three races being counted to decide the division.

As the original qualifying racing finished, four boats from the UK had made it through to the girls' Gold fleet:

Joanna Freeman and Hannah Mitchell   Imogen and Hermione Stanley
Anna Burnett and Flora Stewart   Rebecca Kalderon and Rosie Sibthorp

In the boys' fleet, five GB boats were competing in the Golds:

Ben Palmer and Konrad Weaver   Phil Sparks and Ben Gratton
Mike Wood and Hugh Brayshaw   Matt Rainback and Simon Foskett
Tim Gratton and Ed Riley

As both of the fleets progressed through the finals racing, in the women's World Championship it became evident that one of just four boats was likely to take the title. In the end, New Zealanders Alexandra Maloney and Bianca Barbarich-Bacher took the event on the last day, having started at second overall in the morning. With scores of first, fourth and sixteenth, it was just about enough to push them past the Italian pairing of Camilla Marino and Claudia Soricelli whilst the third-placed USA boat, sailed by Sydney Bolger and Caitlin Beavers, took third with an eighth, second and third. Pre-race event favourites, Martine Grael and Daniela Adler, had the best of the final day with a second, third and sixth, but it was too late to make amends for an error earlier in the week which essentially ruled out their chances.

P	Nat	Helm / Crew	1	2	3	4	5	6	7	8	Pts
1	NZL	Alexandra Maloney, Bianca Barbarich-Bacher	1	6	6	33	16	1	4	16	50
2	ITA	Camilla Marino, Claudia Soricelli	2	DSQ	12	10	7	13	1	14	59
3	USA	Sydney Bolger, Caitlin Beavers	11	4	15	42	18	8	2	3	61
4	BRA	Martine Grael, Daniela Adler	3	DSQ	7	28	13	6	3	2	62
5	ESP	Carlota Massana, Ana Lobo	9	12	3	9	35	16	13	13	75
6	GBR	Imogen Stanley, Hermione Stanley	16	9	21	12	BFD	5	6	7	76
7	GER	Cornelia Oczycz, Johanna Steiner	19	7	8	17	24	10	17	6	84
8	GER	Lisa Schweigert, Lisa Frisch	4	OCS	9	20	30	2	9	11	85
9	ITA	Sara Amemdola, Giulia Paolillo	10	23	17	23	23	4	11	4	92
10	GER	Nadine Böhm, Caroline Tiegel	23	1	1	39	29	11	8	26	99

World 420 Championship; Women

The men's final racing was equally enthralling, although there was more separation in the fleet after the first and second boats. Antonios Tsimpoukelis and George Karonis of Greece had no need to finish the final race to secure their World Championships ahead of Francisco Lardies and Finn Drummond who had travelled from New Zealander. This Kiwi pair finally finished three points behind the Greeks, but they applied pressure throughout the week. Third position was taken by GB's Ben Palmer, sailing with Konrad Weaver, whilst fifth was another GB boat, sailed by the ISAF World Youth Champions, Phil Sparks and Ben Gratton.

P	Nat	Name	R1	R2	R3	R4	R5	R6	R7	R8	R9	R10	Pts
1	GRE	Antonios Tsimpoukelis, George Karonis	3	25	1	2	5	2	7	1	5	DNF	26
2	NZL	Francisco Lardies, Finn Drummond	4	1	OCS	5	1	3	20	4	6	5	29
3	GBR	Ben Palmer, Konrad Weaver	13	9	11	7	6	7	10	2	BFD	4	56
4	ITA	Davide Ortelli, Leonardo Zaggia	15	14	9	3	2	1	1	7	8	29	59
5	GBR	Phil Sparks, Ben Gratton	1	17	23	11	4	21	33	12	1	3	70
6	ITA	Giovanni Meloni, Alessandro Gemini	8	5	2	22	48	26	8	16	19	1	81
7	NZL	Luke Stevenson, Sam Bullock	14	4	33	OCS	10	6	11	17	11	9	82
8	FRA	Gabriel Skoczek, Thibault Soler	7	3	5	42	23	17	16	20	7	32	98
9	GER	Julian Autenrieth, Philipp Autenrieth	21	2	7	25	37	18	24	3	BFD	11	111
10	ITA	Federico Maria Maccari, Rocco Vitali	25	15	36	6	30	60	4	10	14	12	116

World 420 Championships; Men

420 National Championships

Mountbatten Sailing Centre, Plymouth   23 - 28 August 2009

As the school holidays came to an end, the 420 class celebrated another great summer with a fleet of sixty four boats at their National Championships, hosted by the Mountbatten Sailing Centre in Plymouth. At the end of the first day (with winds of about fourteen knots) Josh Pistol and Rosie Sibthorpe led with two first places for the day, together with a sixth. In hot pursuit, amongst others, were Rebecca Kalderon and Piers Strong from Itchenor SC, who had won the final race of the day (Kalderon being Sibthorpe's normal helm!)

Conditions for Day Two were quite similar, but Pistol was pulled up in the early race under the black flag. Tim Gratton and Ed Riley from Hayling Island took the first gun of the day, ahead of Anna Burnet and Fiona Stewart. Kalderon and Strong similarly found themselves on the black flag 'board' after the second race of the day, whilst Ben Palmer and Konrad Weaver took the winner's gun to strengthen their position, followed by James Hayward and Tim Carter. The third race on Day Two was at least clear at the start and was again won by Gratton and Riley who finished the day with a third to leave them in overall lead as night fell. Kalderon and Strong finished the day with a third and second in the final two races, to put themselves in second position overall, whilst third was taken by Anna Burnet and Fiona Stewart, who scored two fourth places and a final race win for the day.

Thirty knot winds precluded any racing from taking place on the Wednesday, but service was resumed on Thursday when four races were held. By winning the final race of the day, Rebecca Kalderon and Piers Strong put themselves back at the top of the leaderboard by two points from Tim Gratton and Ed Riley. Ben Palmer and Konrad Weaver finished in third, ahead of another of the day's race winners, Mike Wood and Hugh Brayshaw, whilst Pistol and Sibthorpe won the other two races on the day, but added them to an eleventh and their second black flag of the week. With the gales back for Friday, no further racing were possible, and this left Rebecca Kalderon and Piers Strong as the new 2009 National Champions, ahead of Gratton and Riley.

P	Helm	Crew	R2	R3	R4	R5	R6	R7	R8	R9	R10	R11	Pts
1	R Kalderon	P Strong	3	1	6	65	3	2	9	2	15	1	42
2	T Gratton	E Riley	25	2	1	7	1	3	8	16	4	2	44
3	B Palmer	K Weaver	2	3	65	1	6	10	14	4	3	5	48
4	M Wood	H Brayshaw	65	5	9	3	2	6	12	7	1	6	51
5	A Burnet	F Stewart	9	9	2	4	4	1	13	17	6	4	52
6	A Vose	C Alton	4	15	5	10	8	5	5	9	13	7	66
7	J Freeman	H Mitchell	11	4	4	5	10	4	26	11	12	10	71
8	J Sparks	M Rainback	12	19	3	14	32	18	11	5	8	3	93
9	J Hayward	T Carter	28	7	25	2	11	11	3	15	14	8	96
10	J Pistol	R Sibthorp	1	6	65	6	5	7	1	1	11	65	103

IBI Sailing

The Junior & Youth Class Dinghy Specialists

Optimists, Cadets, 420s & 470s in stock. Laser & Topper parts. Repairs & Event photos

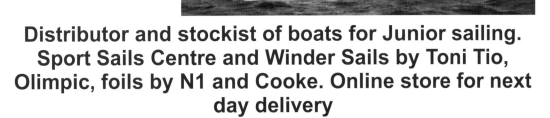

Distributor and stockist of boats for Junior sailing. Sport Sails Centre and Winder Sails by Toni Tio, Olimpic, foils by N1 and Cooke. Online store for next day delivery

Chichester/Ashford UK: 01233 812992 or 07710 130212
Dublin Ireland: 00 353 862 584493
email **sales@ibisailing.co.uk**   www.ibisailing.co.uk

The Dinghy & Smallcraft Review
2009~2010

53

Fireball

Type	Dinghy
Crew	2; 1 on trapeze
PN	982
Length	4.93 m
Beam	1.37 m
Weight	79.5 kg
Sail area M&J	11.43 sq m
Spi type	Symmetric
Spi area	13.01 sq m
Designer	Peter Milne
	www.fireball-dinghy.org.uk

Photo courtesy of Annie Porter

Designed by the late Peter Milne, the Fireball is a fast, easily-sailed two-man dinghy with one man on trapeze. There is a symmetric spinnaker that gives the boat excellent down-wind performance, and the manageable rig ensures that the boat can be sailed by men and women alike. The class has annual World, European, and National Championships, an excellent UK racing circuit and, with nearly 15,000 boats having been built, there is a ready supply of good used dinghies.

Fireball World Championships

La Rochelle, France   22 - 28 August 2009

Following the European Championships, which was a "tune-up" event for the Worlds, one hundred and one boats from ten countries competed for the World Fireball Championships hosted by La Rochelle. The first day provided a beautiful hot day with light breeze, and Chips Howarth and Vyv Townend moved through to the lead after the first lap which was a position that they held to the finish, to start the week strongly. On the final beat there was a certain amount of place changing with Matt Burge and Richard Wagstaffe moving into second, and Dave Wade and Ben McGrane in third.

The second day was cloudier, and sailed with a rising sea breeze. The second race was led by Matt Burge and Richard Wagstaffe until the last leg when a tacking duel with Howarth and Townend saw the lead change before the gun. Martin Lewis and Richard Bailey took third place. The home team of Ludovic Alleaume and Etienne Perdon took the second race of the day ahead of fellow Frenchmen Martin Peculier and Thomas La Seach, with Mike Senior and Andy Thompson in third and Howarth and Townend in fourth. The third race of the day saw something of a duel between Howarth and Alleaume, with Howarth and Townend taking the victory, and the overall lead ahead of the Frenchman in the overall standings. Alleaume and Perdon found the third day a lot tougher, and could manage just a twentieth and sixteenth against Howarth and Townend's second and third, to drop down to fourth in the overall standings. The British pairing, however, had now strung together a series of six results all in the top four, to lead overall after discard by twenty eight points. Second overall, after a third and fourteenth, were David Edwards and Simon Potts, with Matt Burge and Richard Wagstaffe having a good day with a first and fourth, lifting them back to third overall.

On Thursday, just one race was fitted in, and this started after four failed attempts, and eleven boats were black-flagged. With a breeze that peaked at nine knots, it was inevitably a tense race, and was led around the first mark by DJ Edwards and Simon Potts who held their position to the finish from Martin Peculier and Thomas La Seach, with Tom Gillard and Francis Rowan in third. Howarth and Townend started badly, but climber their way up to sixth in the course of the race, to maintain their hold on the championship. Edwards and Potts entered the final day in second position, with Matt Burge and Richard Wagstaffe in third place, with the possibility of up to three races still to complete

With three races still to sail and twenty knots of breeze, it was possible that the title could still be wrestled away from Howarth and Townend. However, a fourth and a fifth place in the first two races of the day left them in an unassailable position, and they did not bother to compete in the final race. Dave Wade and Ben McGrane took the first race, whilst Derian and Andy Scott won the second and UK Champions Matt Burge and Richard Wagstaffe took the final heat, which was enough to assure them of second place overall ahead of Dave Edwards and Simon Potts.

P	Nat	Helm	Crew	R1	R2	R3	R4	R5	R6	R7	R8	R9	R10	Nett	P Tot
1	GBR	C Howarth	V Townend	1	1	4	1	2	3	6	4	5	OCS	21	129
2	GBR	M Burge	R Wagstaff	2	2	41	28	1	4	17	6	7	1	40	109
3	GBR	D Edwards	S Potts	12	3	12	6	3	14	1	2	3	OCS	42	158
4	FRA	L Alleaume	E Perdon	4	18	1	2	20	16	18	7	22	8	74	116
5	GBR	V Horey	R Gardner	13	10	38	13	12	8	14	3	2	OCS	75	215
6	GBR	M Lewis	R Bailey	5	4	15	3	16	17	12	12	9	OCS	76	195
7	GBR	M Senior	A Thompson	15	29	3	7	21	DNF	9	9	17	3	84	215
8	IRL	T Gillard	F Rowan	16	22	27	23	7	1	3	5	DNF	11	88	217
9	GBR	A Smith	J Mildred	25	BFD	11	11	15	2	21	8	24	2	94	221
10	GBR	A Hemming	S Chesney	29	14	23	5	4	5	20	11	OCS	13	95	226

Photo courtesy of IFCA

2009 Fireball World Champions Chips Howarth and Vyv Townend

Fireball European Championships

Société des Régates Rochelaises, La Rochelle   15 - 21 August 2009

The Europeans were set as a warm-up event for the World Championships, and opened in warm and sunny conditions with a reasonable breeze. With two races scheduled for the first day, the fleet finally got underway with the aid of the black flag with Ludovic Alleaume and Etienne Perdon leading at the first mark. They were passed by Chips Howarth and Vyv Townend who took the gun, with Dave Wade and Ben McGrane coming in third. Howarth and Townend again looked to take the gun in the second race, only to find that they had been one of ten boats to receive the black flag treatment, handing the result to Vince Horey and Rob Gardner with Wade and McGrane again coming through in third.

On the second day Howarth and Townend again made the most of things to take victory ahead of Vince Horey and Rob Gardner, with Wade and McGrane in third position. In the next heat Howarth and Townend again looked to be the winners only to find that they had fallen foul of the black flag for the second time, leaving Martin Lewis and Richard Bailey as the winners, ahead of Verner and Winklerin second and Kubovy and Cap in third. Lighter conditions greeted the third day of the Europeans, with Race Five starting in six knots of breeze. Bart Meyendonckx and Francu De Roeck from Belgium led at the first mark, but it was Tom Gillard and Francis Rowan battled hard with Vince Horey and Rob Gardner took first and second position, with Howarth and Townsend pulling through to third on the final beat. Similar conditions in Race Six saw Kevin Hope and Russell Thorne lead from start to finish. Matt Findlay and Richard Anderton finished in second, ahead of Eva Skoreova and Viktor Tkadlec, with Horey and Gardner gaining fifth to hang onto the overnight lead.

Results on the final day were slightly 'unstable', with both wins being taken by Dave Wade and Ben McGrane, who finished the day lying in twenty first position overall! The Championship winners were Vince Horey and Rob Gardner, despite a third and a twenty seventh position in the final races, whilst the Czech team of Martin Kubovy and Martin Cap finished second overall, having added a fourteenth and a tenth to their tally. Tom Gillard and Francis Rowan from Ireland finished the meeting in third position whilst Martyn Lewis and Richard Bailey rounded off the pre-Worlds warm-up in fourth position.

P	Nat	Helm	Crew	R1	R2	R3	R4	R5	R6	R7	R8	Pts
1	GBR	Vincent Horey	Rob Gardner	14	1	2	BFD	2	5	27	3	54
2	CZE	Martin Kubovy	Martin Cap	6	8	5	3	31	11	14	10	57
3	IRL	Tom Gillard	Francis Rowan	9	7	14	5	1	6	28	25	67
4	GBR	Martyn Lewis	Richard Bailey	10	11	7	1	16	OCS	3	21	69
5	CZE	Jaroslav Verner	Pavel Winkler	37	10	12	2	5	17	16	16	78
6	GBR	Tim Rush	Sam Brearey	25	9	9	10	13	18	12	8	79

Fireball Nationals

Weymouth and Portland National Sailing Academy   23 - 29 May 2009

A top quality entry of sixty three Fireballs arrived at Weymouth to sample the Olympic facilities, and determine the results for their National Championships for 2009.

Having undergone a fairly rigorous measurement and registration schedule on the Saturday, Sunday dawned with a forecast of a pleasant eleven knot breeze. However, this did not materialize as a solid breeze and finally, after three hours of searching, the fleet returned to land to prepare for the strenuous social programme. Monday was much the same again, with no opportunity for racing, and the prospect of a reduced race programme looming large. The third day gave some relief with an adequate breeze, and the opportunity to fit four races into the score card. By the end of this day, the leaders were Tom Foskett and Tim Needham, having scored an impressive two firsts, a second and a third. With current Champions, Dave Wade and Ben McGrane in second position on level points, there was a five point gap to third overall, Andy Smith and Jonny Mildred.

With the fleet still playing catch-up on races, it was disappointing to see no racing yet again on Day Four, but four races were held on Day Five, with one team dominating racing; that of Matt Burge and Richard Wagstaff, who won each and every race on the day, lifting them into second overall behind Wade and McGrane with just one day to sail. This pair continued their stunning form for the final day, taking another first and second result and with it the title by two points from the consistent Wade and McGrane. David Edwards and Simon Potts finished in third place, with early leaders Matt Findlay and Richard Anderton in fourth position.

P	Helm	Crew	R1	R2	R3	R4	R5	R6	R7	R8	R9	R10	Tot	Pts
1	M Burge	R Wagstaff	4	6	9	14	1	1	1	1	2	1	40	17
2	D Wade	B McGrane	1	3	1	2	3	3	5	3	3	64	88	19
3	D Edwards	S Potts	5	4	3	4	2	4	3	2	1	64	92	23
4	M Findlay	R Anderton	2	7	5	6	9	8	2	20	7	4	70	41
5	A Smith	J Mildred	6	2	4	3	6	11	11	4	6	10	63	41
6	T Foskett	T Needham	3	1	2	1	7	10	23	19	18	17	101	59
7	M Lewis	R Byne	12	12	6	5	14	2	22	13	5	5	96	60
8	V Horey	J Hunt	14	5	8	10	10	12	6	6	11	14	96	68
9	T Jeffcoate	M Hogan	16	10	7	11	4	5	17	9	21	9	109	71
10	T Rush	R Thorne	9	13	12	15	5	6	18.	14	29	3	124	77
11	P Popple	G Tilson	8	8	10	8	13	23	7	17	8	15	117	77
12	R Kearney	D Hynes	7	14	14	9	12	13	19	29	10	7	134	86
13	B Priest	T Saunders	13	13	13	7	18	7	8	12	20	21	128	87
14	D Scott	A Scott	17	17	11	12	8	15	14	7	23	11	135	95
15	A Pearce	G Henwood-fox	15	16	1	17	20	16	15	21	9	2	147	106

Firefly

Type	Dinghy
Crew	2; Sit out
PN	1162
Length	3.66 m
Beam	1.42 m
Weight	74 kg
Sail area M&J	8.36 sq m
Spi type	None
Designer	Uffa Fox
	www.fireflysailing.co.uk

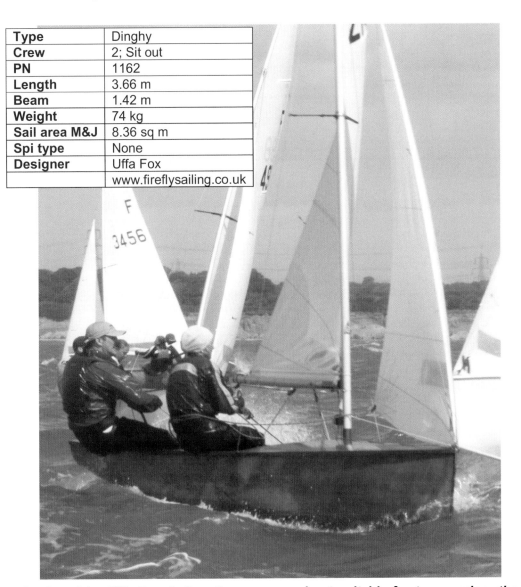

Designed by Uffa Fox, before the war, as a boat suitable for team racing, the Firefly did not go into production until after the war ended. The Firefly dinghy is still viewed as one of the very best team racing boats, and continues to be used for many of the most prestigious events. It was also used in the 1948 Olympic Games, hosted in the UK. The boat is suited to light-weight teams, and the class annually organizes an enjoyable, closely fought and very popular National Championships, together with a full open meeting programme.

Firefly National Championships

Hamble River Sailing Club   15 - 22 August 2009

Sixty three Firefly teams attended the sixty third National Firefly Championships, hosted at Hamble River SC on the edge of Southampton Water.

The first race (which was held over four laps of triangle and sausage, in a Force three to four breeze) was dominated by past champions Steve Tylecote and Sally Wilson who stretched a lead of up to half a leg for much of the race although the distances closed back in towards the end of the race as the chasing pack made progress. Their pursuers were led by five time champion Stuart and Jane Hudson who had pulled their way through from mid teens earlier in the race, and Ben and Jenny Vines who finished close behind in third.

As the fleet prepared for the second day, it appeared that they could expect light winds, but the breeze actually grew in time for the race. Tylecote and Wilson again made the most of the start and led most of the way around for a win ahead of Ben and with Barney Smith and Alannah Witherby battling away for the lead for much of the race, but retaining third place at the finish. The line start for Race Three caused the first general recall of the week. This race showed the first sign of fallibility for Tylecote and Wilson, who crossed the line in fifth position. This race was won by Stuart and Jane Hudson, with Rob and Mel Sherrington in second, and Dave Chisholm and Alice Gardner in third, ahead of the Vines.

The third day saw fickle breezes which were not reinforced by the promised sea breeze, and therefore the tide grew in importance. Steve Tylecote and Sally Wilson again made the most of conditions, adding another first place to their collection, and underlining their overall lead. Nigel Wakefield and Emily Saunderson took second spot, whilst Steve Greaves and Caroline Edwards made a big impression, picking up seven positions on the final beat by hitting the right hand side.

Wednesday's race for the Sir Ralph Gore Trophy saw perfect conditions with bright sunshine, and Tom Mallandine, sailing with Jamie Dick, rounded the windward mark in the lead, with Steve Tylecote and Sally Wilson in hot pursuit. Whilst the two battled for three hours, Tylecote could never quite get clear of Mallindine, and he had to be happy with second position, whilst Mallandine and Dick took the trophy, and the rest of the top ten all finished within three minutes of one another.

Having been in the driver's seat for much of the week, results were turned upside down on Thursday when Steve Tylecote packed up his boat and withdrew to fulfil a prior appointment as best man at a wedding. This left him short of a result as the Thursday sailing was cancelled due to thirty knot winds. This left the title wide open to anyone in the top ten.

In a tense final day, two races were completed and things were wide open. Stuart and Jane Hudson led until the final race but capsized, allowing Ben and Jenny Vines to take over first spot. Their capsize allowed Jamie and Jo McEwen into the lead, until they also fell in, leaving Rob and Mel Sherringham upright to take the win. This left Nigel Wakefield and Emily Saunderson as the new Champions, ahead of Steve Greaves and Caroline Edwards, with the Hudsons in third.

P	SN	Helm	Crew	R1	R2	R3	R4	R5	R6	R7	Pts
1	3674	Nigel Wakefield	Emily Saunderson	6	6	6	2	15	3	2	25
2	1867	Steve Greaves	Caroline Edwards	5	8	9	3	5	2	12	32
3	3850	Stuart Hudson	Jane Hudson	2	14	1	16	12	1	3	34
4	2649	Alex Davey	Jonquil Brookes	15	5	7	13	6	5	4	40
5	3119	Roger Morris	Amy Morris	7	26	14	9	3	6	5	44
6	3617	Rob Sherrington	Mel Sherrington	63	14	2	17	7	4	1	45
7	2144	Ben Vines	Jenny Vines	3	2	4	6	14	22	33	51
8	888	David Chisholm	Alice Gardner	4	16	3	23	25	9	8	63
9	498	Mark Tait	Penny Hooper	8	10	8	14	17	7	24	64
10	3924	Tom Mallindine	Jamie Dick	63	4	20	12	1	21	9	67
11	3037	Steve Tylecote	Sally Wilson	1	1	5	1	2	63	63	73
12	3023	Barney Smith	Alannah Witherby	63	3	25	8	24	10	6	76
13	3615	Jamie McEwen	Georgie Sutcliffe	19	12	19	7	16	8	14	76
14	3708	Lizzie Edwards	Ruth Verrier-Jones	17	13	13	4	19	15	15	77
15	2659	Ben Lumby	Liz Evans	20	9	18	5	4	27	23	79

Flying Dutchman

Type	Dinghy
Crew	2; one on trapeze
Length	6.07 m
Beam	1.78 m
Weight	130 kg
Sail area M&J	18.6 sq m
Spi type	Symmetric
Spi area	21 sq m
Designer	Conrad Gircher & Van Essen
	www.sailingsource.com /sailfd/GBR

Designed by van Essen, the Flying Dutchman is a classic beauty, offering excellent performance, and whilst its development has suffered from de-selection from the Olympic Games, the class still retains an enthusiastic following throughout the world. There is a well supported international race circuit, and an enthusiastic class association.

Flying Dutchman World Championships 2009

Royal Yacht Club, Holland   2 – 8 August 2009

Despite the fact that the International Flying Dutchman class celebrated its 2008 World Championships in Napier, New Zealand, in early January, the 2009 Worlds took place in Holland in August, commencing at Medemblik with ninety seven boats entered from eighteen countries. Initially racing was split into two sections for the qualifying races, and the week got off to a wet and variable start, with two races in each section completed on the first day.

The undoubted mastery of the fleet prior to this event had been shared between Szabolcs Majthény and András Domokos of Hungary (who started their defence of the title with an exemplary three first places and a second in their section), and ex Olympic Champions, Jorgen and Jacob Boysen-Möller of Denmark (leading the other group with three firsts and a ninth). Whilst the Hungarians had won the World Championships at the turn of the year in the absence of the Danes, the Boyson-Möllers had been victorious at the previous year's European Championships when the two had met.

As the week progressed, it again became evident that the regatta was to be a battle between these two; once again it was the Danes who came out on top. Winning five races during the week, in comparison with four for Majthény, the closeness of the racing went right through to the final day when Boysen-Möller's second place was just enough to take the title away from Majthény's fourth position, by just two points. Third position was taken by Dutchmen Bas and his brother Mark van der Pol who were only one point further back, before a small gap to fourth place and top German, Hans-Peter Schwarz.

The Silver Fleet was won by Christian von Mulert and Peter Mulhausree of Germany.

P	Nat	Helm / Crew	R1	R2	R3	R4	R5	R6	R7	R8	R9	Pts
1	DEN	Jorgen Boysen-Möller, Jacob Boysen-Möller	1	1	9	1	1	4	1	5	2	11
2	HUN	Szabolcs Majthény, András Domokos	1	1	1	2	1	3	6	8	4	13
3	NED	Bas van der Pol, Mark van der Pol	3	2	2	1	2	1	9	9	3	14
4	GER	Hans-Peter Schwarz, Roland Kirst	2	4	8	3	3	2	8	4	5	23
5	NED	Enno Kramer, Ard Geelkerken	4	4	1	5	2	1	23	17	29	34
6	GER	Jörn Borowski, Andreas Berlin	6	6	4	5	14	9	19	3	10	43
7	GER	Dirk Bogumil, Michael Lisken	16	13	12	6	9	3	13	1	1	45
8	ESP	Ginés Romero, Alvareo Moreno	3	3	OCS	12	3	2	18	26	7	48
9	ITA	Roberto Cipriani, Stefano Morelli	2	7	14	2	7	6	37	11	25	49
10	GER	Kunze Andreas, Seebauer Josef	6	2	5	13	5	10	10	30	DNF	51

Flying Dutchman National Championships

Royal Torbay Yacht Club   12 – 14 June 2009

The Flying Dutchman class joined the 505s for their National Championships held on the English Riviera in June, with the small and select band experiencing a variety of conditions during the three days of their event.

Early leaders were John Williams, crewed by Alex Rogers, defending the title that they won in 2008, but it was evident that sailmaker Toby Barsley-Dale, sailing with Gareth Russell, was hoping to influence the final destination of the title. In the first race on Day Two, Williams and Rogers sailed around at the front of the fleet, only to be greeted by silence as they had been over the line at the start, gifting the victory to Barsley-Dale, who took strength from this turn of events and proceeded to take the next win as well, as Williams and Rogers capsized the boat.

The final day opened with a certain tension at the head of the fleet. Williams could not afford any more disasters, whilst Barsley-Dale needed to make the most of any chances. By winning the first race on the final day, Barsley-Dale put himself in the driving seat, needing just a second place to take the title, whilst Williams was always going to be up against it in the last heat. He took the lead, with his opposition in second, but the distance back to third was too great, and there was nothing that Williams could do to bring the third boat into play. With all of his efforts to accomplish this, Williams actually lost the lead and the race to Barsley-Dale, who took a deserved title in this beautiful boat. Third position in the overall reckoning went to Pete Doran sailing with Richard Phillips.

P	Helm	Crew	R1	R2	R3	R4	R5	R6	R7	Pts
1	Toby Barsley-Dale	Gareth Russell	2	3	1	1	3	1	1	9
2	John Williams	Alex Rogers	1	1	8	4	2	2	2	12
3	Peter Doran	Richard Phillips	3	4	2	5	1	5	3	18
4	Rosie Pye	Neil Pye	4	2	5	6	8	3	4	24
5	Tony Lyall	Colin Burns	5	5	3	3	5	4	5	25
6	Julian Bridges	Peter Hadfield	6	6	4	2	4	7	6	28
7	Dawn Barsley-Dale	Jamie Whitaker	7	7	8	8	8	6	7	43

GP 14

Type	Dinghy	Weight	133 kg
Crew	2; Sit out	Sail area M&J	9.55 sq m
PN	1127	Spi type	Symmetric
Length	4.27 m	Spi area	38.36 sq m
Beam	1.54 m	Designer	Jack Holt
			www.GP14class.org.uk

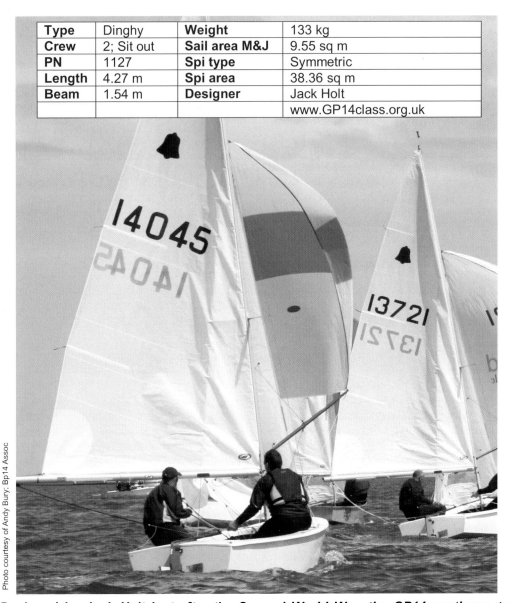

Designed by Jack Holt just after the Second World War, the GP14 continues to offer sailing across the board, from the experienced racer down to the beginner looking for a stable, easy-to-sail boat in which to practise. Raced at every level, from World Championship downwards, this two-man sit-out boat is best known as a competitive dinghy, but it has built up a large following amongst the training and cruising fraternity, as it is a stable and forgiving dinghy.

GP14 Nationals

Llandudno Sailing Club   3 - 5 July 2009

The first July weekend saw over 100 boats attend the 2009 GP14 National Championships at Llandudno with racing commencing on Friday and running through for three days.

The class were using courses incorporating a beat, run, triangle, and beat up to the finish in preference to their more traditional format. The first points race initially saw a close battle between the reigning GP14 World Champions, Ian Dobson and Andy Tunnicliffe, with Team GBR 470 sailor (and Fireball whiz) Matt Mee, crewed by Chris Robinson, helping to set the early pace. Matt Mee took the winning gun, with Dobson in hot pursuit, whilst third position went to Simon Potts and Drew Nickless.

The second race started promptly with a reducing breeze, but there was still sufficient for the class heavy-weather experts, Carl Jeffs and Jim Toothill, to do battle with Mee and Robinson who were again in position to score good points. Mee and Robinson hung on to take the race victory, with Jeffs and Toothill in second position, and a former World and National Class Champion Ian Southworth sailing with Dave Hayes returning to the fleet and gaining a third.

Saturday morning saw competitors launch in a weakening breeze, and racing had to be postponed. Eventually wind settled in and a course was quickly laid. Leaving the gate early was preferable, as these boats were swept up to the mark, whilst later starters were proven to have over-stood. Mee and Robinson, following by Southworth and Hayes, Justin Jones and Lucy Evans, and Potts and Nickless were the boats to make the most of this to finish in that order, just before the breeze switched off for the day, causing various anomalies amongst the remaining finishers. For the rest of the day the wind proved too unreliable to get another race underway, and the fleet eventually returned home to enjoy the social programme in readiness for the final day.

An earlier start was made and the plan for three races on the final day was the schedule required to complete the event. In the first race Dobson and Tunnicliffe did their best to get back on track with a first place whilst Mee and Robinson earned a penalty at the penultimate mark, which dropped them from second position to fourth, with Southworth and Hayes in second and Potts and Nickles in third.

With the second race of the day completed in a Force five, neither side of the beat was particularly favoured, and the leaders emerged as Mee and Robinson once again, with Dobson and Tunnicliffe second.

A number of competitors struggled to make the start of Race Five, apparently pushed back by the tide. The leaders converged on the windward mark from both the left and right hand side of the beat, with Mee and Robinson and Dobson and Tunnicliffe up in the vanguard. Realising the need to keep their chances of championship success alive, Dobson and Tunnicliffe attempted to sail Mee and Robinson outside the top positions. Whilst this course of action gave Tim Jones and Christian Birrell the race win, Mee and Robinson's second position was still enough to secure the 2009 UK National Champion crown and an early shower.

It looked as though no more racing would take place as the gradient wind seemed to be failing against an attempted sea breeze. However, Race Six finally got underway. Dobson and Tunnicliffe sailed into an early lead and took the bullet, in spite of the huge shifts in wind direction that caused much place changing behind. As beats became reaches and reaches became beats sailors did their best to hold on to positions. Mike Senior and Luke Shaw moved from second to third ahead of Dave and Jackie Gebard on the second beat (or was it a reach) and managed to hold that position on the final beat. This result ensured that Dobson and Tunnicliffe had secured second overall in the Championship, a great recovery after a disappointing first two days by their standards, ahead of Southworth and Hayes, whose impressive return saw them finish in third.

P	Helm	Crew	R1	R2	R3	R4	R5	R6	Pts	Nett
1	Matt Mee	Chris Robinson	1	1	1	4	2	DNS	63	9
2	Ian Dobson	Andy Tunnicliffe	2	5	7	1	3	1	19	12
3	Ian Southworth	Dave Hayes	7	3	2	2	9	4	27	18
4	Simon Potts	Drew Nickless	3	4	4	3	8	15	37	22
5	Tim Jones	Christian Birrell	6	6	6.	15	1	6	40	25
6	Mike Senior	Luke Shaw	5	7	17	5	6	2	42	25
7	Carl Jeffs	Jim Toothill	4	2	5	16	13	7	47	31
8	Justin Jones	Lucy Evans	17	12	3	8	5	5	50	33
9	Dave Gebhard	Jackie Gebhard	9	14	8	DSQ	4	3	92	38
10	Adam Parry	Owain Hughes	11	9	39	11	11	11	92	53
11	Neil Davies	Hannah Davies	13	21	37	7	7	12	97	60
12	Bill Kenyon	Ben Ditchburn	8	15	36	10	17	10	96	60
13	Josh Gebhard	Kieran Parslow	15	17	22	9	10	13	86	64
14	Chris Jones	Robert Temple	12	11	10	14	33	19	99	66
15	Paul Owen	Chris Warburton	18	13	26	6	15	24	102	76

Graduate

Type	Dinghy
Crew	2; Sit out
PN	1165
Length	3.82 m
Beam	1.42 m
Weight	84 kgs
Sail area M&J	11 sq m
Designer	Dick Wyche, 1952
	www.graduatedinghy.com

Photo courtesy of Graduate Assoc

The Graduate dinghy suits people of all ages in any combination – mother and daughter, father and son, married couples, grandparents; this is a boat for all seasons and for everyone to enjoy. Renowned for its safe handling, many clubs are again looking at the Graduate for use in their youth training programmes, whilst used boats offer an economic introduction for racing and cruising alike.

News: 2008 has been a successful year of development for the Graduate class; the new mainsail which was introduced at the end of 2007 has much improved both the handling of the boat and its performance. A shortage of good used boats has encouraged a new builder to develop an all epoxy FRP boat which was launched in the course of 2009 to much acclaim, with the assistance of Rooster Sailing, who are working on the promotion and marketing side. The boats are available in various forms as composite, or all wooden construction.

Graduate National Championships

Chipstead Sailing Club   23 - 25 May 2009

A fleet of thirty two Graduates contested the 2009 National Championships, hosted by Chipstead SC. With the event scheduled over three days, the very light breezes of Day One ensured that racing got off to a tense start, but it was the new model Graduate, sailed by Stephen Cockerill and Liam Gardner, which took the first win and led overnight at the end of the day.

The second day of racing also saw a light, shifty breeze, but the race officer managed to get three good races in before the end of the day, with Cockerill and Gardner earning two more race wins and a second. They were not having things entirely their own way, though, as John and Jamie Clementson from the host club earned two second place results to stay in the running, with Island Barn's Graham Hughes and daughters Bradley and Sophie closing the penultimate day in third position overall.

The promise of more wind for the final day was not convincing, but in the end there was sufficient to allow two good races, and a satisfactory end to the event. With two more race wins, Steve Cockerill and Liam Gardner took the title with a race to spare, giving the new version of the Graduate a healthy and successful test! John and Jamie Clementson held onto second overall with a second position and a sixth, whilst Graham and Bradley Hughes finished in third place overall; never having been outside of the top five in any race.

P	SN	Helm & Crew	Club	R1	R2	R3	R4	R5	R6	Pts
1	3000	S Cockerill & L Gardner	SBSC	1	1	2	1	1	1	5
2	2873	J & J Clementson	CSC	5	2	1	2	2	6	12
3	2771	G & B Hughes	IBSC	2	3	4	5	3	5	17
4	2839	A Warren & L Dobson	CSC	4	5	10	3	6	4	22
5	2974	D Wilson & S Wilson	BSC	6	8	5	4	7	14	30
6	2926	D Sword & I Sword	LTSC	8	33	6	10	5	2	31
7	2962	R Cherrill & S Jane Critchley	CSC	3	4	7	9	8	15	31
8	2880	S Eaton & C Pritchard	WOSC	11	7	3	6	15	8	35
9	2878	D Ivens & L Johnson	BSC	10	6	9	8	9	9	41
10	2799	L & R Gibbons/H Forward	CSC	12	10	8	7	20	10	47

Gull

Type	Dinghy
Crew	2; Sit out
Length	3.35 m
Beam	1.44 m
Weight	88 kg
Sail area M&J	6.5 sq m
Spi type	Symmetric
Spi area	5.57 sq m
Designer	Ian Proctor
	www.gulldinghy.org.uk

Since its original design by Ian Proctor over 50 years ago, the Gull has evolved into the current-day version, the GRP Gull Calypso. This retains the chined hull form of the original wooden boats, but with a practical, low-maintenance deck moulding that maximises the space in this little dinghy. The Gull is perfect for novices, and can readily be sailed single-handed, with one crew, or even three-up on occasion.

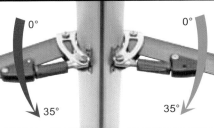

The Dinghy & Smallcraft Review
2009~2010

Heron

Type	Dinghy
Crew	1 or 2; Sit out
PN	1363 (1343 s-handed)
Length	3.43 m
Beam	1.37 m
Weight	63.7 kg
Sail area M&J	6.5 sq m
Spi type	Symmetric
Spi area	6.36 sq m
Designer	Jack Holt, 1949
	www.herondinghy.org.uk

The Heron is a stable boat with a traditional wood frame and ply skin; it is also made with a frameless ply epoxy, GRP or FRP hull, or a composite GRP hull and wooden deck. The Heron may have a Gunter or Bermudan rig, and spars may be of wood or aluminium. The cockpit layout may vary within the rules, and fittings are a matter of owner's choice. The Heron may be sailed with a jib, full genoa, or mini genoa (79% of full genoa). The class is quite active with three Championship Opens, Nationals, Southerns, Northerns, and five other Opens, including one in Kinvara, Ireland.

Hornet

Type	Dinghy	Weight	126 kg
Crew	2; 1 on trapeze	Sail Area M&J	15.42 sq m
PN	973	Spi Type	Symmetric
Length	4.88 m	Spi Area	12.3 sq m
Beam	1.4 m	Designer	Jack Holt
			www.hornet.org.uk

The hull and rig of the Hornet is a one-design, but the cockpit and internal layout is unrestricted, which gives room for owners to develop their own ideas. There is also a degree of flexibility in sail design. The Hornet is a class performance boat, offering excellent racing up to international level, but at a reasonable cost!

Hornet National Championships

Herne Bay Sailing Club   5 - 6 September 2009

A change of venue at short notice caused a slightly reduced attendance, but a fleet of sixteen boats attended the Championships at Herne Bay, and they enjoyed good racing and reasonable winds.

Saturday's racing benefited from fifteen knot breezes, and a nice chop. Peter Bennett and John Shelton from Shoreham came through a tight battle to take the win, and to establish their intent for the weekend. In fact they obviously found the conditions to their liking as by the end of the day they had established a line of first places on the scorecard, and were to continue that trend on Sunday until the title was won. Then, in the sixth race, with the pressure off, Bennett and Shelton could only manage second!

Runners-up in the overall rankings were Dave Edge and Martin Arnison from Weston. They had the same (but more frustrating) line of consistent results in the first five races, with five second places, and a blip in the final heat. However, whilst these leading scores make it look as though every race had a foregone conclusion, in reality there were always four or five boats interchanging positions and battling; but the same boats managed to scrape through at the end each time!

This Championships marked the twenty fifth anniversary of the first time that Peter Bennett won the title, which says something about the longevity of both Bennett and the Hornet!

P	Helm	Crew	Club	R1	R2	R3	R4	R5	R6	Pts
1	Peter Bennett	John Shelton	SSC	1	1	1	1	1	2	5
2	Dave Edge	Martin Arnison	WSC	2	2	2	2	2	6	10
3	Mark Styles	Clint Styles	DSC	3	9	5	6	3	3	20
4	Eric Styles	Alex Church	DSC	5	7	8	5	4	1	22
5	Harry Ashworth	Ruth Walker	BSC	4	6	3	4	5	DNF	22
6	Dean Saxton	Rob Smith	MSC	7	3	6	3	7	5	24
7	Steve Cooke	Alistair Hardy	SSC	6	5	7	8	6	4	28
8	Kevin Burt	Barry Miller	NSC	8	4	4	7	8	7	30
9	Chris Brealy	Gary Danielwicz	HBSC	9	8	DNF	9	9	8	43
10	Graham Dare	Anne Stinton	TBSC	10	10	13	14	10	9	52

International 14

Type	Dinghy	Sail area M&J	18.58 sq m
Crew	2; On trapeze	Spi type	Asymmetric
Length	4.27 m	Spi area	Unlimited
Beam	1.82 m	Designer	Various
Weight	74.25 kg		www.international14.org

Photo courtesy of Annie Porter

The International 14 is a high-performance class, suited to the fittest and most competent sailors. The class has fleets throughout Europe and the USA, and also a very strong following in the southern hemisphere, with competition up to World Championship level. The International 14 is a restricted class, giving some freedom of design, and this has ensured that the boat has continued to develop. The national fleets throughout the world meet for regular World Championships.

International 14 European Championships

Scheveningen, Netherlands   29 May - 1 June 2009

The International 14s held their European Championship off Scheveningen in the Netherlands over a long weekend at the end of May. A total entry of some twenty six boats competed in the event, held principally in lightish winds, and there was little that anyone could do to defeat the pairing of Alister Richardson and Daniel Johnson, who led from the first race, right through the regatta, and had no need to compete in the final race with a set of six wins, two second places and a sixth.

Five points adrift in second was Douglas Pattison, sailing with Mark Tait, who never dropped outside the top four places for the entire event, enabling them to take second overall ahead of Tom Heywood and Ed Clay, with the first non-GB entrants Oliver Voss, sailing with Kens Holscher, finishing in fourth position.

P	SN	Name	1	2	3	4	5	6	7	8	9	10	Pts
1	GBR 1537	A Richardson D Johnson	1	2	1	1	2	1	1	6	1	DNS	16
2	GBR 1500	D Pattison M Tait	2	4	2	3	3	4	2	1	3	1	21
3	GBR 1484	T Heywood E Clay	4	1	4	4	1	2	3	7	6	3	28
4	GER 91	O Voss J Holscher	8	3	3	2	4	3	4	DNS	13	8	48
5	GBR 1536	J Simpson G Rollerson	3	6	6	6	11	11	8	14	2	4	57
6	GBR 1534	C Turner A Ovington	11	5	5	11	12	5	6	DNS	4	2	61
7	GBR 1496	R Pascal M Pascal	7	7	10	9	6	8	14	4	5	6	62
8	GER 28	G Borkenstein E Dietrich	6	11	7	12	8	12	10	8	7	7	76
9	GER 100	S Ritsche D Entzminger	5	DNS	11	5	5	16	9	10	10	10	81
10	GBR 1520	K Nurton D Ash	9	16	9	DNS	DNS	6	7	3	9	5	91

International 14 POW Week

Restronguet Sailing Club   6 - 11 September 2009

Forty International 14s competed in the Prince of Wales Cup Week, held in Cornwall in early September. The week is broken down into two phases with the single race Prince of Wales Cup for the National Championships, and the Points Week for the overall week's racing. The conditions was good throughout the week, although a touch light at times, but it enabled everyone to experience the best in 14 sailing, with both events being taken by multi-Champion Roger Gilbert, crewed by ex RS 800 National Champion, Ben McGrane, both relative newcomers to the class.

POW CUP

Held on the Wednesday in sunny conditions with a northerly twelve to fifteen knot breeze, the race was led at the first mark by Rob Greenhalgh and Simon Marks, and they began to extend their lead to two minutes. On the fifth beat, Roger Gilbert and Ben McGrane made the most of the shifts to pull through and close right up to Greenhalgh and Marks, with Tom Heywood and Ed Clay also closing in to make a three way race, which Gilbert and McGrane finally won, to take the POW Cup, and the national title.

P	Helm	Crew	Design	Year
1	Roger Gilbert	Ben McGrane	Ovington/Morrison	2009
2	Tom Heywood	Ed Clay	Bieker 4	2003
3	Robert Greenhalgh	Simon Marks	Bieker 5	2007
4	Mark Upton-Brown	Phil Kennard	RMW/Morrison	2006
5	Andy Partington	Tom Partington	Ovington/Morrison	2009
6	Douglas Pattison	Mark Tait	RMW/Morrison	2004

POW WEEK

With a wide variety of conditions throughout the rest of the POW week, Gilbert and McGrane continued to excel. Having won the first race, they had a disappointing seventh on Day Two, but were unchallenged thereafter, finishing their campaign with a second and two wins, not needing to compete in the final race to take the week's victory. Second overall was Ed Clay, sailing with Tom Heywood in a six-year-old boat. Third place overall went to Alistair Richard and Dan Johnson, the previous year's POW Cup winners. They finished the week level on points with Andy and Tom Partington, who were the previous year's Points Week winners, and just one point behind Clay and Heywood.

P	SN	Helm	Crew	R1	R2	R3	R4	R5	R7	R8	Total	Nett
1	1541	Roger Gilbert	Ben McGrane	1	7	3	2	1	1	DNF	51	15
2	1484	Ed Clay	Tom Heywood	3	4	2	7	2	5	4	27	20
3	1537	Alistair Richardson	Dan Johnson	5	6	1	3	5	8	1	29	21
4	1540	Andy Partington	Tom Partington	4	2	5	4	4	4	3	26	21
5	1500	Douglas Pattison	Mark Tait	6	3	4	8	6	7	6	40	32
6	1526	Mark Upton-Brown	Phil Kennard	2	8	9	5	3	6	DNF	69	33
7	1538	Martin Jones	Neale Jones	DNF	15	6	6	RAF	2	2	103	67
8	1495	Charles Duchesne	Will Broom	DNC	14	17	13	10	14	5	110	73
9	1539	Paul Ravenhill	Doug Walker	7	20	15	15	13	13	DNF	119	83
10	1529	Andy FitzGerald	Harvey Hillary	DNC	5	10	11	11	11	DNF	121	84

2009 POW Cup and Points winners Roger Gilbert and Ben McGrane

The Dinghy & Smallcraft Review
2009~2010

ISO

Type	Dinghy
Crew	2; 1 on trapeze
PN	926
Length	4.74 m
Beam	1.75m - 2.15 m
Weight	95 kg
Sail area M&J	16.5 sq m
Spi type	Asymmetric
Spi area	21 sq m
Designer	I Howlett & J Caig, 1992
	www.isoracing.org.uk

The ISO is a fast, two person asymmetric boat with a single trapeze, suitable for light and heavy crew, and for less-experienced racers at club level. The class has a very enthusiastic racing circuit in the UK and abroad, supported by an award winning website with a huge amount of information. The ISO is becoming more established in Europe, following a series of annual European Championships, and also offers National and Inland Championships in the UK. Financially the boat is extremely good value in comparison with other classes, and there is an active second-hand market.

ISO National Championships

Lee-on-the-Solent Sailing Club   5 - 6 September 2009

Thirteen ISO dinghies joined the Buzz fleet to share their National Championships at Lee-on-the-Solent SC in early September, and enjoyed a weekend with good breezes and fine conditions.

The event was largely dominated by two boats from local club Emsworth Slipper. Andy and Vicky Gould took the Championship title with a combination of first and second places, with a final race fourth to discard. Gould had last won the title in 2001 and had since been runner-up on a number of occasions, but had been absent for the previous year's Championships. He was in close contention with Mike Lillywhite and Mark Riddington who had also had a combination of firsts and seconds, but were also counting a third, and discarding a seventh. Going into the final race, Lillywhite was still in a position to win the Championships, but to do so he really had to win the race. In the event he was not able to do better than gain a third ahead of Gould, but two points away from the title!

Third position overall was taken by George Chambers and Jonny Wells from Essex Yacht Club, who won the final race, and added that result to a string of third place finishes to end up four points in arrears of Lillywhite and Riddington, but seven points clear of Dave Poupard and Rachael Hughes from Calshot .

P	Helm	Crew	Club	R1	R2	R3	R4	R5	R6	Pts
1	Andrew Gould	Vicky Gould	ESSC	1	1	2	1	2	4	7
2	Mike Lillywhite	Mark Riddington	ESSC	2	7	1	2	1	3	9
3	George Chambers	Jonny Wells	EYC	3	3	3	4	3	1	13
4	Dave Poupard	Rachael Hughes	CSC	4	4	4	3	7	5	20
5	Marco Moniardini	Pete Lindley	CVST	5	9	DNF	6	4	2	26
6	Mick Pullin	Mark Pullin	HSC	6	2	5	10	8	11	31
7	Bob Ladell	Gary Hill	KGSC	DNF	6	6	5	11	6	34
8	Colin Snook	Alison Rewitt	CSC	7	5	8	7	9	8	35
9	Lyndon Gommersall	Gareth Sellors	BGSC	DNF	8	7	8	6	7	36
10	Ian Moss	Will Everitt	WSC	8	DNF	DNF	9	5	9	45

High Performance Sailing
www.isoracing.org.uk

Javelin

Type	Dinghy	Weight	118 kg
Crew	2; 1 on trapeze	Sail area M&J	15.79 sq m
PN	926	Spi type	Symmetric
Length	5.36 m	Spi area	15.79 sq m
Beam	1.68 m	Designer	Peter Milne
			www.javelinuk.com

Designed by the late Peter Milne, the Javelin is a two-man, single trapeze performance boat. The Javelin is a boat that is only available to be built in GRP. Offering high performance, but on a fairly forgiving platform, the Javelin can be sailed by the young and not-so-young equally successfully. In addition to the being sailed in the UK, the boat is also popular in a number of areas of Europe, and the association holds a regular National and European Championships.

Javelin European Championships

Southwold Sailing Club   19 - 24 July 2009

Twenty one Javelins contested the 2009 European Championships, including a number from Germany and Holland.

The week began with a Force four to five breeze, dropping off at times, whilst Day Two was a bit lighter, but shifty! Sailing on Day Three was lost through too much wind, and the forecast looked as though strong winds would be the order of the day for the entire week, but it was still an excellent event.

2009 European Champions are Richard and Kathryn Smith, sailing *Solidsilver*. They were the National Champions last year, while the Europeans were taken by Brian and David Earl (who were second this year). In a nine race series, the Smiths only took two race victories but, after discards were brought into play, their counting results were all in the top three, which is pretty impressive.

The Earls, stalwarts of the class for so many years, were no less impressive; also taking two of the race wins, the rest of their results, including discards, were in the top five, and in the end they were only pipped to the title by two points, having a gross points score exactly the same as the Smiths.

Third and fourth overall were both taken by German competitors, Thomas Broeker and Volkmar Prehn, taking third place (and two race victories) whilst Jens and Jan Schlittenhard finished in fourth, with two race wins, ensuring that the trophies were spread as widely as possible!

P	Helm	Crew	Nat	R1	R2	R3	R4	R5	R6	R7	R8	R9	Pts	Nett
1	R Smith	K Smith	GBR	2	2	1	4	2	1	3	3	7	25	14
2	B Earl	D Earl	GBR	1	3	4	2	1	4	2	5	3	25	16
3	T Broeker	V Prehn	GER	3	13	5	1	AVE	2	7	1	4	40.5	20.5
4	K Schlittenhard	J Schlittenhard	GER	1	1	2	3	7	9	DNF	2	1	69	25
5	Malte Riesner	J Meachen	GBR	7	4	6	6	10	6	6	11	5	61	40
6	P Borck	H Haake	GER	9	6	9	13	11	14	1	4	2	69	42
7	G Johnson	R Johnson	GBR	10	7	14	7	8	3	4	9	8	70	46
8	B Fisher	R Fisher	GBR	8	5	7	14	6	10	8	8	6	72	48
9	T Greenaway	O Boyes	GBR	6	9	16	5	3	7	9	DNF	DNS	99	55
10	A De Jong	M vanden Heuvel	NED	5	8	11	16	5	11	13	6	9	84	55

Javelin National Championships

Glossop and District Sailing Club   28 - 31 August 2009

The Javelin National Championships were hosted by Glossop and District SC over the August bank holiday. With a mixture of strong winds for the Saturday and more shifty and gusty winds on the Sunday, the event provided a good test, and competition at the front of the fleet was largely between the usual suspects!

On the Saturday, Brian and David Earl managed to lead around the front mark, but as the race progressed they were passed by the European Champions, Richard and Kathryn Smith, and this was pretty much the same pattern for the second Saturday race with the Smiths once again taking first place, having slipped past the Earls on a gybe.

Sunday's first race saw the Earls in better shape, leading initially and this time sailing off to win the race. The second race of the day saw the Smiths in control, and taking a comfortable win, leading to Sunday's last race in which the Earls knew that they needed to beat the Smiths to have a chance at the title on the last day. With the wind having eased slightly the Earls led from the start with the Smiths in close pursuit, and on the final lap the Smiths managed to get into the lead to win, with the Earls dropping to third behind Andy Downie and Jane Partington. This virtually confirmed the Smiths as National Champions; a position that was underlined as Monday dawned with extreme conditions, and no possibility of further racing.

P	SN	Helm	Crew	R1	R2	R3	R4	R5	R6	R7	Pts
1	568	Richard Smith	Kathryn Smith	1	1	2	1	1	1	1	5
2	558	Brian Earl	David Earl	2	2	1	2	3	2	DNS	9
3	566	Ben Fisher	Richard Fisher	3	3	4	3	4	3	2	14
4	543	Andy Downie	Jane Partington	7	6	3	4	2	5	3	17
5	565	Gavin Johnson	Rosie Johnson	4	4	5	11	7	4	4	21
6	546	Roger Partington	Steven Tinsley	5	5	7	8	5	7	5	27

Kestrel

Type	Dinghy
Crew	2; Sit out
PN	1041
Length	4.75 m
Beam	1.70 m
Weight	120kg
Sail area M&J	12.69 sq m
Spi type	Symmetric
Spi area	11.1 sq m
Designer	Ian Proctor
	www.kestrel.org.uk

The Kestrel has the distinction of being the first sailing boat to be built in this country entirely of glass-reinforced plastics. The first Kestrel was exhibited at the Boat Show in January 1956. She is a very powerful boat, with excellent upwind performance. The boat is enthusiastically raced and cruised throughout the UK and overseas. A modernized internal layout in the 1990s gave the class a new lease of life and the boat now boasts good turnouts for championships.

Kestrel National Championships

Filey Sailing Club, Yorkshire   1 - 4 August 2009

Eighteen Kestrels competed in the 2009 National Championships at Filey Sailing Club in a breezy championships, held over seven races. In a competitive Championships, the club did everything that they could to ensure the competitors enjoyed their stay, with excellent race management, and enjoyable socials. The Kestrels have already pencilled themselves back in to visit again in 2012!

On the water, the sailing was dominated by past champion Dusty Miller, sailing with John Ellingham. With six wins out of seven races, and discarding a third position, his performance was pretty dominant, and the title was richly deserved. The battle for second and third was a bit more intense. Stewart and Dave Murdoch started the weekend with a second, first and second set of results to put themselves clear of Paul and James Jarvey, but the Jarvey's then spend the rest of the week whittling away at the Murdochs' points score, finishing just two points in arrears at the end of the event.

David Hearsom and Gareth Fay won the battle for fourth position overall, with Liam Pike and Al Luxford in fifth spot, just one point further back.

P	Helm	Crew	R1	R2	R3	R4	R5	R6	R7	Tot	Nett
1	Dusty Miller	John Ellingham	1	3	1	1	1	1	1	9	6
2	Stewart Murdoch	Dave Murdoch	2	1	2	4	3	2	4	18	14
3	Paul Jarvey	James Jarvey	3	2	3	5	2	3	3	21	16
4	David Hearsom	Gareth Fay	5	4	5	3	5	4	2	28	23
5	Liam Pike	Al Luxford	4	5	4	2	4	5	6	30	24
6	Malcolm Worsley	Dannielle Worsley	10	8	7	7	12	6	5	55	43
7	Ian Hunter	Trevor MacDonald	7	7	10	6	8	9	10	57	47
8	Duncan Wilson	Callum Wilson	9	9	8	9	7	17	8	67	50
9	Alasdair Hood	Campbell Morrison	13	6	12	12	6	8	9	66	53
10	Steven Worf	Lin Worf	11	10	18	8	10	7	7	71	53

Lark

Type	Dinghy	Weight	95 kg
Crew	2; Sit-out	Sail area M&J	9.75 sq m
PN	1073	Spi type	Symmetric
Length	4.07 m	Spi area	7.4 sq m
Beam	1.65 m	Designer	Michael Jackson
			www.larkclass.org

Photo courtesy of Speed Sails

Although a one-design class, the Lark class rules cater for a choice of many fittings, including foils and sails. The design of the Lark is suited to a wide range of crew weights, typically from 18 stone up to 25 stone, and with 2,500-odd boats produced, the class continues to grow throughout the UK, and is raced widely both at sea and on inland waters. The Lark class is famous for its social events, in particular the National Championships social programme and the Laying Down supper held annually at the Winter Championships – an event not to be missed!

Lark National Championships

Brixham Yacht Club   25 - 31 July 2009

Shifting, gusty breezes and gloomy looking weather were the order of the day as fifty five crews started their National Championships, hosted by Brixham Yacht Club. Gate starts, and trapezoid courses were scheduled for the first day's racing and, with a windy week forecast, it was concluded that the racing would be largely between the two heavy weather experts in the class, Alan Krailing and Ed McArdle, and Steve Hall and Simon Haighton. The first race underlined this, with Hall and Haighton sailing into a large lead, whilst Krailing and McArdle pulled up to a sound second after a poor start.

By the start of the second race, Krailing and McArdle got the better of the first leg and led at the windward mark ahead of Team Videlo, Fish and Condie, with Hall and Haighton in hot pursuit, sailing into second after adept spinnaker work on the line.

The second day of the event saw the full range of weather conditions, including sun and hail! However, the two front-runners from Day One of the meeting continued to be the main protagonists. By the end of the day, Alan Krailing and Ed McArdle had four points, discarding a ninth place, whilst Steve Hall and Simon Haighton were three points behind, discarding an eighth. Third overall were Chris Fish and Beth Condie with twelve points, two points clear of Harry Pynn and Helen Krailing in fourth.

Day Three saw just one Championship Race, and this time it was Hall and Haighton who were destined to take the win, with Krailing and McArdle in second and Emma Harris and Becky Priest in third. This consistency continued to open the gap in the overall scores from these two boats back to the pack, with two points separating the two at this stage.

Day Four was one of disappointment, with a squall that blew through in the morning, followed by heavy rain and light breeze with a huge wind-shift. In the end the racing was abandoned for the day as the fleet sailed for the windward mark with spinnakers flying!

With better conditions, the Race Committee managed to get the racing back on schedule on Thursday, despite the wind being reluctant to play ball. The force three to four was swinging all over, but the tricky conditions didn't get the better of Hall and Haighton who managed to take the first race win on the day ahead of Emma Harris and Becky Priest and Chris Fish and Beth Condie. With increased breeze in Race Six, Fish and Condie sailed into a healthy lead which they held to the finish. Behind, the struggle was on for second position, with Krailing and McArdle improving to take the position, and Matt White and Harriet Steer in a good third place and right on the pace.

In the third race of the day (Race Seven) a huge shift turned the fleet around. This left the Videlos with a lead that was never challenged, with Simon and Sara Cox in second, and Smashie Bennet and Nicola Booth in third. This left the main protagonists, Krailing and McArdle and Hall and Haighton, battling around tenth spot. Krailing and McArdle managed to improve their position to fifth, but Hall and Haighton's ninth looked to be a discard, and with only one race to go, the gap between the first two was just 1.75pts.

Chris Fish and Beth Condie chose the shifts well and rounded first, with Emma Harris and Becky Priest picking up on the better breeze on the right to round in second. Behind, Krailing and McArdle rounded with a slight advantage. They then managed to creep into second and pip Emma and Becky on the line behind Fish and Condie. Try as they might, Hall and Haighton could get no higher than fourth, taking the runner's up position for the week and leaving **Krailing and McArdle** to regain the title, last won by them in 2006.

Whilst Fish and Condie actually had no need to go sailing on the final day (as nothing could shift them from their third overall) the race for fourth overall was interesting with Harris and Priest having to beat Pynn and Krailing over the line and beat the Videlos by seven places. Both of these, they managed!

P	Helm	Crew	R1	R2	R3	R4	R5	R6	R7	R8	R9	Total	Nett
1	A Krailing	E McArdle	2	1	1	9	2	2	5	7	2	30.50	14.50
2	S Hall	S Haighton	1	2	4	8	1	6	9	1	4	35.25	18.25
3	C Fish	B Condie	4	3	6	5	11	1	6	3	1	39.50	22.50
4	E Harris	B Priest	8	5	7	10	3	7	12	2	3	57	35
5	S Videlo	C Videlo	6	4	34	6	5	52	1	6	9	122.75	36.75
6	H Pynn	H Krailing	9	8	3	3	7	5	17	5	7	64	38
7	R Bennett	N Booth	12	6	2	22	4	23	3	13	8	93	48
8	S Cumley	N Cumley	3	10	8	7	10	13	24	8	11	94	57
9	S Hydon	I Videlo / H Showell	16	7	12	1	8	20	20	11	10	104.75	64.75
10	H Hewat	R Johnson	7	9	13	4	12	9	25	23	14	116	68

Laser 2000

Type	Dinghy	Weight	100 kg
Crew	2; Sit out	Sail area M&J	11.78 sq m
PN	1089	Spi type	Asymmetric
Length	4.44 m	Spi area	9.86 sq m
Beam	1.85 m	Designer	Phil Morrison
			www.laser2000.org.uk

Photo courtesy of Will Tremlett www.h2ophotos.org.uk

The Laser 2000 offers excellent performance for the experienced sailor, but is also a boat suitable for the less-experienced. It is popular as a training boat with sailing schools, holiday companies and the armed forces, and also as a day-sailing and racing dinghy. The Laser 2000's versatility ensures that the boat continues to grow as one of the most popular of the modern dinghy classes. The strength of the class and its association is such that boats attract premium second-hand values, and the well supported racing circuit visits clubs throughout the UK, with the 2009 Nationals being hosted at Hayling Island.

Laser 2000 National Championships

Hayling Island Sailing Club   27 – 31 July 2009

Eighty three Laser 2000s celebrated their tenth anniversary National Championships. With winds generally in the fifteen to twenty knot range, and sometimes venturing above that, the fleet found Day One to be a somewhat testing affair, and with equally strong breezes for the second day, the decision was made to hold racing inside Chichester Harbour, with three additional races completed.

On Day One Matt and Clare Sergeant gained the first race victory ahead of Dave and Scott Adams from Broadstairs SC with Rob and Katie Burridge from Weir Wood SC. However, by the time the racing recommenced the change in conditions obviously suited Jon Holroyd and Jane Rusbatch better, as they added a second, third and first to their set of results to lead overnight from past Flying Fifteen World Champions Mike Hart and Sally Kilpatrick, who added a third, first, third. The aptly named Sergeants, representing Army Sailing, lay in fourth position at this stage, level on eleven points with Jasper and Laura Barnham from Snettisham Beach SC.

After a lay day, Thursday proved something of a benefit for Mike Hart and Sally Kilpatrick with three races held, and three bullets added to their score. This gave them a clear lead going into the final day, ahead of Matt and Clare Sergeant, from Jon Holroyd and Jane Rusbatch, with Dave and Scott Adams only two points off a top three finish. Three more races were completed in Hayling Bay on the last day of the Championships to decide the event. By adding a second, third and finally another race win, Hart and Kilpatrick took the Championships in great style with all counting results of third or better in their score despite what had been a fairly a testing week. Matt and Clare Sergeant had a poor final day, dropping them to sixth overall, with Holroyd and Rusbatch finishing in second, and Rob and Katie Burridge in third.

P	Helm	Crew	R1	R2	R3	R4	R5	R6	R7	R8	R9	R10	Tot	Nett
1	M Hart	S Kilpatrick	4	3	1	3	1	1	1	2	3	1	20	13
2	J Holroyd	J Rusbatch	8	2	3	1	3	OCS	4	4	4	7	119	28
3	R Burridge	K Burridge	3	9	6	7	10	10	DNC	1	2	3	134	41
4	D Adams	S Adams	2	4	5	6	2	DNC	2	14	11	12	141	44
5	A Hulley	S Payne	13	22	18	4	8	5	11	3	1	2	87	47
6	M Sergeant	C Sergeant	1	8	2	DSQ	5	2	3	20	15	16	155	52
7	C Jordan	G Jordan	9	1	7	12	12	4	12	7	8	10	82	58
8	B Dawber	S Denyer	6	7	38	24	11	OCS	9	10	6	6	200	79

Laser 4000

Photo courtesy of Digigraphics

Type	Dinghy	Weight	80 kg
Crew	2; 1 on trapeze	Sail area M&J	14.7 sq m
PN	908	Spi type	Asymmetric
Length	4.64 m	Spi area	17.1 sq m
Beam	1.5 m	Designer	Phil Morrison, 1994
			www.laser4000.org.uk

The Laser 4000 was one of the first of the new generation of asymmetric dinghies, introduced in 1994. With one crew on trapeze, and a large asymmetric spinnaker, the boat offers excellent performance, and with a weight equalisation system, appeals to a range of sailors. The class holds a European and National Championship, and a full open meeting circuit each year.

Laser 4000 Europeans

Bandol, France   24 - 27 June 2009

Twenty three boats competed in the 2009 Laser 4000 Europeans at Bandol in France, with competitors from four different countries taking part.

Racing for the first three days was dictated by the predominantly light winds which came and went, leaving the fleet drifting aimlessly mid-race at times. As a final twist, the last day was sailed in winds up to force five, just to ensure that the event saw a wide spectrum of conditions!

At the end of the event, it was Andy Palmer-Felgate, crewed by Chris Gould, who took the title by just one point from Huw Powell and Kevin Barnard; Palmer-Felgate gaining four wins and five seconds in his tally, whilst Powell earned five wins and two seconds in the course of the event. They were following in third position overall by Douglas and Hilary Baker, with fourth going to Alistair Hodshon and Sue Ogg, ahead of Jon Modral and Charlotte Heffernan in fifth.

With the British boats being dominant this year, the top overseas competitor were the Italians Federico Rigotti and Paolo Battini who finished ninth overall, whilst Reunan Leger and Yannick Massus rounded up the top ten.

P	Helm	Crew	R1	R2	R3	R4	R5	R6	R7	R8	R9	R10	R11	Pts	Tot
1	A Palmer-Felgate	C Gould	2	1	1	1	2	2	1	2	4	3	2	12	21
2	H Powell	K Barnard	4	5	5	2	1	1	2	1	5	1	1	13	28
3	D Baker	H Baker	6	2	2	3	3	4	4	3	6	2	5	23	40
4	A Hodshon	S Ogg	9	8	3	4	5	7	9	9	2	5	3	37	64
5	J Modral	C Heffernan	1	6	7	7	7	3	7	OCS	1	6	DNC	38	93
6	D Reaney	A Watkins	3	9	4	13	6	11	3	6	3	4	11	38	73
7	T Linell	G Lincoln	7	3	9	5	4	9	6	5	DNF	12	4	43	88
8	G Holden	B Holden	5	4	14	12	15	13	13	4	7	8	7	60	102
9	F Rigotti	P Battini	18	12	6	6	12	20	15	7	8	9	10	70	123
10	R Leger	Y Massus	14	10	12	11	8	10	16	12	11	7	5	75	117

Laser 4000 National Championships

Beer Sailing Club   12 - 15 September 2009

Laser 4000s from as far afield as Loch Lomond ventured to Beer Sailing Club for the National Championships in mid September, and the class was pleased to welcome an influx of new owners taking advantage of the low secondhand boat prices, and an upsurge of interest in the class.

Racing on the first day was exciting, once the fleet had been launched through the large swell, and Huw Powell and Kevin Barnard quickly got to grips with the conditions to take two races wins and a second on the first day, whilst second at the end of the day, and winners of the second race were Mark Cotgrove and Ian Gotts.

On the second day, both the swell, and the wind were reduced, and the first race was won by David Marchant and Alayne Seymour who were pursued by Iain Reynolds and Adam Brushett. The following race was delayed after a general recall, as the wind disappeared, only to return ninety minutes later as a shifting northerly. Powell and Barnard took another victory with Cotgrove and Gotts in pursuit with Nick Alp and Jo Morrison in third. The final race of the day was taken by Chris Gould, crewed by past championship winning crew Bonnie Moody.

The third day saw stronger (and increasing) winds, with the first race of the day being won by Chris Webber and James Baldwin. The next race went to Powell and Barnard once again, and with the wind blowing its hardest, the final race of the day Webber and Baldwin took another race win.

With the final day blown off with 30 knot gusts, Powell and Barnard were crowned National Champions, ahead of Cotgrove and Gotts, with Webber and Baldwin third and Gould and Moody in fourth at the end of an excellent meeting.

P	Sail No	Helm	Crew	Club	Pts
1	4597	Huw Powell	Kevin Barnard	Red Wharf Bay	11
2	4	Mark Cotgrove	Ian Gotts		15
3	4223	Chris Webber	James Baldwin	OLYC	19
4	4516	Chris Gould	Bonnie Moody	Oxford Uni	27
5	4502	Toby Linnell	Gareth Lincoln	Northampton	46
6	4536	Hugh Watson	Susanna Bickford	Emsworth	49

Laser 5000

Type	Dinghy	Weight	109 kg
Crew	2; both on trapeze	Sail area M&J	21.16 sq m
PN	846	Spi type	Asymmetric
Length	5 m	Spi area	33 sq m
Beam	1.9 m	Designer	P Morrison, 1994
			www.laser5000. lasersailing.com

Photo courtesy of Laser 5000 Class Assoc

The Laser 5000 is a powerful racing boat sailed by a crew of two on trapeze, and utilising an adjustable rack/weight system to compensate for variations of crew weight. Designed in 1994, the boat was a contender to be the Olympic high-performance dinghy, but was beaten to the selection by the 49er. The 5000 is strongly constructed and, whilst no longer available new, it does offer excellent value on the second-hand boat market, providing great sailing and incredible performance for the price.

Laser 5000 Nationals

Warsash Sailing Club   13 - 14 June 2009

Hosted by Warsash SC, the Laser 5000s returned to their spiritual home for the 2009 National Championships, held over a June weekend with a pleasant (if slightly light) forecast. With just a Force two on the Saturday, and even lighter breezes to start the Sunday, it was obviously going to be a weekend of finesse, although a building sea breeze on the Sunday gave all a chance to stretch their legs!

Defending champions, Thomas Sauvel and Alistair Farman retained the title that they won at Weston SC 2008, with an impressive three wins on the trot, having started the event slightly less vigorously than normal. They battled against Taff Owens and Andy Mount who started the weekend with a win, and the tussle was quite intense as the two boats entered the final showdown. Owens and Mount appeared to have blown their chances with a late capsize whilst waiting for the start, but they were back up and running just in time. Meanwhile, as the fleet progressed up the course, Sauvel's boom snapped, leaving him a spectator for the rest of the race, and with the final rankings very much in the hands of others. Owens and Mount finished in second position, which left both them and Sauvel on eleven points, with the title going back to Sauvel on count-back after a close shave!

Behind the creditable challenge of Owens and Mount, third position went to Mark and Nicky Rushdon to conclude a great championship.

P	SN	Helm	Club	R1	R2	R3	R4	R5	R6	Pts
1	5231	Thomas Sauvel	GWSC	2	6	1	1	1	DNC	11
2	5233	Taff Owens	WSC	1	5	2	2	4	2	11
3	5249	Mark Rushton	GWSC	3	4	3	3	2	1	12
4	5269	Paul Burns	GWSC	5	1	4	4	5	3	17
5	5301	Niall Furguson	DWSC	4	2	5	6	3	4	18
6	5291	Gavin Webb	RSC	DNC	3	6	5	6	DNF	27

Laser II

Photo courtesy of Annie Porter

Type	Dinghy	Weight	79 kg
Crew	2; 1 on trapeze	Sail area M&J	11.52 sq m
PN	1035	Spi type	Symmetric
Length	4.39 m	Spi area	10.2 sq m
Beam	1.42 m	Designer	F Braithwaite
			www.laser2sailing.org.uk

The Laser II is a two-man boat which is sailed with the crew on trapeze. There is a conventional-style spinnaker which is stored in an integral chute for ease of handling. The Laser II is an international class, with over 10,000 boats registered, and offering World and European Championships, as well as a national circuit.

Laser II World Championships

Weymouth and Portland Sailing Academy   18 - 25 July 2009

Thirty seven competitors travelled to Weymouth from all over Europe for the 2009 World Laser II championships, the thirtieth anniversary of the event. With the first day's racing held in Force three to four winds, the Committee held three excellent races, with class stalwart Nigel Skudder, sailing with Keith Hills, earning two wins and a second ahead of old rivals Lisa Buddemeier and Matthais Duwel. The second day's racing, in winds of up to twenty five knots, was run inside Portland Harbour, with the race team again working to maximum efficiency. Skudder and Hills continued their early mastery of the event with two wins and a third place, but the consistency of the chasing German crews of Buddemeier and Matthias Duwel, and Marian and Daniel Scheer meant that the event was still wide open, but with even stronger winds forecast time alone would tell how the week would progress.

Over the next two days, in continuing boisterous conditions the Race Officer managed to fit in another five races, leaving Skudder and Hills "fencing" with Buddemeier and Duwel with neither pulling sufficiently far ahead to be able to relax, and just three points dividing their positions. The Scheers were comfortable in third position, now some twelve points behind Skudder, but twenty three points clear of fourth placed Mike and Diana Croker. With two races scheduled for the final day, the title position was tight, but very much in Skudder's hands. Whilst only three points clear, Skudder and Hills were discarding a second and third position. Therefore, for Buddemeier and Duwel to take the title, they needed to beat Skudder in both of the final races and, moreover, they actually needed to win both races, whilst keeping Skudder out of the leading positions if at all possible. With a steady Force five in the first race Nigel Skudder and Keith Hills gave another display of heavy airs sailing to take a well earned victory ahead of Lisa Buddemeier and Matthias Duwel, who also finished as runners up in the overall event. These two boats then sailed for home to leave the fleet to race for the minor placings in the last race of the week; David Annan and Amanda Childs took the opportunity to win the final race to make up for gear failure in the first race of the day. This took them up to sixth overall, whilst second spot in this final race left Marian and Daniel Scheer well clear in third spot overall, ahead of the second UK team of Mike and Diana Croker.

P	Nat	Helm / Crew	R1	R2	R3	R4	R5	R6	R7	R8	R9	R10	R11	R12	R13	Pts
1	GBR	N Skudder K Hills	1	1	2	1	3	1	2	1	2	1	2	1	DNC	15
2	GER	L Buddemeier M Duwel	2	2	1	2	2	3	1	2	1	2	3	3	DNC	21
3	GER	M Scheer D Scheer	4	3	5	4	1	2	3	4	3	3	1	2	2	28
4	GBR	M Croker D Croker	3	7	3	17	5	6	4	8	7	9	4	6	10	62
5	NED	S Harkema C Gerlach	5	5	6	3	4	4	10	12	9	6	10	5	6	63
6	GBR	D Annan A Childs	11	9	16	5	8	8	7	5	5	4	5	DNC	1	68

Laser Stratos

Type	Dinghy	Weight	170 kg (c/b)
Crew	2 or 3; Generally sit out	Sail area M&J	14.53 sq m
PN	1084	Spi type	Asymmetric
Length	4.94 m	Spi area	12.54 sq m
Beam	2.00 m	Designer	Phil Morrison
			www.laserstratos.org.uk

Designed by Phil Morrison, the Stratos has been supplied in either centreboard or keel format, the latter providing an already stable dinghy with a little extra security. The boat has become popular amongst training establishments, as well as with the general public, because it does offer a large cockpit space (big enough to seat 5 or 6) with a manageable rig.

Laser Vago

Type	Dinghy	Sail area M&J	12.09 sq m
Crew	2; 1 on trapeze	Spi type	Assymetric
Length	4.2 m	Spi area	12.07 sq m
Beam	1.56 m	Designer	Jo Richards
Weight	106 kg		www.vago.lasersailing.com

The Laser Vago was created to stimulate. Unmatched handling and exhilarating performance are harnessed in its uniquely stunning, modern design. The Laser Vago is a versatile single-trapeze boat, with a multi-functional concept and interchangeable horsepower. The design encompasses many design features found on individual boats; the magic of this Richards design is that the Vago carries the majority of these features, without compromise.

Laser Vago National Championships

Felpham Sailing Club   4 - 5 July 2009

A select band of Laser Vago sailors competed for their Coastal Championships at Felpham SC in Sussex, in an event that was dominated by the local team of Martin and Emma Keen, from Arun YC, who maintained results in the top two for the entire weekend.

It was an event that saw conditions from force two to four over the duration, with slightly lighter breezes on the initial day when Race Officer Chris Grosscurth set forty five minute races on a windward/leeward layout. In the lighter wind events, the tide also took its effect, and the fleet had to be wary that it did not drift off the course in a lapse of concentration!

The 2008 Champion, Martin Rawling, sailed the event with local crew Richard Keen from Arun YC, but despite the wind increasing to Force four to five on the second day, they were never quite able to get on terms with the leaders, to finish the event with a set of results, all in the top three for second overall. Third overall went to Ed and Tim Deacon, whilst fourth was taken by Richard and Abi Bentley from the home club.

Pos	Helm	Crew	Club	R1	R2	R3	R4	R5	R6	Nett
1	Martin Keen	Emma Keen	AYC	1	2	1	1	2	1	6
2	Martin Rawling	Richard Keen	SISC	3	1	3	2	1	2	9
3	Ed Deacon	Tim Deacon	SESCA	4	3	2	7	4	4	17
4	Richard Bentley	Abi Bentley	FSC	2	4	6	3	3	6	18
5	Paul Noble	Suzie Rodgers		8	6	7	5	5	3	26
6	Stuart McTavish	Katie Hill	OSC	7	8	5	4	6	5	27

Lymington River Scow

Type	Dinghy
Crew	1 or 2; Sit in
Length	3.45 m
Beam	1.5 m
Weight	100 kg
Sail area M&J	6 sq m

The Lymington River Scow was first produced in the 1800s but boat-builder John Claridge has given the class a new lease of life by producing the boat in modern materials. The class is now widely sailed and raced by young and old alike, and has been taken on as a training boat by some clubs. The rig is a balanced lug, and has an optional jib to allow for two-person sailing. At the annual Championships, which generally are held at Lymington, the class races in both single handed and crewed sections, and generally a fleet of 50 odd boats compete in this friendly class.

Merlin Rocket

Type	Dinghy
Crew	2; Sit out
PN	1018
Length	4.27 sq m
Beam	2.18 sq m
Weight	98 kg
Sail area M&J	10.55 sq m
Spi type	Symmetric
Spi area	7.43 sq m
Designer	Various
	www.merlinrocket.co.uk

The Merlin Rocket combines the boat handling and tactical racing of the traditional designs with the thrills and excitement of the modern "fast in a straight line" designs. Upwind, the high aspect rig means that in light and medium wind conditions the Merlin Rocket is one of the highest pointing dinghies around. It is the bane of the trapeze boat sailor. On the reaches, the long spinnaker pole and the new 10m^2 spinnaker are a powerful combination, ensuring that close-reaching under spinnaker remains one of the strengths and thrills of Merlin Rocket sailing.

Merlin Rocket National Championships

Whitstable Yacht Club   16 - 21 August 2009

Fifty seven boats attended the Merlin Rocket National Championships, hosted by Whitstable Yacht Club; one of the most popular and well-visited venues.

The first race was held in classic conditions with fourteen knots of wind and a slight sea. After several false starts the black flag was brought into play and Richard Whitworth and Sally Townend led around the windward mark from Willie Warren and Chris Robinson. Down the run Matt Biggs and Rob Kennaugh closed in on the leaders, and held station for some time before eventually pulling through to gain the lead, which they did to the end. Whitworth and Townend held onto second position, ahead of Glen Truswell and Olly Turner in third.

The second day of the Championships was scheduled for two races, and provided tricky conditions. After a general recall the black flag was introduced! The fleet got away in a five knot breeze, and was led by Andy Davis and Ellie Bremner at the first mark, from Alex Jackson and Holly Scott who had unfortunately fallen foul of the black flag and were disqualified. As the race headed towards its conclusion a forty degree shift came through, necessitating setting a new windward mark, and lifting Glenn Truswell and Olly Turner into contention. On the final beat, with ten boats all in contention for the win, it was Truswell and Turner who inched their way to the win, ahead of Andy Davis and Ellie Bremner, with Tom Stewart and Liam Dempsey in third.

Wednesday's conditions were difficult with the breeze coming off the land with the associated "bends" and shifts. The points race was held in four to six knots of breeze, and the black flag was introduced after two general recalls. Tom Stewart and Liam Dempsey led at the first mark from Simon Blake and Phil Dalby, and on the second beat Stewart and Dempsey came under pressure from Andy Davis and Ellie Bremner, as well as overall leaders Glen Truswell and Olly Turner. Truswell managed to drift into the lead whilst Richard Whitworth and Sally Townend slipped into second and they finished in this order.

Efforts to race on Wednesday came to nothing as the wind would not cooperate. However, whilst the racing was held over to Thursday, unfortunately a number of boats had been black flagged in the effort to start, and this penalty would ensure that these boats were excluded from the re-run race.

Thursday's conditions were fresh and breezy, and enabled the Race Officer to hold two races and to get back on schedule. The first race was won by Andy Davis and Ellie Bremner ahead of Jon Gorringe and Peter Horn, with Richard Whitworth and Sally Townend in third. Championship leaders Truswell and Turner had their worst race of the week with a sixth. However, a second place in the next race reversed their

Startline activity at the 2009 Merlin Championships

The Dinghy & Smallcraft Review
2009~2010

fortunes, and left them one point clear of Whitworth and Townend. Andy Davis and Ellie Bremner were six points further back, in third overall entering the final day, and Tom Stewart and Liam Dempsey a further two points in arrears, in fourth spot overall.

With a steady Force four gusting five, Richard Whitworth and Sally Townend led the race from Andy Davis and Ellie Bremner and David Winder and Pippa Taylor with Glen Truswell and Olly Turner in fourth. The leaders capsized as they caught a wave, recovering to twenty third with Truswell and Turner picking up places to second. Whitworth and Townend got back to within striking distance of Truswell and Turner but they could not break through and second position for the Starcross boat was sufficient to give them a well deserved Championship.

P	Helm	Crew	Club	R1	R2	R3	R4	R5	R6	Pts
1	Glen Truswell	Olly Turner	SSC	3	1	1	6	2	3	10
2	Richard Whitworth	Sally Townend	HLSC	2	7	2	3	1	6	14
3	Andy Davis	Ellie Bremer	CSC	6	2	6	1	5	1	15
4	Mike Calvert	Christopher Downham	ASC	5	5	4	4	4	7	22
5	Tom Stewart	Liam Dempsey	NSC	4	3	3	7	6	9	23
6	Jon Gorringe	Peter Horn	PYC	9	8	15	2	9	4	32
7	Chris Lewns	Tom Pygall	WYC	11	4	12	8	12	5	40
8	William Warren	Chris Robinson	SYC	7	9	7	59	17	2	42
9	Simon Blake	Phil Dalby	CRSC	8	10	11	13	8	8	45
10	David Winder	Pippa Taylor	HLSC	10	11	5	5	15	59	46
11	Matt Biggs	Rob Kennaugh	BSC	1	6	8	59	20	15	50
12	Steve Goacher	Andy Tunnicliffe	RWYC	13	27	21	9	3	10	56
13	Pat Blake	Jill Blake	CRSC	18	17	10	10	11	12	60
14	Will Rainey	Kelly Miller	CRSC	14	21	17	14	10	11	66
15	Dan Parsons	Hamish Kilburn	WYC	19	15	14	11	21	13	72

Miracle

Type	Dinghy	Weight	59 kg
Crew	2; Sit out	Sail Area M&J	8.9 sq m
PN	1178	Spi Type	Symmetric
Length	3.89 m	Spi Area	7.4 sq m
Beam	1.59 m	Designer	Jack Holt / Barry Read
			www.miracledinghy.org

The Miracle was designed by Jack Holt and Barry Read. The Miracle is a hard chine design, aimed at home-building, although it is now possible to buy GRP and composite professionally built boats. The boat is ideal as either a training or racing boat, and is well suited to younger crews as she is easily handled ashore and afloat. This two man sit-out boat is available with a spinnaker, and this gives it a nice turn of foot. The Championships each year attract people of all ages and both sexes, but are particularly popular with families, and husband and wife, or fathers sailing with child crews are often seen at the front of the fleet.

Miracle Nationals

Ullswater Sailing Club   2 – 7 August 2009

Fifty eight Miracle dinghies participated in the National Championships, which took place in the Lake District in early August, with the entry showing a healthy increase over the 2008 Championships.

Sunday's race took place in bright conditions with a good breeze and was won by Eamon and Lauren Cuthbert from Leigh and Lowton Sailing Club, with Sam Mettam and Geoff Phillips from Hayling Island Yacht Club taking second place. Mettam and Phillips appeared to take victory in the second race, but were disqualified under the black flag, leaving Martyn and Rebecca Lewis from Draycote Sailing Club as the winners. The third points race, held on Tuesday, again saw Mettam and Phillips in control, and this time making no mistakes in gaining the victory.

On Tuesday grey skies, rain and blustery conditions met the crews. Some helms struggled in the strong gusts and there were several capsizes. Sam Mettam and his crew were first over the line followed by the Lewises in the first race, with the positions being reversed for Race Two of the day.

Conditions were much improved for Wednesday and Thursday's racing. Competition was fierce during the four races sailed, with Sam Mettam winning two races and Martyn Lewis winning the third race and coming second in the other rounds. Thus, as the final day dawned, only two points separated Sam Mettall and his rival, Martyn Lewis and the final race on Friday was eagerly anticipated. Unfortunately, conditions for racing were somewhat disappointing with very hot sun but no wind and, after several postponements, the Race Officer made the inevitable decision that conditions were not suitable for racing, and the final race was abandoned.

P	Helm	Crew	Club	R1	R2	R3	R4	R5	R6	R7	R8	R9	Nett
1	S Mettam	G Phillips	HISC	2	BFD	1	1	2	1	3	10	1	11
2	M Lewis	R Lewis	DSC	3	1	4	2	1	2	2	3	2	13
3	P Hewitt	C Hewitt	DSC	4	8	2	5	5	3	1	18	3	23
4	E Cuthbert	L Cuthbert	L&LSC	1	10	13	6	4	4	5	5	7	32
5	M Huett	G Huett	DSC	5	3	8	3	7	5	18	7	6	36
6	D Southwell	R Southwell	L&LSC	8	6	9	4	6	8	4	19	4	40
7	R Pye	H Pye	DSC	6	2	14	8	10	11	11	1	5	43
8	A Jones	H Jones	DSC	11	4	3	10	3	DNF	13	6	18	50
9	D Raines	M Raines	RYA	10	5	5	13	15	6	8	16	19	62
10	P Bailey	H Bailey	GSC	15	11	7	9	11	7	7	22	13	65

Mirror

Length	3.3 m
Beam	1.4 m
Weight	61.4 kg
Sail area M&J	6.53 sq m
Spi type	Symmetric
Spi area	5.2 sq m
Designer	Jack Holt / Barry Bucknell
	www.ukmirror sailing.com

Originally designed for home construction, the Mirror is responsible for bringing sailing to the masses with over 70,000 boats now built, many produced from kits or plans. With the advent of Bermudan rigs, and competitive GRP boats, the racing side of the class is going from strength to strength, and the pottering side continues to be an attraction for many. The Mirror is suitable for single-handed sailing, or for racing with a crew, and the class association actively supports all aspects of Mirror sailing.

Mirror World Championships

Pwllheli   27 July – 1 August 2009

With three races completed, and three different winners, on the first day of the World Championships, the fleet promptly got into gear. Leading after the first day were Chris and Jessica Rust, with Ed and Beth Grey in second position, having won the first race of the day, whilst third overall were Hugo Sloper and Emma Spruce. The final race of Day One was won by Andy and Tom Smith, who also had a second in the first three results, but a disappointing third race pulled them down the rankings.

Day Two saw strong winds and huge seas and, after deliberation, it was inevitable that racing would be cancelled for the day, and the race committee decided that four races should be scheduled for Wednesday. Sure enough, the following morning dawned with light and shifty breezes, which quickly settled down, and peaked at eight knots. The light breezes, combined with tide and the black flag, mean that twenty odd competitors had "earned" a BFD in their scores by this point in the week. Chris Rust, the overnight leader, could only record an eleventh and seventh which dropped them down to second overall, whilst Charlotte Fitzgerald and Annie Sibthorp gained the overnight lead with two fourth places, and Charlotte's sister, Izzy, sailing with Emily Peters, won the first race of the day after a long and tight battle, whilst the second race win was earned by Hugo Sloper and Emma Spruce.

Day Four of the Mirror World Championships benefited from excellent conditions which permitted four more competitive races with big seas and breezes that grew to over twenty knots at times. Each of the day's heats saw a different winner; the Rusts took the first race in a tussle with Ross Kearney and Katy Jones and Andy and Tom Smith. Tom Lovesey and Millie Pugh dominated the second race from the Smiths, whilst the Barry sisters took the third race after a sustained challenge from Izzy Fitzgerald and Emily Peters. The day's final race saw Kearney and Jones get into their stride and sail off to a huge winning margin, with second spot taken by Charlotte Fitzgerald and Annie Sibthorp after a hard fought battle with the Rusts, and the Smiths.

With four more races behind them and the first discard now in play, the overall leader board looked a bit different. Andy and Tom Smith's consistency through the day took them to the head of the table, with Chris and Jessica Rust twelve points in arrears, one point clear of Izzy Fitzgerald and Emily Peters, who in turn were five points clear of sister Charlotte, sailing with Annie Sibthorp, in fourth position.

Despite the Smiths' twelve point lead, with the potential for three more races during the next day the 2009 Mirror World Championship was far from over and any one of the top six boats had a realistic chance of making a late charge.

As so often happens, the more anticipation builds towards the end of the week, the better the chance of an anticlimax, and that was the case here, with the strong overnight winds failing to moderate on Friday morning, and leaving no choice but to abandon racing and leave the results as they had been at the end of Thursday, with Andy and Tom Smith taking the title from Chris and Jessica Rust. Third overall and winner of the Oceanair 2009 Mirror Junior World Championships were Izzy Fitzgerald and Emily Peters, ahead of sister Charlotte, crewed by Annie Sibthorp, who were also runners up in the Junior Worlds; appropriate really, given that their father, International 14 sailor Andy Fitzgerald, runs Oceanair!

P	SN	Helm	Nat	R1	R2	R3	R4	R5	R6	R7	R8	R9	Tot	Nett
1	70513	A & T Smith	GBR	16	2	1	9	6	3	2	8	4	51	35
2	70537	C & J Rust	GBR	2	3	7	11	7	1	14	13	3	61	47
3	70559	I Fitzgerald E Peters	GBR	8	9	5	1	11	25	4	2	8	73	48
4	70502	C Fitzgerald A Sibthorp	GBR	7	1	11	4	4	10	21	14	2	74	53
5	70506	R Kearney K Jones	IRL	14	BFD	2	8	20	2	5	4	1	154	56
6	69776	E & M Barry	GBR	5	10	13	3	5	8	12	1	15	72	57
7	70504	H Sloper E Spruce	GBR	4	4	8	15	1	7	9	25	16	89	64
8	70574	M Newman M Bond	GBR	3	BFD	4	6	10	19	11	6	6	163	65
9	70519	T Lovesey M Pugh	GBR	12	BFD	3	14	18	4	1	5	13	168	70
10	70356	D Conlon C Bond	GBR	9	6	16	25	15	9	3	7	10	100	75

Photo courtesy of Paul Todd/OutsideImages.co.nz

Action at the Mirror Worlds

Mirror National Championships

Pwllheli   23 - 26 July 2009

One hundred and nine Mirrors competed in the 2009 National Championships by way of a tune-up regatta for the World Championships, to be held at Pwllheli at the end of July. There was little opportunity for pre-event sailing, however, as the wind kept the bulk of the fleet ashore until racing got underway.

During the first race, with winds building to over twenty five knots and one and a half metre seas, the current European Champion, Chris Rust, and his sister Jessica led at the windward mark, pursued by past World Champions Ross Kearney and Katy Jones from Ireland with the 2008 National Champions, the Barry sisters in third. Kearney and the Rusts had a luffing match, which ended up with the former taking a quick swim, and the Rusts sailed on to the winning gun, with Paul and Austin Taylor from Australia in second, and Kearney and Jones in third.

Lighter conditions prevailed on Day Two of the Mirror Nationals. In the first heat, Ross Kearney and Katy Jones rounded the windward mark first followed by Charlotte Fitzgerald and Annie Sibthorpe who took the lead downwind and went on to win the race from Liam Wilson and Jessica Stout and Christopher Rust and sister Jessica. Race Three saw the winning gun go to Tom Lovesey and Milly Pugh, ahead of Hugo Sloper and Emma Spruce, with Kearney and Jones in third, and it was again Lovesey and Pugh who dominated the third race of the day to win ahead of Emma and Martina Barry, with Paul Taylor and his son Lawson coming in third.

The final day of Nationals sailing before the Worlds started in earnest saw another four heats, which proved just enough for Ross Kearney and Katy Jones to show their form, and to take the title by three points from Tom Lovesey and Milly Pugh, with Charlotte Fitzgerald and Annie Sibthorpe in third position. Kearney's final day score was actually only bettered by one boat, Andy and Tom Smith, who finished in fourth overall.

P	Helm	Crew	Nat	R1	R2	R3	R4	R5	R6	R7	R8	Pts
1	Ross Kearney	Katy Jones	IRL	3	6	3	5	1	3	8	7	28
2	Tom Lovesey	Milly Pugh	GBR	4	14	1	1	10	4	6	5	31
3	Charlotte Fitzgerald	Annie Sibthorp	GBR	7	1	5	6	11	6	14	1	37
4	Andy Smith	Tom Smith	GBR	DNC	11	7	7	5	10	1	2	43
5	Millie Newman	Mitchell Bond	GBR	6	15	4	12	3	13	4	3	45
6	Emma Barry	Martina Barry	GBR	DNC	10	10	2	8	1	2	14	47
7	Izzy Fitzgerald	Emily Peters	GBR	8	4	13	16	14	2	3	4	48
8	Paul Taylor	Austin Taylor	AUS	2	13	9	3	2	21	29	6	56
9	Hugo Sloper	Emma Spruce	GBR	5	BFD	2	11	6	16	13	9	62
10	Guy Wilkins	Clare Peterson	GBR	9	5	19	13	7	5	10	18	67

National 18

Type	Dinghy
Crew	3 man; 1 trapeze
PN	957
Length	5.49 m
Beam	2.36 m
Weight	200 kg
Sail area M&J	21.32 sq m
Spi type	Symmetric
Spi area	17.5 sq m
Designer	Ian Proctor, 1968
	www.national18.com

Photo courtesy of Dave Kneale

The National 18 is a restricted class, established in 1938. The original clinker-built boat, Ace, was designed by Uffa Fox. Since then over two hundred and fifty wooden boats have been built. Since the late Ian Proctor designed a GRP version in 1968, about one hundred and twenty glass-built boats have been added, racing on level terms with the wooden boats. This is a challenging big dinghy sailed by a network of big-hearted friends, some of them fourth-generation 18 sailors.

News: During 2009, the matter of carbon spars is again being considered, having previously been dismissed in 2005. The second "prototype" spar has now been passed around the Irish boats for more than 12 months, and with some 50% of the racing fleet based in Cork, their approval is imperative if the proposal is likely to be accepted. In addition there are various amendments being considered to separate the jib and spinnaker halyard entry points further (and therefore to avoid compromising the spar strength), and also some talk about increasing spinnaker luff length by 210mm subject to further testing. The previously considered option of increasing the luff by 450mm provided an over-powerful and cumbersome sail, and was therefore finally discounted.

National 18 National Championships

Portland   2 - 7 August 2009

An entry of twenty six national 18s attended their 2009 National Championships, a small increase from 2008, but a promising sign given the economic situation!

Colin Chapman, Martin Almond and Morgan O'Sullivan of Royal Cork YC defended their National Championship title when the event was hosted in Portland during August, winning the trophy by six points. It was a close-fought Championship, with any one of four boats capable of taking the title at the end of the regatta, with three races held on the last day of the event.

Second overall was Colin Barry, sailing with Dickie Mac and Dan O'Connell from Monkstown Bay SC, whilst Findhorn member, Phil Hermiston, sailing with Alistair Davis and Martine Cruden, took third spot with two wins in the final three races, which he added to his tally including all three race victories from Wednesday.

During the week long event, it had been a competition of variable conditions. All racing was lost on the Tuesday as gales blew through the area. Early leader was Dave O'Connell, sailing with Kevin Horan and Shane O'Connell, but Chapman's steady progress through the week proved too much once he had recovered from being over the line in the first race. Hermiston, who probably had the potential to win the event this year, was really pressurized throughout by receiving two discards on the first day; without these, and with an average third race result, his positions were definitely of Championship-winning potential for the rest of the week.

P	Helm	Crew	Crew	R1	R2	R3	R4	R5	R6	R7	R8	R9	R10	Tot	Nett
1	Colin Chapman	Martin Almond	Morgan O'Sullivan	OCS	1	1	10	3	3	1	7	2	2	57	20
2	Colin Barry	Dickie Mac	Dan O'Connell	5	2	7	RTD	2	2	3	2	3	OCS	80	26
3	Phil Hermiston	Alistair Davis	Martin Cruden	OCS	DNC	14	1	1	1	2	1	1	7	82	28
4	David O'Connell	Kevin Horan	Shane O'Connell	1	5	2	7	9	5	4	9	4	1	47	29
5	Stuart Urquhart	Richard Urquhart	Ross Young	OCS	3	3	8	8	10	8	8	6	3	84	40
6	Bryan Hassett	Fred Cudmore	Sandy Rimmington	OCS	6	8	2	5	4	RTD	6	1	5	102	48
7	Mick Kneale	Phil Hardisty	Daniel Kneale	3	10	4	6	6	13	7	11	8	4	72	48
8	Peter O'Donovan	Robbie O'Sullivan	Colm O'Connell	2	4	10	5	4	9	18	4	11	OCS	9	49
9	Jessica Berney	Olivia Trench	Kim Waterfield	4	7	5	9	7	6	6	13	7	8	72	50
10	Kevin Davidson	Stephen Laurie	Greg Davidson	6	9	13	11	14	8	10	3	13	9	96	69

Photo courtesy of Dave Kneale

Action at the National 18 Championships

Sailboat Performance Hardware

Take a look at the majority of sailing dinghies in the world and you'll fnd products designed and manufactured by Allen, from state-of-the-art dynamic bearing block systems, to a simple 'u' bolt.

We have been in the performance hardware business since 1956 and are passionate about producing hardware capable of achieving the best results.

If you would like to discuss anything, call us on tel: +44(0)1621 774689 or email: sales@allenbrothers.co.uk

www.allenbrothers.co.uk

allen

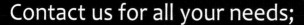

National 12

Type	Dinghy
Crew	2; Sit out
PN	1097
Length	3.66 m
Beam	1.98 m
Weight	70 kg
Sail area M&J	10.4 sq m
Spi type	None
Designer	Various
	www.national12.org

Photo courtesy of Tom Gruitt/N12 Assoc

The National 12 is a well established two-person, two-sail racing dinghy. With a sail area of around 10.4 sq metres ($8.4m^2$ measured) and a light hull there is ample power to drive the fast and responsive hull. The National 12 is a development class, which allows for hulls and rigs to be changed or modified within the class rules. The different hull designs allow helm-crew combinations between 16 and 23 stone to be competitive.

National 12 Burton Week

Thorpe Bay Yacht Club   23 - 26 May 2009

Burton Week, the National Championship of the National 12 class, was this year held at Thorpe Bay YC from 23 - 26 May, and the long awaited return to this venue, together with the abbreviated format for the event, ensured it was a great success; with the eighty boat entry the best for fifteen years.

Amongst the entries was a new Paradigm 2 design straight from the box, a selection of vintage boats competing in the classic section, and Jo Richards' *Dead Cat Bounce* with a collection of technical developments that Jo had been pondering since his last foray into the Nationals.

The opening race was won by 2008 Champions, Graham Camm, and Zoe Ballantyne. In their wake, Richards, with crew Sophie Mackley, took second, with Tom Stewart and Elisabeth Ross in third. That was to prove the only light at the end of the tunnel for Richards' opposition, as he and Mackley took *Dead Cat Bounce* to victory in the other 6 races, despite always being pushed hard.

Monday was Burton Cup day after which the event takes its name. By the terms of the deed of gift for this trophy, donated in 1937 by Sir William Burton, the race must be sailed around a course that cannot be shortened but consists of four triangles, with each leg being at least one mile long, followed by a final beat. The day dawned with a little more breeze which gradually built as the fleet launched. By the appointed start time it had reached force six. These conditions proved to be to the liking of Kevin Iles and Jane Wade from the home club, who narrowly led at the first mark from Steve Norbury and Andy Hill. However, by the end of the first lap it was Stewart and Ross who had a good lead of over two hundred yards from Richards and Mackley. Over the next couple of hours the wind slowly dropped to little more than a Force one at the finish and Richards and Mackley relentlessly ground away at Stewart and Ross to pass them just before the final leeward mark to go on and take their fourth win of the series.

With the winds returning on he final day, and a bracing Force five to six blowing, Richards and Mackley again established a lead which they held to the end of the race, to win the week long event. To rub salt into the wound, they stayed out for the final race which again they won, to underline the strength of their campaign. Second overall were Stewart and Ross who had a "wobble" in Races Three and Four but otherwise were clear of Anthony and Jo Gifford in third place overall. They in turn were four points clear of Kevin Iles and Jane Wade, whilst defending Champions, Graham Camm and Zoe Ballantyne had hit the highlights early with their first race win, and found conditions for the rest of the week somewhat testing.

Jo Richards and Sophie Mackley in the all-conquering *Dead Cat Bounce*

P	SN	Helm	Crew	R1	R2	R3	R4	R5	R6	R7	Pts
1	3519	Jo Richards	Sophie Mackley	2	1	1	1	1	1	1	6
2	3513	Tom Stewart	Elizabeth Ross	3	2	12	9	2	2	6	24
3	3514	Antony Gifford	Jo Gifford	12	14	2	2	3	4	9	32
4	3512	Kevin Iles	Jane Wade	9	9	6	13	7	3	2	36
5	3494	Jon Ibbotson	Charlotte Stewart	14	15	7	3	5	5	3	37
6	3436	Steve Sallis	Joanne Sallis	8	4	4	7	17	7	78	47
7	3492	Graham Camm	Zoe Ballantyne	1	6	11	8	11	11	16	48
8	3516	Steve Norbury	Andy Hill	5	78	13	12	4	10	4	48
9	3441	Ian Gore	Penny Yarwood	34	7	10	14	6	8	8	53
10	3485	Gavin Willis	Sabrina Willis	4	5	8	6	18	22	78	63
11	3450	Richard Williams	Lindsey Iles	11	78	28	4	10	6	5	64
12	3515	John Meadowcroft	Katy Meadowcroft	37	11	3	5	8	31	10	68
13	3455	Caroline Martin	Andy Douglass	10	13	9	16	9	20	15	72
14	3483	Jon Brown	Max Duce	6	10	5	11	28	18	78	78
15	3501	Keri Harris	Theo Harris	16	3	14	17	16	26	19	85

Osprey

Type	Dinghy	Weight	134 kg
Crew	2; 1 on trapeze	Sail area M&J	13.94 sq m
PN	938	Spi type	Symmetric
Length	5.32 m	Spi area	17.19 sq m
Beam	1.75 m	Designer	Ian Proctor
			www.ospreysailing.org.uk

The Osprey is a high-performance two-man dinghy, used largely as a racing boat, but with a forgiving nature that allows comfortable day sailing as well. The boat is equally well-suited to open-sea sailing, or use on large lakes – anywhere with the space for this elegant boat to go through her paces. The introduction of the Mark IV variant in the past three or four years has revitalized the class, with growing attendance at the National Championships, and an exciting open meeting circuit.

Osprey National Championships

Mounts Bay Yacht Club   26 - 29 July 2009

A fleet of forty three Ospreys travelled to Mounts Bay for their National Championships, in what is one of the best loved Osprey venues. Held over four days, the event was initially dominated by local boats, particularly *Lethal Weapon*, sailed by Colin Stephens and Michael Greig, who took three wins in the first four races, to lead convincingly half way through the event. Dinghy legend Andy Barker (a frequent winner of this Championship in the past), sailing with Peter Greig in *Georgia,* had a retirement in Race Three due to equipment problems, but otherwise was positioned in second place overall after the second day, one point clear of Richard and Mark Hartley, the previous year's runner-ups, who were counting two third places and two fourths. Reigning Champions Martin Cooney and Peter Frith had a good second day with two second position finishes, but were also counting two eighth positions from the first day.

Day Three saw Mounts Bay at its best, with a Force five, and huge rolling seas. The conditions suited Martin Cooney and Peter Frith, and they put together two race wins to bring them up to second overall behind Colin Stephens and Michael Greig, who added two second places to their consistent set of results. Whilst their tally of results had all but given the Championships to Stephens and Greig, mathematically the event was still open between these two boats, with everything on the final race. Third place was also wide open, with Andy Barker and Peter Greig level on points with Richard and Mark Hartley. The final day presented something of a contrast, rain and miserable conditions, with a dying breeze. After the race was held for a while, the fleet was eventually set off and Colin Stephens and Michael Greig did their lap of honour to win the last heat, and with it to complete an impressive display of Osprey sailing. Martin Cooney and Peter Frith put up a great defence, after a disappointing start, to finish in second position, ahead of Andy Barker and Peter Greig in third, and the class builders Richard and Mark Hartley in fourth.

P	SN	Helm	Crew	Club	R1	R2	R3	R4	R5	R6	R7	Pts
1	1116	Colin Stephens	Michael Greig	MBSC	3	1	1	1	2	2	1	6
2	1290	Martin Cooney	Peter Frith	PYC	8	8	2	2	1	1	3	9
3	1299	Andy Barker	Peter Greig	MBSC	1	3	DNF	5	5	3	2	14
4	1342	Richard Hartley	Mark Hartley	CSC	4	4	3	3	3	DNF	7	17
5	1206	Rob Larke	Robin Hobson	SSC	7	2	9	8	4	DNF	DNF	30
6	1317	Rob Shaw	Ian Little	KWSC	2	6	8	15	10	8	6	30
7	1296	Jeremy Williams	Roger Curnow	MBSC	5	7	6	4	11	DNF	13	33
8	1339	Adam Ellery	Christopher Ryan	MBSC	12	DNC	5	7	6	5	15	35
9	1311	John Batt	Nick Broomhall	BSC	9	5	14	DNF	12	4	9	39
10	1085	George Odling	Simon Spears	RSYC	11	12	7	9	7	10	DNF	44

RS Feva

Type	Dinghy	Weight	63 kg
Crew	2; Sitting out	Sail area M&J	8.6 sq m
PN	1189	Spi type	Asymmetric
Length	3.64 m	Spi area	7 sq m
Beam	1.42 m	Designer	Paul Handley
			www.rs-association.com

The RS Feva was designed to cope with a number of tasks, from single-handed sailing and training, all the way up to full-blown international racing. Manufactured in an advanced form of rotomoulded polyethylene, the boat is very rugged, but its simple-to-sail layout requires minimal maintenance. The Feva class has now been granted international status, and there is a full racing programme, with a lively multi-national fleet at this year's World Championships. The RS Feva is a very popular junior training dinghy.

RS Feva European Championships

Lake Garda   25 July - 1 August 2009

Hosted by the Acquafresca Yacht Club at Brenzone on the eastern shores of Lake Garda, the Feva Europeans started in beautiful, sunny weather, with a fleet of some eighty boats. The racing was held in four flights with each flight racing each other twice during the qualification series. That means that Gold and Silver fleets would be decided at the end of Day Two, before there would be three days of final fleet racing to decide the real prizes.

After Day One, with three races, Ollie Cooper and Callum Ellis led the way, but a disappointing second day left them down in fifth, whilst Cathy Lear and Francine Counsell maintained their form for the second day, despite scoring an OCS to earn them an early discard. However, they were still in the top three overall, whilst Robert Baddeley and James Taylor were the big winners on Day Two, with two race wins to lift them to the top of the scoring charts! On the International front, Ireland's Conor Lyden and Peter Stokes were top non-GB boat in fourth place, and Italians Alessio and Mattia Bellico were in seventh at this stage of the regatta.

As the fleet reached the end of the qualification races, they all moved on to the eight race finals. With two days of the finals racing completed, and just one still to go, Owen Bowerman and Charlie Darling found themselves at the head of the field in the Gold fleet with a consistent string of top six results; and some ten points clear of Conor Lyden and Peter Stokes. Third were Alice Kent and Lucy Childs, whilst fourth at this stage were Ollie Cooper and Callum Ellis.

The Silver fleet was being led by Amanda Hallgren and Kevin Olsson from Sweden with three wins and a second (and discarding an OCS) in the finals. Irelands Brendan Lyden was second, holding off the Italian Filippo Mazzantini.

An early start was promised for the final day and with the day came some breeze! Initially only the Gold fleet were sailed, because of the wind strength, and they sailed three straight heats whilst the Silvers joined in for two and then added a third as the Gold went ashore.Twelve year olds Owen Bowerman and Charlie Darling, who started with a ten point lead, found the conditions difficult and faded to fourth overall at the end of the day. Olly Cooper and Callum Ellis added a first, seventh and fifth to their scoreline to just take the title from Alice Kend and Lucy Child who added a fifth, first and thirteenth. Conor Lyden and Peter Stokes added the International face to the podium in third place, despite two poor final-day races, and Italians Alessio and Mattia Bellico rounded off the top six.

P	Nat	Helm	Crew	R1	R2	R3	R4	R5	R6	R7	R8	R9	Pts
1	GBR	O Cooper	C Ellis	3	2	2	DNF	12	4	1	7	5	24
2	GBR	A Kent	L Childs	7	1	29	3	7	3	5	1	13	27
3	IRL	C Lyden	P Stokes	6	9	1	12	1	2	23	17	4	35
4	GBR	O Bowerman	C Darling	2	3	6	1	2	1	21	DNF	DNF	36
5	ITA	A Bellico	M Bellico	10	7	4	5	6	26	DNF	9	1	42
6	GBR	J Hawkins	C Thomas	8	4	DSQ	6	9	11	9	19	10	57
7	ITA	N Scarpa	B Favaro	18	15	9	8	28	9	DNF	11	2	72
8	ITA	F Zamboni	D D Mosto	9	16	11	10	23	18	10	10	6	72
9	GBR	R Allan	T Allan	11	13	19	9	16	OCS	3	8	18	78
10	GBR	C Warren	H Derbyshire	26	14	14	7	5	10	12	5	17	79

Gold Fleet

P	Nat	Name	Crew	R1	R2	R3	R4	R5	R6	R7	R8	R9	Pts
1	SWE	A Hallgrenb	K Olsson	41	1	OCS	1	1	2	4	8	10	58
2	GBR	L Gibbons	H Forward	50	4	9	2	3	12	1	4	1	65
3	IRL	B Lyden	M Cudmore	42	5	4	8	7	1	10	3	5	67
4	GBR	H Jones-Warner	J Poyner	51	2	24	6	2	11	6	1	2	70
5	ITA	F Mazzantini	A Docetta	45	3	8	3	4	16	7	11	7	77

Silver Fleet

Photo courtesy of RS Assoc. Copyright Anemoi

The Feva Europeans fought out against a stunning Lake Garda backdrop

RS Feva Nationals

Weymouth and Portland National Sailing Academy   23 - 25 May 2009

A seventy two boat fleet of RS Fevas attended their National Championships at the Weymouth and Portland National Sailing Academy over the late-May bank holiday weekend. Despite a first day of fickle winds and massive shifts, the race team managed to get three races in before the breeze finally disappeared for good.

As the first day's racing closed, the fleet was divided into Gold and Silver, with the overall leaders being the 2008 World and National Champions, Tim Gratton and Chris Taylor, with three excellent race wins, and they were certainly enhancing their positions amongst the event favourites, with Will Lowes and Hugo Tucker, and Debbie and Tommy Darling in hot pursuit. With little wind about on Day Two, racing was delayed until 16.00hrs when it was possible to fit in one race before close of play. This was a tense affair initially, with many of the bigger names pinned back in the fleet. As they came towards the end of the race, however, the Darlings, and Gratton and Taylor gravitated forward and, with a tussle down the last run, Gratton and Taylor pulled through to take another winning gun, and pushed themselves into a strong position going into the last day. However, with four possible races due on the final day, there was still a great deal of work to do and their lead of four points from the Darlings, and five points from Owen Bowerman and Charlie Darling was not enough to allow them to relax before the final day.

As it transpired, the final day appeared to have produced the weather that everyone had been hoping for, with fifteen to twenty knot winds, but as they prepared to set sail, the sunshine appeared, and the wind dropped, and the fleet sat around for two hours before returning to shore! A final start deadline was set for 16.00hrs and as time passed, a slight breeze appeared and built up to five knots, so the fleet relaunched for another try. The course was laid, and then laid again, and finally once again before it became apparent that things were not liable to progress and the event was curtailed and the fleet returned home for the prize-giving, with the previous day's results dictating the awards.

This left Tim Gratton and Chris Taylor as successful defending champions in what was to be their last Feva event before moving on. Second position overall was Debbie Darling sailing with son Tommy, whilst Owen Bowerman made up the successful Hayling Island top three, sailing with Charlie, another of the Darling family!

Gold	SN	Helm	Crew	Club	Q1	R2	Pts
1	2686	Tim Gratton	Chris Taylor	HISC	2	1	3
2	1	Debbie Darling	Tommy Darling	HISC	3	4	7
3	3105	Owen Bowerman	Charlie Darling	HISC	6	2	8
4	2915	Cathy Lear	Francine Counsell	OSC	5	5	10
5	1226	Will Lowes	Hugo Tucker	WYC	3	8	11
6	3307	Robert Baddeley	James Taylor	BSC	6	6	12
7	380	Niall Houston	Syd Mclean	HISC	10	3	13
8	1518	Peter Curtis	James Curtis	IBSC	7	9	16
9	3000	Hugo Jones-Warner	James Poyner	HISC	14	7	21
10	576	Will Acres	Ed Bowman	ESC	15	10	25
Silver	SN	Helm	Crew	Club	Q1	R1	Pts
1	2617	Jacob Barnett	Emma Barnett	RTYC	33	4	37
2	3018	Tristan Bracegirdle	Sam Barker	CCSC	38	1	39
3	1434	Jim Sowden	Jamie Tarrant	HSC	39	2	41
4	2890	Joshua Potts	Peter Budden	HHSC	36	6	42

RS Vision

Type	Dinghy
Crew	2; Sit out
Length	4.6 m
Beam	1.75 m
Weight	125 kg
Sail area M&J	12.2 sq m
Spi type	Asymmetric
Spi area	12.6 sq m
	www.rs-association.com

The RS Vision is a boat designed to suit the family end of the market, capable of being raced or cruised, and with a crew of two, or with space for up to four or five adults when you are off for a picnic! The boat is provided in a range of specifications, from the basic simple to reef version, up to the racing boat with gennaker included.

RS Vision National Championships

Mayflower Sailing Club, Plymouth   25 - 26 July 2009

The first RS Vision National Championships were hosted by Mayflower Sailing Club in Plymouth, as part of the Port of Plymouth Regatta. With an exclusive but widespread entry, the event was dominated by Matt and David Hogben from Herne Bay SC. After an initial shudder, when they collect a third place result, they made light work of the two ensuing races to end up with a total of five points, one clear of runners-up Dan and Hannah Jaspers from Emsworth Slipper SC, who finished with three second positions, for a six point total.

David and Steven Lloyd from Oxford were delighted to win the first race of the weekend, and adding that result to their third and fifth positions left them clear in third place overall, with Garry and Esther Butterfield from Sandwell Valley SC, finished in fourth position with a third and two fifth places.

Whilst the nature of racing in the Vision may not be as high pressure as in some classes today, it is particularly good to see that every boat entered at the Nationals was sailed by two family members, a good sign for the continued success of the boat in the future.

P	Helm	Crew	Club	R1	R2	R3	Total	Nett
1st	Matt Hogben	David Hogben	HBSC	3	1	1	5	5
2nd	Dan Jaspers	Hannah Jaspers	ESSC	2	2	2	6	6
3rd	David Lloyd	Stephen Lloyd	OSC	1	3	6	10	10
4th	Garry Butterfield	Esther Butterfield	SVSC	5	5	3	13	13
5th	Janet Beal	Jen Beal	WSC	4	4	7	15	15

RS Q'BA

Type	Dinghy
Crew	1 or 2; Sitting out
Length	3.53 m
Beam	1.42 m
Weight	58 kg
Sail area M&J	8.3 sq m
Spi type	None
Designer	LDC/Racing Sailboats
	www.rs-association.com

The RS Q'Ba continues the long line of RS success in their training/general purpose dinghy range, a rotomoulded hull providing all of the toughness that this type of dinghy requires, but incorporating the fore-thought of design that is now expected. The Q'Ba is ideal for one or two adults or youngsters to learn the essentials of sailing in a safe fashion, and with the option of a more powerful rig (the "Pro" rather than the "Sport" rig), it provides the option of a little more performance and responsiveness.

RS 200

Type	Dinghy
Crew	2; Sit out
PN	1059
Length	4 m
Beam	1.83 m
Weight	114 kg
Sail area M&J	11.52 sq m
Spi type	Asymmetric
Spi area	8.29 sq m
Designer	Phil Morrison
	www.rs-association.com

The Morrison-designed RS 200 is the perfect choice for lightweights; it responds to finesse rather than physique, and allows parents, youngsters, couples, and friends to share the excitement of asymmetric sailboat racing. The boat has been a huge success in the dinghy racing world, and is now a regular competitor in club racing throughout the UK. It also offers a national race circuit where the sailing is good, and the socials are better.

RS 200 Nationals

Looe Sailing Club   16 - 20 August 2009

Looe SC welcomed one hundred and thirty RS 200s to their Championship; one of the few classes that reached their entry limits in 2009, and with a host of renowned names to ensure that the racing would be good.

With ten races scheduled for the week, the first day was greeted with testing light winds which were shifting all around. 470 star Jo Glanfield, sailing with Kate McGregor for the week, led for much of the race only to be pipped into second at the end by Ian Martin and Chris Catt, whilst Geoff Carveth and Emma Clarke rounded off the first three. The second race saw a reversal of fortunes, with Frances Peters and Claire Lasko getting the best of the wind to take first gun after Robbie Burns and Vicki Simpson crossed the line first to an ominous silence after starting on the wrong side of the start mark! Pete Vincent and Tess Nicholls finished in second, with Dave and Jan Hivey in third position.

The second day saw a light breeze blowing across the course, and a hint of sunshine. The first race got away without incident, and James Stewart, crewed by Toby Lewis, led throughout to take the first gun ahead of South Africans Roger Hudson and Taariq Jacobs, with Dave and Jane Hivey in third position. Following promptly, the fourth points race was held in largely similar conditions, with Jo Glanfield and Kate MacGregor grabbing the win at the last moment from Andy and Jill Peters, with James Peters and Alan Roberts just a half boat length further behind.

Day Three showed Looe off to its best advantage, with eight to twelve knots of breeze and blue skies. Geoff Carveth and Emma Clarke rounded the windward mark in the lead and sailed on to a comfortable win with Ian Sharps and Kate Nicholls winning the race for second from Tom Morris and Emma Porteous. The conditions remained the same for the sixth race too and once again it was Carveth and Clarke who took the initial lead, but they were passed on the final lap by Robbie Burns and Vicki Simpson, who sailed on to the win from Chris Martin and Juliet Charles, with James Peters and Alan Roberts in third. This meant, with six races finished, that three boats had opened up something of a lead; Geoff Carveth and Emma Clarke on twenty five points, ahead of Ian Martin and Chris Catt on thirty with young James Peters, sailing with Alan Roberts, just one point further back.

After three days of light breezes, a good fifteen knots was blowing over the course on the fourth day and Geoff Carveth and Emma Clarke showed that they liked the conditions, leading at the top mark, and retaining that position to the finish ahead of James Peters and Alan Roberts, whilst Dave and Jane Hivey added yet another third to their tally for the week. Before the second race of the day was started, the breeze had died considerably once again, and it took four attempts to get the start boat away.

Carveth and Clarke again led at the first mark, with Peters and Roberts in hot pursuit. Peters crept past Carveth with a little extra wind, and then applied a tight cover to the finish to ensure that they took the victory, with Joe Glanfield and Kate MacGregor coming through to third position. Going into the last day (with a forecast of twenty-odd knots!) Carveth and Peters were just three points apart, with Ian Martin and Chris Catt a further six points behind.

The final day was a classic, final day showdown with plenty of breeze. After one false start, the fleet got away at the second attempt. Initially, the left looked good, but a 20 degree right hand shift saw the leaders come in from that side. James Stewart and Toby Lewis led at the windward mark and sped off downwind, establishing a lead they held to the end. Behind, Geoff Carveth and Emma Clarke were in second, which would be good enough to win the championships as James Peters and Alan Roberts, the main challengers, were well down the fleet. However, Peters and Roberts picked up some great shifts on the second beat to round the last windward mark just a few boat lengths behind Carveth and Clarke, but, with just one downwind leg left, it was too little too late and Carveth covered Peters to ensure he couldn't get past. This allowed Dave and Jane Hivey to sneak through to second in the race, with Ian Martin and Chris Catt in third.

Overall, Geoff Carveth and Emma Clarke were worthy champions, showing good consistency across a range of conditions.

P	Helm	Crew	R1	R2	R3	R4	R5	R6	R7	R8	R9	Pts
1	G Carveth	E Clarke	3	12	130	5	1	4	1	2	4	20
2	J Peters	A Roberts	5	53	5	3	15	3	2	1	5	24
3	I Martin	C Catt	1	15	4	4	28	6	4	6	3	28
4	D Hivey	J Hivey	37	3	3	42	7	9	3	10	2	37
5	R Hudson	T Jacobs	8	6	2	32	14	27	18	17	6	71
6	J Stewart	T Lewis	18	10	1	20	23	28	5	22	1	77
7	S Dunn	S Craig	42	130	7	39	6	8	7	8	7	82
8	M Heather	E Cowell	13	8	26	8	32	10	12	52	9	86
9	R Burns	V Simpson	23	130	22	30	4	1	10	12	16	88
10	C Martin	J Charles	4	18	58	45	11	2	17	7	33	92
11	A Peters	J Peters	29	22	21	2	16	19	14	4	18	94
12	J Glanfield	K Macgregor	2	36	33	1	18	7	34	3	58	98
13	M Saul	S Hartley	11	130	12	48	17	16	15	21	17	109
14	J Boyce	S Tozer	35	23	15	52	8	35	6	14	10	111
15	D McLean	B Hyde	10	4	130	24	43	22	37	5	12	114

RS 400

Type	Dinghy
Crew	2; Sit out
PN	952
Length	4.52 m
Beam	2 m
Weight	129 kg
Sail area M&J	14.76 sq m
Spi type	Asymmetric
Spi area	13.94 sq m
Designer	Phil Morrison
	www.rs-association.com

The RS 400 is the first boat that RS produced and is still one of the most successful. It is a two man, sit-out boat with asymmetric spinnaker and offers fast, vice-free sailing. The foam sandwich construction ensures that the boat is responsive, yet strong, and the pivoting centreboard allows the boat to be raced in shallow or deep waters equally comfortably.

RS 400 National Championships

Mounts Bay Sailing Club   23 - 28 August 2009

A fleet of sixty six RS 400 dinghies competed for the National Championships, in a week that started with good breeze and rolling waves, and was briefly visited by Hurricane Bill.

The Championship title was awarded to Dave Hivey and Emma Clarke who were leading from the first day, when they collected two race wins, and never dropped below fifth in any race during the week, taking three race wins in total. This marked the end of a good fortnight in Cornwall for the pair; the previous week Hivey had come fourth in the RS 200 Nationals whilst Emma Clarke crewed for Geoff Carveth to win the RS 200 Championship.

Second overall in the title race were Richard Brown and Keith Bedborough. After a slightly tense start, they strung a set of results together that did not drop out of the first three to show excellent consistency, and to miss out on the title by only one point. By contrast, Michael Sims and Andrew George started very well, and tailed off on the last day to gain two discards, and to allow Brown and Bedborough to pip them for the runners-up position.

Fourth position overall was taken by the strong partnership of James Stewart, sailing with the 2008 RS 200 National Champion Roger Gilbert. Of all of the competitors, they were the fastest 'finishing', winning the final two races and seeming to improve their results throughout the week.

It was an enjoyable week and, with the rolling seas for which Mounts Bay is so famous, it offered spectacular sailing for those competing and watching.

P	Helm	Crew	R1	R2	R3	R4	R5	R6	R7	R8	R9	Total	Nett
1	David Hivey	Emma Clarke	1	1	3	2	1	5	5	2	5	25	15
2	Richard Brown	Keith Bedborough	8	9	2	1	4	3	1	3	2	33	16
3	Michael Sims	Andrew George	2	5	1	4	7	1	3	DNF	11	101	23
4	James Stewart	Roger Gilbert	7	4	6	17	8	4	2	1	1	50	25
5	Dave Jones	Mark Hogan	4	3	4	3	6	6	6	5	3	40	28
6	Jim Downer	Jon Price	6	6	7	16	13	8	4	4	4	68	39
7	Joshua Metcalfe	Iwan Basten	9	2	5	6	3	7	8	DNF	9	116	40
8	Howard Farbrother	Nathan Pinch	14	10	14	10	2	9	7	8	6	80	52
9	Chris Martin	Dan Martin	3	7	DNF	DNF	15	2	9	10	10	190	56
10	Phil Kennard	Paul Smalley	22	8	8	15	26	15	13	6	7	120	72

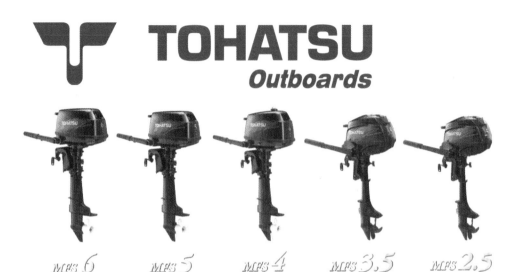

TOHATSU
Outboards

MFS *6*   MFS *5*   MFS *4*   MFS *3.5*   MFS *2.5*

A comprehensive range of four stroke and direct injection outboards from 2.5hp - 115 hp; something for everyone.

Tohatsu 5.5

"The perfect coaching boat"

RS 500

Type	Dinghy
Crew	2; 1 on trapeze
PN	960
Length	4.43 m
Beam	1.58 m
Weight	77 kg
Sail area M&J	10.5 sq m
Spi type	Asymmetric
Spi area	14 sq m
Designer	Phil Morrison, 2006
	www.rs-association.com

Photo courtesy of Annie Porter

The RS 500 is designed to suit everyone, from youngsters up to the most experienced sailor. With a choice of two rigs, the RS 500 is designed to provide continuity and to avoid the normal break between youth and senior boats. The boat is easy to sail, and yet sensitive to tune and adjustment, so you have to try to make the very best of the potential.

RS 500 European Championships

Lake Garda, Italy   2 - 6 August 2009

A fleet of twenty six RS 500s took to the waters of Lake Garda for their inaugural European Championships, an event supported by large fleets from Italy and Great Britain, and also with entries from Sweden and the Netherlands.

Despite having lost the first day through lack of winds the Committee soon got the programme back on schedule, with the event front runner proving to be Alex Taylor and Bryan Mobbs from GB, who gained eight race wins. This left them ahead of a battle of three Italian boats after three days of racing; Ruggero Tita and Giacomo D'Andrea, Filippo Barison and Veronica Luppi, and Veronica Maccari and Valentina Balbi.

The final day of racing saw the play-offs for second and third hotly contested between Team Italy. Alex Taylor and Bryan Mobbs had already won the regatta the previous day with a race to spare so they enjoyed the Garda views and climate on shore whilst the rest of the fleet took to the water. It was a day for the girls with Veronica Maccari and Valentina Balbi winning the last race of the series with Federica Zamboni and Delia Da Mosto in second. A sixth in the last race was enough to secure second overall for Filippo Barison Pier and Veronica Luppi. Meanwhile, a fifth in the final race gave Holly Watson and Eilidhl McIntyre sixth overall; a creditable result for the young British team who teamed up just for the event.

P	Nat	Helm / Crew	R1	R2	R3	R4	R5	R6	R7	R8	R9	R10	R11	R12	Pts
1	GBR	A Taylor B Mobbs	1	1	3	4	1	1	1	1	1	2	1	DNS	13
2	ITA	F Barison V Luppi	16	9	1	2	5	OCS	3	2	3	1	2	6	34
3	ITA	R Tita G D'Andrea	3	2	10	3	2	2	4	OCS	8	3	5	8	40
4	ITA	V Maccari V Balbi	DNS	19	11	1	4	3	2	4	2	10	4	1	42
5	ITA	E Marini S Balestrero	6	8	7	9	10	5	8	6	4	11	3	7	63
6	GBR	H Watson E Mcintyre	8	3	4	11	13	4	11	9	6	7	13	5	68
7	GBR	K Gerald W Martin	10	10	12	12	6	9	9	8	5	4	6	9	76
8	GBR	I Tedbury P Tedbury	2	5	14	8	7	7	12	3	9	18	17	10	77
9	ITA	F Corica J Guagliardo	9	DNS	8	7	9	OCS	7	7	7	9	12	4	79
10	ITA	M Brioschi E Roccatagliata	5	4	9	10	OCS	6	10	OCS	10	5	10	11	80

RS 500 Nationals

Arun Yacht Club, Littlehampton   29 - 31 August 2009

Eighteen RS 500s visited Arun Yacht Club, in Littlehampton to participate in their National Championships held over the August bank holiday.

The event was dominated by Alex Taylor and Bryan Mobbs from Budworth Sailing Club, the 2009 European Champions, who won five of the nine races and added two second places in their counting score to take the title by six points from Chris and Nikki Catt of Downs Sailing Club who also had only top three results to count in their points tally, discarding their first two results of fifth and fourth. Third overall was taken by Amy Hulley, crewed by the experienced Rob Burridge from Weirwood Sailing Club, who started the event strongly, but tailed off slightly with two fifths at the end, which cost them any chance of gaining second place overall.

Conditions for the long weekend were fairly breezy but the club location ensured that launching and recovery was fairly sheltered. Five races were held on the first day, but the strong conditions only allowed a single race on Day Two, with a final four races on the last day when conditions had cooled down to some degree.

Amy Hulley won the prize for top lady helm and also for top youth.

P	Helm	Crew	Club	R1	R2	R3	R4	R5	R6	R7	R8	R9	Total	Nett
1	Alex Taylor	Bryan Mobbs	BSC	1	2	1	1	1	1	3	4	2	16	9
2	Chris Catt	Nikki Catt	DSC	5	4	3	3	3	2	1	2	1	24	15
3	Amy Hulley	Rob Burridge	WSC	2	1	2	2	6	DNC	2	5	5	44	19
4	Tim Wilkins	Heather Martin	SSC	3	3	4	4	2	5	4	1	3	29	20
5	Jeni Tod	Kate Tod	LTSC	6	8	7	10	8	4	5	3	4	550	37
6	Jon Holmes	Matt Purdon	ESSC	12	9	8	5	4	3	10	9	8	680	46
7	Jack Munnelly	Jack Holden	AYC	11	7	5	8	7	7	11	8	9	73	51
8	James Tanner	Lucinda Blain	BSC	7	10	10	7	DNF	DNC	6	6	7	91	53
9	Richard Morley	Sue Morley	BDSC	15	12	11	13	9	8	7	7	6	88	60
10	Riki Hooker	Emma White	HSC	9	6	6	6	5	DNC	DNC	DNC	DNC	108	70

RS 800

Type	Dinghy	Weight	110 kg
Crew	2; Both on trapeze	Sail area M&J	16.5 sq m
PN	822	Spi type	Asymmetric
Length	4.8 m	Spi area	21 sq m
Beam	1.88 – 2.89 m	Designer	Phil Morrison
			www.rs-association.com

Photo courtesy of Mark Bloomfield

The RS 800 is a strong yet light, exciting two-man, twin-trapeze boat, having been produced in epoxy foam sandwich. Because of this light weight, the boat doesn't need an enormously big rig to power it, and therefore you can have excellent performance without the need for a large or particularly strong crew. The RS 800 benefits from the active RS Association, with an excellent range of events and socials.

The Dinghy & Smallcraft Review
2009~2010

RS 800 National Championships

Tenby, South Wales   29 - 31 August 2009

A breezy forecast for the August bank holiday weekend tempted forty RS 800s to make the trip to Tenby in South Wales for the National Championships. Two races on Day One of the event, in fifteen to twenty knots of wind, gave everyone an exciting start to the racing, with Justin Deal and Ollie Page making the most of the day to lead with two third places by evening. Laurie Fitzjohn-Sykes and Daniel Allin were second overall with a seventh and a second followed by Alan Olive and Guy Fillmore with two fifth places. Several notable competitors (not least Pete Barton and Roz Allen, and Charlie Room and Tom Jeffcoate, together with Race One winners Andy Jefferies and Adam Broughton) were seen pitch-poling in the testing conditions, to the detriment of the scoresheets!

Day Two was unfortunately lost through gales. Consequently, despite very strong winds again on Day Three, every effort was made to get some racing underway, and after a four hour postponement, two short races were planned. Steve Wilson and Jamie Stewart found the conditions to their liking and led both races. In the first, however, they were caught out by a wave and had to be satisfied with finishing seventeenth! Laurie Fitzjohn-Sykes and Daniel Allin made the most of the day and managed to score a first and second, which moved them to the top of the overnight leader-board.

With even stronger winds on the final day, no further racing was possible, and Fitzjohn-Sykes and Allin were the worthy new RS 800 National Champions in a somewhat abbreviated series, with Wilson and Stewart in second and Deal and Page in third.

P	Helm	Crew	Club	R1	R2	R3	R4	Pts
1	Laurie Fitzjohn-Sykes	Daniel Allin	DSC	7	2	1	2	5
2	Steve Wilson	Jamie Stewart	HISC	10	1	17	1	12
3	Justin Deal	Ollie Page	LSC	3	3	18	6	12
4	Justin Visser	Ryan Visser	RLYC	16	6	2	7	15
5	Ben Schooling	George Kingsnorth	HSC	14	4	3	10	17
6	Ross McKerchar	Phil Lasko	OSC	8	15	5	5	18
7	Alan Olive	Guy Fillmore	SBSC	5	5	12	12	22
8	Neil Baker	James Hughes	TBYC	15	41	6	3	24
9	Tim Saxton	Nicola Groves	EUSC	11	10	15	4	25
10	Andy Jeffries	Adam Broughton	K&QYC	1	24	7	18	26

Scorpion

Type	Dinghy
Crew	2; Sit-out
PN	1056
Length	4.27 m
Beam	1.45 m
Weight	81 kg
Sail area M&J	9.95 sq m
Spi type	Symmetric
Spi area	11.14 sq m
Designer	Taprell Dorling, 1960
	www.sailscorpion.co.uk

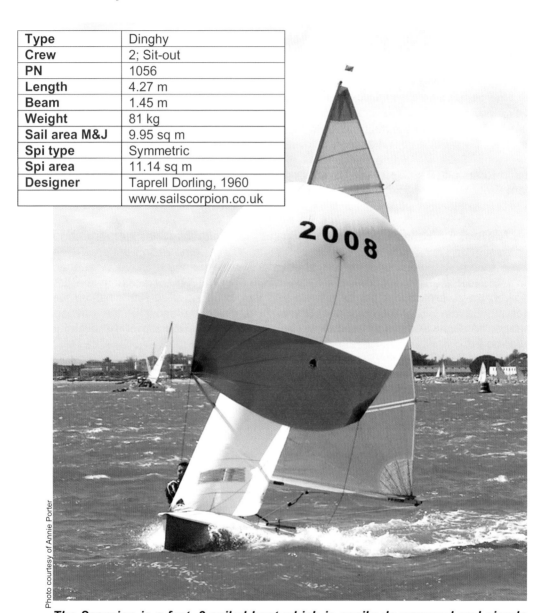

Photo courtesy of Annie Porter

The Scorpion is a fast, 3-sailed boat which is easily de-powered and simple to sail. The class sees great competitive racing at all levels, with many regional open meetings and a week-long Nationals, seeing in excess of fifty boats. The class is fun and friendly, with a good mix of people – male, female, young and old – to make for great socials and excellent racing for all the family.

Scorpion National Championships

Lyme Regis Yacht Club   15 - 21 August 2009

A fleet of fifty one Scorpions spent an enjoyable week at Lyme Regis SC in mid August when they participated in the 2009 National Championships, showing that the Scorpions are maintaining their attendances despite the testing economic times! Reigning National Champion Tom Jeffcoate teamed up with Andy Davies (the third placed helm from 2008) for the event, and started very strongly with two first places in the first two races. The previous year's runners up, John Mursell and Nick Keast opened the event with a second and third place, as did Tim Parsons and AJ Eaton.

On the second day there was less wind and more tide which necessitated the black flag being introduced. Jeffcoate and Smith again had the best of the conditions and led from start to finish from Mursell and Keast whilst Parsons and Eaton gained a third position. Jeffcoate and Davies again took charge of the fourth race and led from the windward mark to gain another gun. Whilst initially with a bit of ground to make up, Mursell and Keast managed to pass Andy McKee and Tarren Jones for second position before the end; as did Steve Hall and Simon Haighton, whilst Kevin Gosling and Max Hayman finished off the top five places. The black flag was reintroduced for the fifth race and this was to see Jeffcoate and Davies knocked off the top step of the podium! With a difficult sea and ten to fifteen knots of breeze the race was won by Parsons and Eaton. Jeffcoate and Davies finished in second, and Hall and Haighton gained another third, whilst Adrian and Rob Smith finished in fourth.

With two more races completed on the penultimate day, Jeffcoate and Davies added another first and second place to their tally to be confirmed as the new National Champions with Parsons and Eaton ten points behind, having earned a fifth and a third on the day. Mursell and Keast held third position going into the final day, two points in arrears, with a margin of twenty one points back to fourth placed David and Mike Hannan, and the overall winner looking likely to come out of the top three. Jeffcoate and Smith did not compete in the final race, leaving the squabbling for the minor placings to others. In the event Hall and Haighton won the race, which left them clear in fourth position overall, with Mursell and Keast second in the final heat, and third overall. Parsons and Easton were third in the final race which left them level on points with Mursell but they got the second overall position on the tie break.

P	Helm	Crew	R1	R2	R3	R4	R5	R6	R7	R9	Pts
1	T Jeffcoate	A Smith	1	1	1	1	2	1	2	52	7
2	T Parsons	A Eaton	2	3	3	6	1	5	3	3	15
3	J Mursell	N Keast	3	2	2	2	6	4	7	2	15
4	S Hall	S Haighton	4	4	52	3	3	52	1	1	16
5	D Hannan	M Hannan	8	7	10	9	5	7	4	4	35
6	A Smith	R Smith	7	5	7	7	4	15	16	5	35
7	K Gosling	M Hayman	5	6	52	5	14	6	6	8	36
8	A McKee	T Jones	12	22	6	4	8	3	10	15	43

12 sq m Sharpie

Type	Dinghy
Crew	2; Sit out
PN	1025
Length	5.99 m
Beam	1.43 m
Weight	230 kg
Sail area M&J	12 sq m
Spi type	None
Designer	J Kroege, 1931
	www.sharpies.org.uk

The 12 sq m Sharpie is the only international class still to sport a gaff. It was designed to revive the flagging German dinghy market in 1931 and was first imported to the UK by the Barnt Green Sailing Club in 1934. The class is now mainly centered on the North Norfolk coast with about 35 boats being regularly sailed. The Sharpie National Championships are held in June, with the European Championships alternating between Great Britain, Holland, Germany, and Portugal. Open meetings are held at the three Norfolk clubs.

12 sq m Sharpie Nationals

Brancaster Staithe Sailing Club   12 - 14 June 2009

Thirty three Sharpies, including two boats from Holland, competed in the 2009 12 sq m Sharpie National Championships, which were raced in tricky conditions over a long weekend.

The National Championship title was won by Chris and Tim Gibbs of Wells SC, defending the title that they won in 2008, despite being unable to pull back on the reigning European Champions, Tom Weller and Jeroen van Veen who took victory in the first race, continued to sail a dominant regatta throughout to win the Open Championship. With conditions over the first two days never rising beyond Force two, scores were inevitably quite high, but as the fleet entered the third and final day, the results for the Nationals looked to be between the Gibbses, James Case and Jimmy Goodley and Martin and Ollie Read. With a slightly later start time, at least there was a Force two to three to help resolve the tangle at the top of the scoreboard.

The Dutch team confirmed their dominance with another win in Race Five before resting for the final heat in which the Gibbs team got a second, followed by a first to confirm their position as National Championships for the sixth consecutive time, whilst the tussle for second and third in the National title race was tight, James Case and Jimmy Goodley ending with a three point margin ahead of Martin and Ollie Read, and Paddy Spink and John Ellison.

P	Helm	Crew	Club	Pts
1	Chris Gibbs	Tim Gibbs	WSC	13
2	James Case	Jimmy Goodley	WSC	18
3	Martin Read	Ollie Read	WSC	21
4	Paddy Spink	John Ellison	BSSC	21
5	Richard Major	Bob Curtis	WSC	25
6	Richard Cracknell	Gemma Nye	WSC	38
7	Jerry Clark	Jonathan Charles	OSSC	45
8	Kiki Spink	Bob Bradshaw	BSSC	47
9	Cliff Nye	James Nye	BSSC	48
10	Brian Lambert	Tim Adams	BSSC	63

Snipe

Type	Dinghy	Weight	125 kg
Crew	2; Sit out	Sail area M&J	11.9 sq m
PN	1117	Spi type	None
Length	4.72 m	Designer	W Crosby
Beam	1.54 m		www.snipe.org.uk

The Snipe was designed in 1931 and, over the years, has become very popular internationally. There are over 30,000 boats around the world, and because of the simplicity of sailing, the boat has become popular with people of all ages.

Snipe Nationals

Paignton Sailing Club   22 - 24 August 2009

The 2009 Snipe National Championships were held at Paignton Sailing Club as part of the Ocean BMW Torbay Week with an entry of seventeen boats, and a seven race series held over three days. The race course was shared with the Vortex National Championships and the Laser meeting, with the Snipes and Lasers sailing on a standard Olympic class.

Conditions remained stable over the three day period, with a shifty force three and a short chop (with a liberal scattering of 'holes' as an extra test). The conditions certainly suited some, with Alan Williams and Liz Pike dominating the racing and winning six out of the seven heats and taking the title comfortably with a race to spare. Behind Williams competition was far more intense, Andy and Carol Gibson finishing in second position overall, whilst the next three competitors (Ian Gregory and Cecile Munoz, Nick McGonigle and Guy Welch, and Ian Knight and Graham Hoy), all finished within one point overall after seven races with the overall results finally determined in the last race.

The class had built a reserve race into the schedule in case of weather problems, and it was decided that this race should be run outside of the championships as a fun event with crews drawing for their helmsmen, or visa versa! This was won by Ian Knight and his borrowed featherweight crew Anne Gregory. The opportunity for a relaxed fun race in the course of the championships was a welcome diversion for many!

P	Helm	Crew	Club	R1	R2	R3	R4	R5	R6	R7	Pts
1	Alan Williams	Liz Pike	BCSC	1	1	1	1	4	1	1	6
2	Andy Gibson	Carol Gibson	RYCB	5	7	2	6	2	4	3	22
3	Ian Gregory	Cécile Munoz	BCSC	4	5	12	5	3	8	4	29
4	Nick McGonigle	Guy Welch	RSC	6	4	10	2	1	7	12	30
5	Ian Knight	Graham Hoy	SSC	8	3	3	12	6	5	5	30
6	Iain Marshall	Richard Marshall	MYC	2	2	13	10	11	2	6	33
7	Brian Gregory	Anne Gregory	BCSC	3	13	11	8	10	3	2	37
8	Phil Hackney	Emma Hackney	BSC	9	6	8	3	9	14	8	43
9	Mark Antonelli	Tracy Norris	BSC	11	9	7	7	7	6	7	43
10	Will Williams	Stephen Williams	BSC	10	10	4	9	5	9	9	46

12ft Skiff

Type	Dinghy	Weight	45 kg
Crew	2; On trapeze	Sail Area M&J	Unlimited
PN	871 Prov	Spi Type	Unrestricted
Length	3.7 m	Spi Area	Unlimited
Beam	1.8 m	Designer	Various; early 1900s
			www.12footskiff.com

Photo courtesy of Garrick Cameron

The 12ft Skiff is a largely unrestricted class, with simple rules governing the maximum length and beam, and minimum weight of the hull only. Rigs are completely unrestricted, with most boats having four or five rigs for different wind strengths, the largest rigs carrying asymmetric spinnakers of up to 60 sq m on 14ft bowsprits. The 12ft Skiff is one of the most challenging, yet rewarding, classes in the world, and is not for the faint-hearted.

12ft Skiff Action "Down Under"

29er

Type	Dinghy
Crew	2; 1 on trapeze
PN	926
Length	4.45 m
Beam	1.77 m
Weight	70 kg
Sail Area M&J	12.5 sq m
Spi Type	Asymmetric
Spi Area	15 sq m
Designer	Julian Bethwaite, 1997
	www.29er.org.uk

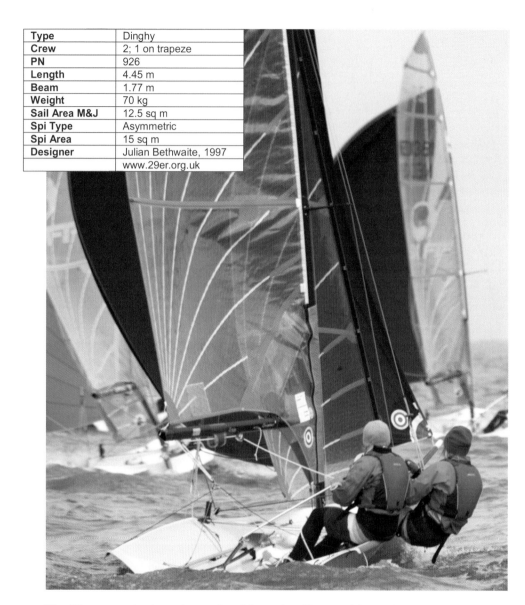

The 29er was designed as a lead into the 49er and has since become a full international class in its own right. Used as the two-person asymmetric boat at both the RYA National Championships and the ISAF Youth World Championships, it is suited to both young teams and small adult teams. A full international and national racing programme is organized by the international and national class associations.

29er World Championships

Riva del Garda, Italy   18 - 25 July 2009

Following straight after the 49er World Championships, one hundred and eighty three 29ers celebrated their World Championships in the classic sailing venue of Riva del Garda, with competitors from the four corners of the world.

The huge fleet was split into four flights for the initial racing, and each flight enjoyed three races on the first day. Overall leaders after the first day of racing were Haylee Outteridge, sailing with Iain Jensen. Haylee's brother Nathan had won the 49er World Championships the previous week, sailing with Iain Jensen, so this was a convenient arrangement for all concerned. Nathan, incidentally, was also sailing in the 29er event, crewing for girlfriend Lauren Jeffries, and lying fifteenth overall after the first day!

Second overall after the first day was another Australian crew, Steven Thomas sailing with New Zealander Blair Tuke, with the Croatians Domagoj Fizulic and Leon Ostrez in third spot, just ahead of the first UK boat, Emsworth based Tom Durham sailing with George Hand, who had a first, second and third to count after the initial day's sailing.

Day Two saw another series of three races per flight, with two teams gaining a one hundred percent record on the day. Steven Thomas and Blair Tuke won all three races in their flight while Americans Judge Ryan and Matt Noble equalled this by winning all their races as well. This left Thomas, the reigning World Champion at the top of the leader-board ahead of Ryan and Noble, whilst first-day leader, Haylee Outteridge continued in third and Tom Durham and George Hand from the UK continued as top Brit in seventh position ahead of Max Richardson and Alex Groves.

Three more fleet races on Day Three with a good eighteen to twenty knots of breeze saw the fleet split into Gold, Silver, Bronze and Emerald. Outteridge and Jensen scored two wins and a second to maintain their challenge, passing the US sailors Judge Ryan and Matt Noble in the process, whilst Thomas and Tuke added a first and second position, although gaining a discard of a seventeenth in the course of the day.

Day Four and Five saw the Australians underlining their high standards, with the top three positions going to them. Steven Thomas and Blair Tuke had a thirty point lead on Haylee Outteridge and Iain Jensen, who had passed Lauren Jeffries and Nathan Outteridge in the course of day. At this stage there were four Australian teams in the top five of the regatta, with Brits Max Richardson and Alex Groves in fourth, and Tom Durham and George Hand continuing a steady week in seventh place as second Brits at this stage, although they fell away slightly on the final day.

As the final day opened, there was still much for which to sail, although the overall Championship had already been won, retained by Steven Thomas and Blair Tuke with a thoroughly steady display, with no results below third, giving them the luxury of sitting back throughout the final two races!

The battle on the final day was between the Outteridge siblings. In the end big brother Nathan with skipper Lauren Jeffries out-sailed his sister to take second overall. Haylee with Iain Jensen as crew finished third overall just two points behind.

Max Richardson and Alex Groves of GBR were the top placing youth team, finishing fourth in the Gold fleet while Ida Marie Baad Nielsen and Marie Thusgaard Olsen of Denmark were the top placing female team.

The fifty four boat Silver fleet was won by Americans Paris Henken with Chris Rast as crew, another 49er Olympic sailor in the front of the boat, whilst the Bronze fleet was won by Sinem Kurtbay and Ville Bergman of Finland with the Emerald fleet winners Casey McDermott and Chantelle Boudreau of Canada.

P	Nat	Helm / Crew	1	2	3	4	5	6	7	8	9	10	11	Pts
1	AUS	Steven Thomas Blair Tuke	1	3	2	2	1	1	1	3	1	DNF	DNF	15
2	AUS	Lauren Jeffries Nathan Outteridge	5	1	9	6	8	2	3	14	14	5	4	43
3	AUS	Haylee Outteridge Iain Jensen	2	2	6	1	21	12	10	1	8	10	5	45
4	GBR	Max Richardson Alex Groves	9	5	10	8	2	10	15	4	4	21	9	61
5	ARG	Pepe Bettini Fernando Gwozdz	6	21	5	17	10	22	4	6	13	6	1	63
6	AUS	David O'Connor Rhys Mara	15	16	7	7	11	3	2	2	22	3	22	66
7	FRA	Kevin Fischer Glenn Gouron	4	12	1	21	7	9	16	13	9	9	13	77
8	ITA	Riccardo Camin Lorenzo Franceshini	13	6	23	24	4	4	6	10	16	7	12	78
9	USA	Maxwell Fraser David Liebenberg	18	11	22	12	5	7	5	11	12	20	2	83
10	USA	Judge Ryan Matt Noble	3	7	3	23	OCS	18	17	16	10	1	10	85
11	NED	Mark Walraven Kaj Bocker	7	4	14	15	14	15	12	18	7	4	8	85
12	GBR	Tom Durham George Hand	8	19	18	4	3	5	24	9	5	18	24	89
13	ARG	Belen Tavella Franco Greggi	20	8	4	25	18	13	14	5	3	12	14	93
14	AUS	Hannah Nattrass Jamie Woods	10	9	15	10	9	20	7	RAF	15	17	7	99
15	GBR	Bleddyn Mon Nick Redding	16	23	13	3	12	DSQ	20	8	2	11	15	100

29er National Championships

Hayling Island Sailing Club   24 - 28 August 2009

A fleet of forty nine 29er dinghies took part in their Nationals, held in conjunction with the 49er Nationals at Hayling Island SC and with some competitors taking part in both events! On the first afternoon the wind continued to increase and this, combined with the strong tide, tested the less experienced. After the black flag was brought in, almost half of the fleet found itself in trouble!

Having competed in the 49er Nationals immediately prior to the 29ers, local boy Tom Durham from Emsworth, sailing with George Hand, swapped boats on the start line and launched into the second event with some verve, gaining a first, second and third on the first day. He following this up with a string of first places that had him in control of the event throughout the week, and when racing was finally abandoned on the Firday, Tom and George were left with the National title, with a healthy eleven point margin. Henry Lloyd Williams, sailing with Sam Batten, also had a good week, winning two races and with three second places to count, to beat leading overseas entrant, Gakl Jaffrezic and Julien Bloyet for second overall. Gear problems for ex Optimist Champion Alex Mothersele, sailing with Hamish Ellis, allowed Erwan Fischer and Julien Thibault to grab fourth overall, with Mothersele completing a good week in fifth.

P	Helm	Crew	R1	R2	R3	R4	R5	R6	R7	R8	R9	R10	Tot	Nett
1	T Durham	G Hand	3	2	1	1	1	1	1	3	DNC	1	64	11
2	H Lloyd Williams	S Batten	1	BFD	6	2	6	2	2	OCS	1	2	122	22
3	G Jaffrezic	J Bloyet	4	5	5	5	4	3	7	6	2	OCS	91	34
4	E ischer	J Thibault	BFD	7	4	6	7	5	4	7	5	15	110	45
5	A Mothersele	H Ellis	2	1	14	12	5	8	9	21	7	7	86	51
6	C Matthews	E Gibbons	6	13	3	7	2	10	14	90	DSQ	6	120	56
7	I Martin	F Hampshire	BFD	3	2	4	19	9	5	8	21	8	129	58
8	A Horlock	T Walton	BFD	19	7	8	16	12	6	2	3	4	127	58
9	H Jones-Warner	R Jones-Warner	BFD	6	BFD	13	11	4	3	1	16	9	163	63
10	J Sivyer	C Esse	BFD	12	DSQ	3	3	23	13	5	4	3	166	66

29er XX

Type	Dinghy	Weight	70 kg
Crew	2; Both on trapeze	Sail area M&J	15 sq m
PN	850	Spi type	Asymmetric
Length	4.45 m	Spi area	19 sq m
Beam	1.77 m	Designer	Julian Bethwaite, 2006
			www.29erxx.org

The 29erXX is basically a 29er on steroids. A taller mast, bigger sails, mast head spinnaker and twin trapeze makes for an exciting, fast, small skiff. For those who want to step up from the 29er but find the 49er too big a step, the 29erXX fills the gap. To ease the transition, the 29erXX rig goes straight onto the 29er hull.

29erXX Gold Cup

Lake Garda   12 - 19 July 2009

The inaugural 29erXX Gold Cup was held at Lake Garda in mid July, in conjunction with the 2009 49er World Championships.

A small but strong entry of fifteen boats (from eight different countries) ensured that racing would be good, and the initial performance suggested that one of the pace-setters was liable to be 2006 29er World Champion Silja Lehtinen from Finland, sailing with Will Howard as crew, who took the lead at the end of the first three races, counting an initial victory amongst his results. The second day saw Lehtinen/Howard strengthen their position further with two race wins and a second position, from Sara Engstrom and Hanna Dahlborg of Sweden, whilst another Finnish crew, Tina Kotamies and Camilla Cedercreutz, filled third ahead of top Brits, Sam Watson and Henry Collinson.

As the week concluded, Lehtinen and Howards domination of the event became more complete, and with a final winning tally of six races from the nine heats sailed, they became comfortable 29erXX Gold Cup winners. Second overall in equally dominant fashion were Sara Engstrom and Hanna Dahlborg, who finished twenty three points clear of US sailors, Jen Morgan-Glass with German Billoch who just came out on top of a very tight cluster of boats with only four and a half points separating third position overall from sixth.

The UK contingent of Sam Watson and Henry Collinson, and Dave Hall and Jessica Smith finished in fifth and sixth positions, just one point apart.

P	Nat	Helm	Crew	R1	R2	R3	R4	R5	R6	R7	R8	R9	Pts
1	FIN	Silja Lehtinen	Will Howard	5	2	1	2	1	1	1	1	1	10
2	SWE	Sara Engstrom	Hanna Dahlborg	1	5	8	1	2	12	2	2	5	21
3	USA	Jen Morgan Glass	German Billoch	6	11	9	3	3	13	4	6	7	44
4	FIN	Tina Kotamies	Camilla Cedercreutz	2	3	11	5	4	6	12	10	4	45
5	GBR	Sam Watson	Henry Collinson	11	1	2	13	5	2	5	9	13	48
6	GBR	David Hall	Jessica Smith	10	6	3	10	7	9	3	5	6	49
7	GER	Karin Marchart	Tina Marchart	8	13	5	9	9	4	8	4	3	50
8	FIN	Mikko Kotamies	Nova Van Der Ende	7	4	6	11	6	3	DNF	7	10	54
9	ITA	George Wills	Alessandra Angelini	9	10	7	12	8	10	9	3	2	58
10	GER	Werner Gieser	Dominik Entsminger	3	8	4	7	10	14	6	8	8	60

Tasar

Crew	2; Sit out
PN	1023
Length	4.52 m
Beam	1.75 m
Weight	68 kg
Sail area M&J	11.43 sq m
Spi type	None
Designer	Frank Bethwaite, 1975
	www.tasar.org.uk

Photo courtesy of Tasar Assoc

The Tasar was designed to be sailed by a man and a woman, and it delivers exciting performance without using either spinnaker or trapeze. The hull has a fine angle at the bow to reduce wave-impact drag, with unusually clean and sharp chines aft to ensure very free planing and outstanding stability. The wide beam and a cockpit designed for comfortable hiking make the Tasar easy, fun and very exciting to sail in winds up to 25 knots.

Tasar Nationals

East Lothian Yacht Club   23 – 25 May 2009

Thirty two Tasars from throughout Europe made the long trip to East Lothian Yacht Club at the end of May for their National and European Championships. Every race victory was taken by Malcolm and Fiona Davis who consequently retained their title from 2008 in great style, taking the European title in the act. The entries were affected slightly by the economic downturn, and also by the timing of the event which was set to permit boats to compete in the Worlds in Japan in September.

Racing during the regatta was held in strong conditions, with wind speed up to thirty five knots, and the scheduled eight race programme had to be shortened to six races as the final day was too lively for competitive sailing.

P	SN	Helm	Crew	Club	Tot	Nett
1	2628	Malcolm Davies	Fiona Davies	PSC	6	5
2	2642	Pete Ellis	Charlotte Birbeck	TMSC	19	13
3	2502	Howard Astley-Jones	Barney Proud	MKSC	35	20
4	405	James Sinclair	Patrick Burns	ELYC	30	21
5	363	Tim Knight	Mayumi Knight	RLYC	30	22
6	2816	Neil Spacagna	Sam Richardson	BSC	41	30
7	298	Constantine Udo	Jan Slotemaker	WSVR	41	30
8	659	Sam Pascoe	Hayley Goacher	WSC	47	34
9	2804	Roop Stock	Mike Hutton-Ashkenny	RLYC	49	39
10	268	Kevan Gibb	Alex Buglass	LSC	57	41

Tideway

Type	Dinghy
Crew	1 or 2 plus children
PN	1447
Length	3.66 m
Beam	1.52 m
Weight	125 kg
Sail area M&J	7.53 sq m
Spi type	None
Designer	L H Walker, 1954
	www.tidewaydinghy.org

A classic cruising dinghy with a fine reputation built in the Swallows and Amazons tradition of safe and fun sailing and designed for stability and ease of handling, Tideways are attractive, safe and fun boats to sail. They are still available in wood but most today are a balance of traditional and modern with high quality fiberglass hulls coupled with wood in the build – mahogany gunwales, thwarts etc and spars of douglas fir. Mostly gunter rigged, all the spars fit within the boat, and with a simple and effective rig. There is an active Tideway Owners Association that arranges meetings around the country each year.

Topper Magno

Type	Dinghy	Weight	60 kg
Crew	1 - 4	Sail area M&J	10.26 sq m
PN	1175	Spi type	Asymmetric
Length	3.94 m	Spi area	8.72 sq m
Beam	1.56 m	Designer	I Howlett / R White
			www.toppersailboats.com

The Magno is designed to suit all the family. The boat is easy to sail, with an exciting yet forgiving hull, which combines well with the easily-controlled rig. She suits the novice as well as the experienced sailor, and offers a suprising turn of speed. The hull shape ensures that the boat is very stable, yet handles very well, and offers a boat that can satisfy a wide range of demands, be it as a single-hander, or with three or four on board.

Topper Omega

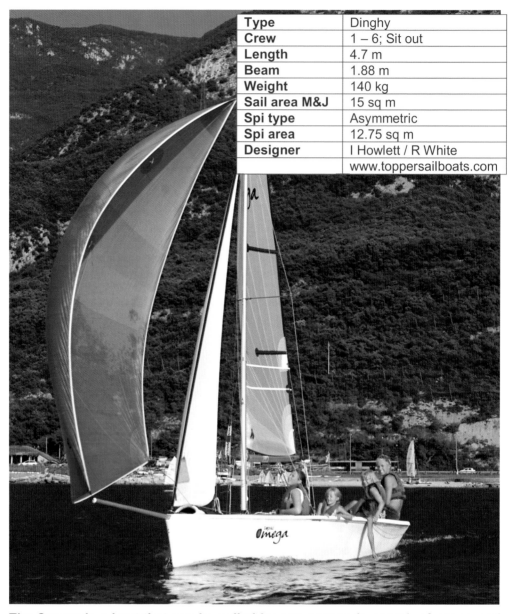

Type	Dinghy
Crew	1 – 6; Sit out
Length	4.7 m
Beam	1.88 m
Weight	140 kg
Sail area M&J	15 sq m
Spi type	Asymmetric
Spi area	12.75 sq m
Designer	I Howlett / R White
	www.toppersailboats.com

The Omega is a boat that can be sailed by one person in search of peace and quiet, or a whole family of up to 6! Given an extremely spacious cockpit and deep topsides, the Omega has become very popular with the dinghy cruising fraternity, but she also is a boat that is suited to club racing, with her easily manageable asymmetric spinnaker, and well thought-out fittings layout.

Topper Xenon

Type	Dinghy
Crew	1 - 4
PN	1075
Length	4.5 m
Beam	2.0 m
Weight	118 kg
Sail area M&J	15.5 sq m
Spi type	Asymmetric
Spi area	12.75 sq m
	www.toppersailboats.com

The Xenon is a high-performance, 2-man hiking boat, ideal for daysailing or for club racing. Because of the economies available by selecting this form of manufacture, the Xenon is an extremely economical way to buy a new club-racing boat, and the boat's pedigree is obvious, as the boat has now been chosen for the prestigious Champion of Champions event in the Endeavour Trophy in the past few years.

3000

Type	Dinghy	Weight	55 kg (was 79 kg)
Crew	2; 1 on trapeze	Sail area M&J	12 sq m
PN	1007/1032	Spi type	Asymmetric
Length	4.4 m	Spi area	13 sq m
Beam	1.46 m	Designer	Frank Bethwaite / Derek Clark, 1996
			www.3000class.org.uk

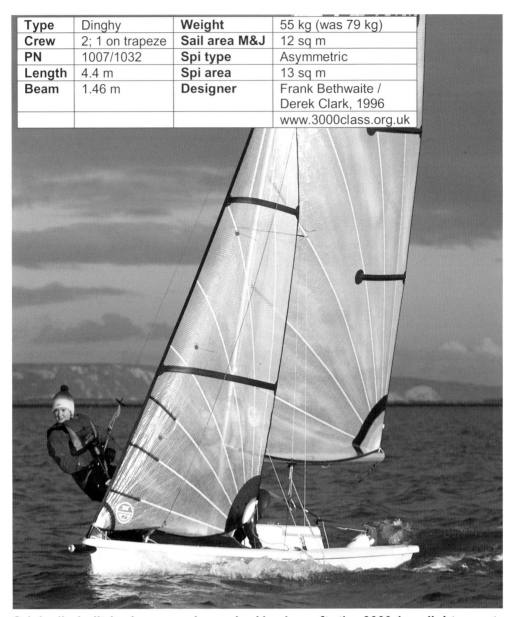

Originally built by Laser, and now by Vandercraft, the 3000 is a light, sporty dinghy with an asymmetric spinnaker and a trapeze. It offers fast, exciting, yet easy sailing, particularly for the lighter sailor couples, parent-child and teenage combinations are common at all 3000 events. A series of open events are organized though the summer, and trial sails are available upon request.

3000 National Championships

Grafham Water Sailing Club   12 – 14 June 2009

A fleet of sixteen 3000s travelled to Grafham Water SC in Huntingdon for the 2009 National Championships. Now that the boat has settled with its new builder, it is good to see that there is a degree of development taking place to define its position in the market, and also a number of brand new boats coming into the fleet to keep competition keen. Amongst other changes this year has been the advent of a Dacron jib, to increase longevity of the sails. The fact that the winning boat boasted one of these sails indicates that it is not only longevity that they can offer. Congratulations to Patrick Shellcock and Harry Batty of Sedburgh School, who won the prize draw for a new genoa at the championships; hopefully it helped them to their eighth overall position!

Winners of the Championships this year were Wilsonians Tony Hunt and Suzanne Hall, successfully defending their title won at Rutland in 2008 with three impressive wins and a second position in the four races. Behind then in the rankings were a number of new faces. Runner-up for the event was Joe Pester, sailing with Lyndi Jones from Ullswater YC in Cumbria, whilst Peter Heyes and Adam Bermingham, and Martin Brown and Max Caston made up the Wilsonian SC "attack", taking third and fourth positions overall.

P	Helm	Crew	Club	R1	R2	R3	R4	Tot	Pts
1	Tony Hunt	Suzanne Hall	WSC	1	2	1	1	5	3
2	Joe Pester	Lyndi Jones	UYC	2	1	3	3	9	6
3	Peter Heyes	Adam Bermingham	WSC	3	5	4	2	14	9
4	Martin Brown	Max Caston	WSC	4	3	5	4	16	11
5	Nick Arran	Patrick, Matthew or Chris Arran	CSC	7	6	2	DNC	32	15
6	Ben Blake	Graham Blake	QMSC	6	4	6	7	23	16
7	Ed Walker	Chloe Tucker	RWSC	5	8	7	5	25	17
8	Patrick Shellcock	Harry Batty	KSA	DNC	9	8	6	40	23

Wanderer

Type	Dinghy
Crew	2; Sit out
PN	1132
Length	4.27 m
Beam	1.75 m
Weight	129.5 kg
Sail area M&J	10.68 sq m
Spi type	Symmetric
Spi area	9.94 sq m
Designer	Ian Proctor, 1980
	www.wanderer.org.uk

The Wanderer is a high-quality, hand-built, GRP-constructed two man dinghy with outstanding long term durability. With either transom or centre-main sheeting, this boat has excellent handling characteristics, which helps even new sailors to become confident and improve their skills. With a total hull weight of less than 130 kg, handling the boat in and out of the water is straight forward. The active and friendly Wanderer Class Owners' Association – focusing on family-oriented activities – organises training, racing, and cruising events throughout the spring, summer, and autumn. The Wanderer can be sailed single-handed, or raced with two up, or sailed with up to four adults, making it an ideal family dinghy.

Wanderer Nationals

Whitstable Yacht Club   10 - 12 July 2009

A fleet of nineteen Wanderers gathered at Whitstable YC to contest the 2009 National Championships, with the new Hartley Laminates Wanderer attracting much attention amongst the fleet, and capturing the title with an impressive five race wins, in the hands of father and son boat builders, Richard and Mark Hartley.

Conditions on Saturday were perfect with a shifting force four SW breeze for the first race, and offered somewhat more stable conditions later in the day. In Race One, past Championship winner, Gavin Barr, sailing with Mark Skipper, kept the pressure on the Hartley's, along with Tim Barr and Ali Nicolson, but whilst the rescue facilities were kept busy, neither team was quite able to better them! Race Two saw new faces in pursuit of the Hartleys in the form of Paul Yeadon and Liz North, who chased Tim Barr and Ali Nicholson throughout to gain a great third position in their first day of Wanderer sailing! For Race Three, Gavin Barr and Mark Skipper were back on the pace, after a capsize off the start in Race Two. They led at the windward mark, but were unable to fend off the Hartleys, and finished the day with another second position.

Originally a passage race had been planned for the Sunday morning, but conditions were not perfect for this, and the fleet reverted to "around the cans" courses. In Race Four, Tim Barr shut out the Hartleys at the Committee boat, but the delay was temporary and they soon took the lead, whilst the fifth race once again saw them complete a clean sweep to take the Championships in a convincing manner.

P	Helm	Crew	Club	R1	R2	R3	R4	R5	Tot	Pts
1	R Hartley	M Hartley	CSC	1	1	1	1	1	5	4
2	T Barr	A Nicolson	T&TSA	3	2	5	2	2	14	9
3	G Barr	M Skipper	WYC	2	5	2	3	4	16	11
4	M Saqui	J Saqui	RLYC	4	4	3	7	3	21	14
5	P Yeadon	L North / A Stanley	PSC	9	3	4	8	10	34	24
6	J Stuart-Smith	T Dodd	WYC	7	7	7	5	5	31	24
7	M Fagg	J Carter	WYC	5	9	13	4	8	39	26
8	M Hamilton	D Oates	CSSA	10	6	6	9	12	43	31
9	W Lowes	I Hender	WYC	11	8	8	6	9	42	31
10	C Partington	J Skipper	WYC	6	20	9	10	11	56	36

Wayfarer

Type	Dinghy
Crew	2; Sit out
PN	1099
Length	4.85 m
Beam	1.85 m
Weight	167 kg
Sail area M&J	13.07 sq m
Spi type	Symmetric
Spi area	13.5 sq m
Designer	Ian Proctor, 1958
	www.wayfarer.org.uk

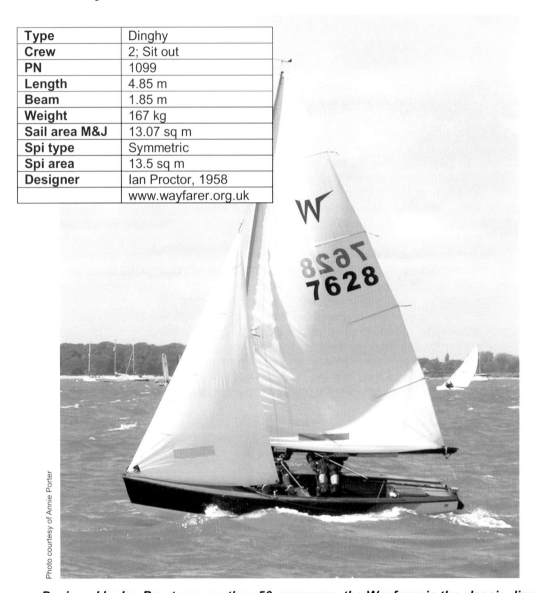

Photo courtesy of Annie Porter

Designed by Ian Proctor more than 50 years ago, the Wayfarer is the classic dinghy, managing to incorporate so many desirable traits; it is easy to sail, but hard to sail well, and is stable, yet surprisingly responsive and rapid. For many years the Wayfarer was the basis for all dinghy training, and still is the choice of many schools. Whilst normally raced by two, five or six can be accommodated for daysailing, and can sail in comfort. The Wayfarer is widely raced, yet is equally at home as a dinghy cruiser, with the famous exploits of Frank Dye giving an idea of the boat's abilities.

Wayfarer National Championships

Falmouth Week, Restronguet Sailing Club   3 - 7 August 2009

The Wayfarer National Championships of 2009 took place as one of the integral race-series within the Falmouth Week Regatta, with sailing based at Restronguet Sailing Club, and courses held within the normal organisation of the event. With a fleet of twenty five boats participating, the racing differed from standard championship sailing in that it followed the Falmouth Week format, giving the competitors the opportunity to visit various parts of the harbour, and different clubs in the course of the event, a format that has previously proven very popular with the class.

The racing provided for two races per day on most days, with a long distance harbour race on Thursday; a total of ten heats. Winner overall, and the winner of six of the races during the week, was past champion Michael McNamara, sailing for this event with Denmark's "Ace" Wayfarer sailor, Jesper Friis, in the absence of his normal crew. He was pushed by Wayfarer newcomer Rob Lyne, crewed by Mark McKechnie, who had only collected his new boat a few days before the event and who immediately confused the pecking order with a string of top three positions. Long time class member Brian Lamb, crewed by Tony Hunt, also showed excellent speed in a new boat, winning one race during the course of the event, and comfortably taking third position ahead of Peter Sigetty Boje and Jonathon Boje of Denmark, the current Wayfarer World Champions.

P	Helm	Crew	R1	R2	R3	R4	R5	R6	R7	R8	R9	R10	Tot	Nett
1	M McNamara	J Friis	1	1	3	1	10	2	1	2	1	1	23	10
2	R Lyne	M McKechnie	3	2	2	4	1	OCS	2	4	5	3	51	21
3	B Lamb	T Hunt	7	6	5	12	2	9	8	1	3	4	57	36
4	P S Boje	J Boje	9	9	OCS	2	3	1	9	3	6	17	84	42
5	G Harris	E Harris	8	3	1	10	4	18	6	5	10	5	70	42
6	L McGrath	S McGrath	4	11	6	5	5	5	3	20	11	6	76	45
7	D Wealthy	A Wealthy	DNC	5	8.5	3	7	4	12	9	7	12	92.5	55
8	J Goudie	S Hall	6	14	13.5	7	9	6	7	11	2	16	91.5	61.5
9	P Kay	C Fuller	11	7	10	6	6	OCS	4	15	8	13	105	65
10	M McKechnie	G Ireland	2	4	15.5	11	11	12	11	13	9	8	96.5	68

Y W Dayboat

Type	Dinghy	Weight	204 kg
Crew	2; Sit out / steel plate	Sail area	12.26 sq m
PN	1200	Spi type	None
Length	4.27 m	Designer	O'Brien Kennedy, 1949
Beam	1.725 m		www.ywdb.co.uk

The Yachting World Dayboat is a classic dinghy which blends stability and seaworthiness with good performance, although it is too heavy to readily plane. It is a very stable family boat for safe day-sailing, and its small foresail can be handled by light crew. It is ideal for a (drying) mooring, but the modern combination trailers make launch, sailing and recovery entirely feasible.

Yachting World Dayboat National Championships

Fishguard Bay Yacht Club   8 - 14 August 2009

Eighteen boats ventured to Fishguard Bay YC for the 2009 National Championships Week, with particularly strong representation from both the Poole Yacht Club and Gravesend Sailing Club. Racing was held across the full range of wind conditions, from relatively calm, up to gusting force seven, and this ensured that the final results were a fair representation. This meant that Peter Hewitt and Alannah Honey had the best week, with four race wins and a second in their results. This dominance meant that the championships were theirs with a day to spare, from Bob and Kath Davis, who came in just one point clear of third place overall, David and Caroline Cake. Each of these three (and indeed all of the top five overall) are members of the successful Poole Yacht Club fleet, whilst sixth overall was taken by the first of the Gravesend boats sailed by Richard and Deborah Twyman.

In 2008 Hewitt could do no better than fourth overall when sailing with his wife, and there is little doubt that he found the conditions more to his liking this year. Additionally, the previous year's Champion, Ron Lovett, was not in attendance in 2009, and therefore not able to challenge Hewitt during the event. However, since his last Nationals victory (in 2005), Hewitt has made a habit of coming in the top three or four places, and this return to form is certainly his just desserts for continuous effort.

P	SN	Helm	Crew	R1	R2	R3	R4	R5	Pts
1	649	Peter Hewitt	Alannah Honey	2	1	1	1	1	4
2	641	Bob Davis	Kath Davis	3	4	7	3	2	12
3	661	David Cake	Caroline Cake	1	7	2	6	4	13
4	635	Wendy Davies	Roy Davies	4	3	5	7	5	17
5	659	Murray Glenister	Theresa Glenister	5	5	3	5	RTD	18
6	612	Richard Twyman	Deborah Twyman	12	2	4	10	3	19
7	565	Tim Parkinson	Diana Parkinson	6	10	6	2	6	20
8	650	Sue Clayton	Howard Clayton	9	6	8	4	RTD	27
9	632	John Lokier	Phil Lokier	7	8	10	9	9	33
10	622	Dave Thompson	Helen de Bie	8	12	11	8	RTD	39

Single-handers

Blaze

Type	Dinghy	Weight	72 kg
Crew	1; Sit out	Sail area M	10.2 sq m
PN	1047	Spi type	None
Length	4.2 m	Designer	I Howlett / J Caig, 1996
Beam	2.48 m		www.blazesailing.org.uk

The Blaze offers significantly high performance (PN 1047), while at the same time remaining simple to sail. The boat brings together high speed and crisp handling in a powerful, easily-driven hull, a fine entry flares into wide planing sections aft for maximum stability and blistering off-wind performance, and all from the security of a really comfortable cockpit. The Blaze class association exists to assist the development, promotion, and organizing of Blaze sailing.

Blaze National Championships

Pembroke Yacht Club   11 - 13 September 2009

Thirty two Blazes travelled to South Wales for the National Championships of this resurgent class. After two failed Championships last year, due to breathless weekends, the event was moved to take advantage of autumnal winds, but yet again the fates were against and the first day was too light for racing, despite everyone's best efforts.

After a very light winds race on Saturday morning everything seemed to be going the same way again as it died, but as everyone arrived onshore a breeze appeared, and then built to the point that the Race Officer was able to hold three more races on Saturday. Sunday was yet again a very light day with a huge void in the middle, but once again the Race Officer managed to fit in racing; one before the wind disappeared, and a final heat after the wind reappeared once again.

The event was finally won by Andy Hewitt, who had a very consistent weekend, including three race wins on the trot on Saturday afternoon. Reigning Champion Christian Smart finished just two points in arrears, after winning both of the Sunday races to join the first race win. Nick Miller's results were all in the top five places, and this was sufficient to gain him third overall ahead of local sailor Chris Holman, who also took the First Youth trophy.

Next year there is no doubt that the class is due for some proper breeze!

P	SN	Helm	R1	R2	R3	R4	R5	R6	Pts
1	760	Andy Hewitt	5	1	1	1	3	2	8
2	763	C Smart	1	3	8	4	1	1	10
3	757	Nick Miller	2	4	4	2	5	4	16
4	751	Chris Holman	4	7	9	3	2	6	22
5	761	Paul Hemsley	6	8	5	6	4	8	29
6	733	Andy McIcor	12	9	6	8	7	DNF	42
7	670	S Smart	15	10	7	5	14	7	43
8	750	Allistar Barbrook	10	6	10	10	11	9	45
9	637	Toby Barsley-Dale	8	14	13	11	18	5	51
10	720	Andy Conway	13	12	3	OCS	10	14	52

British Moth

Type	Dinghy	Weight	45 kg
Crew	One; Sit out	Sail area	8.06 sq m
PN	1183 /1191	Spi type	None
Length	3.35 m	Designer	S Cheverton
Beam	1.27 m		www.britishmoth.co.uk

The British Moth is an 11ft dinghy with superb light-wind performance that is quick to plane, making it sheer excitement in a blow. One design, with a fully stayed rig, scow bow, and hard chine hull built to closely-defined tolerances, the cockpit and controls can be laid to the helmsman's preferences. The rig is fully adjustable to suit the conditions and helm weight, making it suitable for all ages. Carbon fibre masts debut this season. Friendly competitive fleet sailing lakes and rivers.

British Moth news: There is much anticipation about the arrival of new British Moths from John Claridge, the renowned Lymington based boat builder. This, and the possible introduction of carbon spars is leading to increased interest in the class for the future.

British Moth National Championships

Northampton Sailing Club   12 - 15 August 2009

Twenty four boats gathered at Northampton SC for the British Moth National Championships, and the fleet benefited from a variety of weather and winds, but master of all of these conditions proved to be Tim Davison who finished the regatta with an unblemished record of race wins.

Throughout the meeting, Davison was challenged by a variety of competitors; second overall at the end of the meeting was Stephen Seargeant who started with an eighth, but then rapidly improved to finish with a series on second and third positions to take second overall away from Colin Hall. Roger Witts finally finished in fourth overall, but was disappointed to have missed out on the second spot. His series of four second positions was marred by being over the line in one race, and also retiring in one race, thus having to count eighteen points for just one race!

P	Helm	Club	R1	R2	R3	R4	R5	R6	Total	Nett
1	Tim Davison	MSC	1	1	1	1	1	1	6	5
2	Stephen Seargeant	KGSC	8	5	2	3	3	2	23	15
3	Colin Hall	HSC	3	4	3	5	4	7.5	26.5	19
4	Roger Witts	FSC	2	2	OCS	2	2	DNF	51	26
5	Mark Wiltshire	FSC	6	7	4	8	5	10	40	30
6	Jeremy Higson	FSC	4	6	9	7	9	5	40	31
7	Andrew Perrott	CSC	5	10	5	6	6	DNF	50	32
8	Graham Pope	FSC	9	3	6	9	7	DNF	52	34
9	Gary Tompkins	SESC	7	12	7	12	10	6	54	42
10	Ian Edwards	ESC	DNC	11	8	4	8	DNF	74	49

Byte CII

Type	Dinghy
Crew	1; Sit out
PN	1159
Length	3.65 m
Beam	1.3 m
Weight	45 kg
Sail area M	5.6 sq m
Designer	Ian Bruce, 1990
	www.byteclass.org

The Byte CII is a single-hander for the smaller sailor but offers a good competitive weight-spread. As an International class, the Byte offers World and Regional Championships, and is also used in specialist events, being selected for the Youth Olympics as an example. The class in general benefits from the continued involvement of its designer, Ian Bruce, and this interest will ensure that it remains at the front of dinghy development, whilst remaining a one design dinghy.

Byte Nationals

Mumbles Yacht Club   4 - 5 August 2009

Fourteen Bytes travelled to Mumbles for the National Championships, all using the C11 rig. The event was beautifully run and the weather was forgiving as well.

Eight races were run; with one discard; three on Friday, three on Saturday and two on Sunday. On Friday, with a force three to four, Eddie Pope led from start to finish though he was pursued by Gordon Kevan. Kevan led from the first mark of Race Two to take the win, whilst Richard Whitehouse took the final race of the first day to keep the overall positions in abeyance.

Saturday opened with a gentle force two with shifts! Whilst generally preferring heavy winds, Gordon Kevan showed new confidence in the lighter conditions, and won the first and last race of the day, taking an impressive second in the second heat which was won by Eddie Pope.

As they entered the final day, any one of three could have taken the title still, although Gordon's record definitely suggested he was favourite! As it happened, he won the final races to give himself a comfortable margin of five points, from Eddie Pope who was six points clear of Richard Whitehouse.

P	Helm	Club	R1	R2	R3	R4	R5	R6	R7	R8	Total	Nett
1	Gordon Kevan	B&FSC	2	1	3	1	2	1	1	1	12	9
2	Eddie Pope	LSC	1	3	2	2	1	3	2	3	17	14
3	Richard Whitehouse	CSC	3	2	1	11	3	4	3	4	31	20
4	John Futcher	WSC	5	4	4	10	7	2	4	2	38	28
5	Chris Tack	TSC	8	5	5	12	5	5	8	6	54	42
6	Chris Rees	WSC	4	10	DNF	4	4	7	6	8	58	43
7	Michael Radford	WOSC	6	9	6	6	6	9	7	5	54	45
8	Sarah Gregson	FOSSC	7	13	7	3	8	8	9	7	62	49

Comet

Type	Dinghy	Beam	1.37 m
Crew	1; Sit out	Weight	50 kg
PN	1173	Sail area M	6.5 sq m
Length	3.45 m	Designer	A Simmons, 1981
			www.cometsailing.org.uk

The Comet is a light and lively single-handed dinghy. It is a one-design class, overseen by a lively association that promotes racing and pottering alike, and the design features a deeper cockpit than many other designs, in order to offer a more secure feel for the inexperienced or nervous. With a two-part mast and its light hull weight, the Comet is easily car-toppable, and yet offers enough space to sail with two when necessary.

Comet National Championships

Littleton Sailing Club   24 - 25 May 2009

A good entry of twenty nine Comets arrived at Littleton Sailing Club for the 2009 Comet Association Championships, with the event starting in perfect sailing conditions. The first race began in glorious sunshine and a Force two wind. Simon Thompson, C809, led up the first beat until the wind started to die when Eddie Pope, Mark Wilkins and John Windibank all easily passed him. The lead was exchanged with Pope crossing the line first followed closely by Wilkins then Windibank.

Race Two was a frustrating one for the Race Officer, Richard Cranbrook, and the helms. Variable wind, both in strength and direction, made course setting very difficult. The race was eventually started and Wilkins, Windibank, Pope, Annette Walters and Robin Balham all contested the front of the fleet. Wilkins was again beaten into second place by Pope, and Walters finished a close third. Race Three was deferred until Day Two as the wind had now died out completely.

On Day Two the competitors thought they were in for a blow. A Force four to five greeted them with waves on the lake. Regrettably it just a squall and it quickly eased to a Force two and then progressively fell away during the day. Race Three saw Henry Jaggers get away on a port tack at the pin end and he led to the finish. A chasing pack of nine boats swapped places, picking up puffs of wind with Annette just beating Guy Wilkins into third place. Race Four had a delayed start. A group containing Wilkins, Pope, Best, Wilkins and Walter drew away from the pack in what were very light airs. The lead was hotly contested with Pope and Wilkins duelling for first place. Pope picked up a rare puff of wind and covered Wilkins to the line. Best was a close third. With three wins Eddie Pope was a worthy Champion.

P	Helm	Club	R1	R2	R3	R4	Total	Nett
1	Eddie Pope	Littleton	1	1	4	1	7	3
2	Mark Wilkins	Chipstead	2	2	5	2	11	6
3	Annette Walter	WGCSC	13	4	2	5	24	11
4	John Windibank	Chipstead	3	3	16	7	29	13
5	Guy Wilkins	Chipstead	9	6	3	4	22	13
6	Henry Jaggers	Beer	6	10	1	12	29	17
7	Tony Best	Taplow Lake	7	9	8	3	27	18
8	Simon Thompson	Crawley	4	8	6	10	28	18

1st Youth - C212 Laura Glover - Littleton SC
1st Lady - C857 Helen Leivers - Severn SC
1st Xtra - C844 Paul Hinde - Severn SC
1st Veteran - C532 John Coppenhall - Hunts SC
1st Ancient Mariner - C518 Robin Ballam - Crawley Mariners SC

Contender

Type	Dinghy
Crew	1; Trapeze
PN	994
Length	4.67 m
Beam	1.5 m
Weight	104 kg
Sail area M	10.4 sq m
Designer	Bob Miller, 1967
	www.sailcontender.org.uk

Photo courtesy of Digigraphics

The Contender was designed in 1967 by Bob Miller (later Ben Lexcen), and participated in trials to find a boat to take over from the Finn as the Olympic Single-hander. Whilst it won the trials, the move away from the Finn was never made, but the Contender went on to gain international recogition, and a following around the world. Fast and yet manageable, the boat continues to be raced at World Championship level, and the class in the UK still hosts a keenly-fought National Championships.

Contender World Championships

Sanderborg, Denmark   25 - 31 July 2009

A fleet of one hundred and twelve Contenders took part in the 2009 World Championships, hosted at Sanderborg in Denmark. With sixteen countries represented (including a strong entry of eighteen UK based boats), this represented a huge increase over the 2008 entry, when the venue was Canada, and the difficulty in transporting the boats was obviously far more acute. Leaders after two days were Danes Jens Langendorf and Søren Andreasen, both fellow club members from Copenhagen's Hellerup SC, the home of Paul Elvstrom. Whilst Langendorf held a small lead, Andreasen's position was somewhat more tenuous, with third placed Italian Andrea Bonezzi and fellow Dane Bjarke B Johnsen also on sixteen points. Top Brits at this stage were Matt Aston and Graham Scott, in seventh and eighth positions overall, Scott having won Race Three to aid his score.

Day Three saw Johnsen's results of first and second lift him to the top of the leaderboard, with the pre-event favourite Andrea Bonezzi still in second after sixth and third position finishes. Langendorf's fifth and eighth dropped him down to fourth overall, behind club-mate Andreasen who won one of the races, and finished eighth in the other. However, this left the top four boats within four places of one another overall with plenty more racing to be completed.

With a day lost for racing, the final day, with three races scheduled, was likely to be decisive. With a first and second to add to his tally, Andrea Bonezzi picked his way to the World Championship title, having been playing make-up since his first race tenth. Australian Jono Neate did just enough to get into second place, ahead of the Danes Jacob Lunding and Jens Langendorf, whilst Simon Mussell was top Brit in fifth after a great last day; with two race wins and a sixth to add to his score. Mention must be made of Dane Bjarke B Johnsen, leading overall at the end of Day Three and finally finishing in eleventh position with last day scores of twenty first, eigthteenth and OCS; not a great way to end the week!

P	Nat	Helm	R1	R2	R3	R4	R5	R6	R7	R8	R9	Pts
1	ITA	Andrea Bonezzi	10	2	2	2	6	3	1	57	2	18
2	AUS	Jono Neate	1	8	4	7	5	2	3	7	4	26
3	DEN	Jacob Lunding	8	9	4	5	2	15	2	3	3	27
4	DEN	Jens Langendorf	1	4	3	4	5	8	4	13	8	29
5	GBR	Simon Mussell	13	20	12	1	8	1	6	1	1	30
6	DEN	Søren Andreasen	7	1	1	7	1	8	11	4	9	30
7	GER	Christoph Homeier	8	1	8	2	24	5	5	6	6	33
8	AUS	Chris Peile	3	5	DSQ	3	6	6	6	11	19	42
9	GER	Jan von der Bank	7	6	15	8	3	10	9	2	14	45
10	GBR	Graham Scott	9	9	1	6	12	4	13	8	OCS	50

Perfect conditions at the Contender World Championships

Contender National Championship

Highcliffe Sailing Club   19 - 22 September 2009

Fifty three Contenders attended the class's National Championship in mid-September, but were not greeted by the customary autumn winds.

Racing was lost altogether on the first day through absence of wind, and whilst there was just enough to get a race underway on Sunday morning, it was a light and patchy affair, filling in from every quarter. As this race finished the tide took control and no further racing was possible as the class suffered a bit of a log-jam of races going into the third day. With this start in mind, everyone's thoughts went back to the 2008 Nationals when sailing was only possible on the final day, and the event was decided on just three races.

Unfortunately these initial conditions were symptomatic of much of the weekend, with races delayed and rescheduled on a frequent basis. However, in 2009 the Race Committee did manage to fit in a ten race Championship despite the reluctance of the breeze, and this resulted in a very tight finish between the top three boats, all ending within one point.

The title went to Graham Scott, who has been sailing the boat for many years (he first won the nationals in 1991, and last won them in 2007!). With an excellent end to the week, he overhauled boat Stuart Jones (similarly a class stalwart, having won the World Championships in 1993) and Simon Mussell, both of whom could have taken the title had Scott not won the final race.

The previous year's winner, Gary Langdown (from the host club) put up a valiant defence of his title, but the trying conditions didn't work in his favour this time, and he was unable to overcome an early retirement to finally be seventh overall.

P	Helm	Club	R1	R2	R3	R6	R7	R8	R9	R10	Tot	Nett
1	G Scott	RYA	5	3	17	5	3	1	3	1	38	21
2	S Jones	DWSC	2	2	4	1	7	3	2	8	29	21
3	S Mussell	HSC	1	1	34	9	1	5	1	4	56	22
4	M Aston	DWSC	4	4	2	2	5R	9	6	5	37	28
5	T Holden	HSC	3	10	6	10	4	18	7	2	60	42
6	J Browett	DWSC	6	7	7	14	5	8	4	7	58	44
7	G Langdown	HSC	DNF	9	15	6	2	4	9	11	110	56
8	S Bray	PSC	10	6	1	8	16	12	14	18	85	67
9	P Dives	ESSC	14	21	5	4	15	13	13	10	95	74
10	K Paul	WSC	OCS	13	9	7	12	6	16	14	131	77

R signifies redress

VANDER CRAFT

DINGHY TROLLEYS & TRAILERS

Vander Craft has developed a unique range of trolleys and trailers for the dinghy sailing enthusiast.

Trolleys are manufactured as fully-welded round and box tube construction making for an exceptionally strong, yet lightweight trolley. The round tube is formed to make the handles and the main frame, minimising the number of welds required. Unique adjustable gunwale and keel supports ensure an accurate fit.

TROLLEY	Boat Length
VCT200	T-frame
VCT220	3.3m – 4.0m
VCT250	4.0m – 4.6m
VCT275	4.6m – 5.1m

TRAILER	Boat Length
VCB200	T-frame
VCB220	3.3m – 4.0m
VCB250	4.0m – 4.6m
VCB275	4.6m – 5.1m
VCB LASER	Laser Trolley

Sole supplier of trolleys to Ovington Boats and Comet Boats

Vander Craft can provide a trolley & trailer for every class of dinghy as well as the Admiral Range of Powerboat Trailers

Vander Craft suppliers of the Phantom, K1 s/h keelboat, & V-3000

Vander Craft • Unit 28 Flightway • Dunkeswell Business Park
Dunkeswell • HONITON EX14 4RJ

t 01404 891 913 • m 07971 404 617

www.vandercraft.co.uk | www.admiraltrailers.co.uk

Europe

Type	Dinghy
Crew	1; Sit out
PN	1139
Length	3.38 m
Beam	1.41 m
Weight	45 kg
Sail area M	7.1 sq m
Designer	Alois Roland
	www.europeclass.org.uk

The Europe was originally designed under the International Moth rules, with an unstayed mast. As it developed its own identity, the Europe was granted International status, and subsequently gained selection as the Olympic single-handed dinghy for women. Despite the loss of that status, the class continues to grow, with 100+ fleets at the World Championships in 2008, and a lively UK association organizing a variety of events. The boat is suited to the light and agile, but is not particularly well-suited to novices.

Europe World Championships

Brest, France   24 July - 1 August 2009

The combined Europe World Championships were held in Brest with a combined fleet of some one hundred and sixty five boats, ninety seven men and fifty eight women. Following a pre-Worlds regatta which was won by Sven Stadel Seiler, racing got underway in excellent conditions, with the first two races being won in the Women's Division by Sarah Poulsen, whilst Frenchman Thomas Ribeaud had the same excellent start in the Men's Division.

Once in front, Ribeaud was able to sustain the position, however, and, as the week progressed, he comfortably kept control of the fleet from Spaniard Sven Seiler, with Anders Carlson of Sweden taking the Bronze medal position, level on thirty three points with Kim Carlsson, also of Sweden, with the tiebreak deciding it. Ribeaud took six race wins on the way to his victory.

In the women's fleet Sarah Poulsen of Denmark got off to a great start with two wins on Day One, but could do nothing to defeat the highly competitive Anne-Marie Rindom, who took two second places, and then followed by winning six of the next eight races. Fellow Dane Anette Andreasen finished second overall, with Spaniard Ascension Roca de Togores third, and Poulsoen hanging on for fourth overall.

Europe World Championships: Men

P	Helm	Nat	R1	R2	R3	R4	R5	R6	R7	R8	R9	R10	R11	Pts	Tot
1	Thomas Ribeaud	FRA	1	1	3	OCS	1	26	1	7	10	1	1	26	100
2	Sven Stadel Seiler	ESP	5	1	5	2	3	1	8	6	5	17	2	30	55
3	Anders Carlson	SWE	3	11	2	1	1	2	7	1	14	5	27	33	74
4	Kim Carlsson	SWE	4	3	2	5	2	6	5	4	34	2	12	33	79
5	Holger Tidemand	SWE	3	2	1	6	4	1	2	12	13	28	3	34	75
6	Antoine Drogou	FRA	6	4	4	5	9	4	3	2	17	4	11	41	60
7	Oscar Niklasson	SWE	5	8	1	3	3	10	19	8	6	3	31	47	97
8	Jacob Lundqvist	SWE	6	4	3	13	5	5	25	9	19	11	5	61	105

Europe World Championships: Women

P	Helm	Nat	R1	R2	R3	R4	R5	R6	R7	R8	R9	R10	R11	Pts	Tot
1	Anne-Marie Rindom	DEN	2	2	1	1	1	4	1	1	2	1	20	12	36
2	Anette Andeason	DEN	4	3	3	4	3	1	2	2	14	4	3	25	43
3	Ascension De Togores	ESP	3	13	2	5	5	8	3	4	4	9	2	36	58
4	Sarah Poulsen	DEN	1	1	6	3	4	2	19	5	20	8	16	46	85
5	Anna Livbjerg	DEN	5	9	9	11	2	3	5	BFD	5	2	10	50	118
6	Hanna Klinga	SWE	11	12	8	2	23	6	13	7	8	6	1	61	97

Finn

Photo courtesy of Tosca Zambra

Type	Dinghy	Beam	1.5 m
Crew	1; Sit out	Weight	125 kg
PN	1069	Sail area M	10 sq m
Length	4.5 m	Designer	Rickard Sarby
			www.finnuk.org.uk

One of the most physically-testing dinghies, the Rickard Sarby-designed Finn continues to be selected for Olympic sailing, and offers close and tactical racing of the highest level. The boat has an unstayed mast (now generally carbon fibre on the up-to-date boats) and an alloy centre plate. Apart from the Olympics, the class is also going from strength to strength at a more attainable level, with excellent attendance at national events, and a huge following amongst older sailors – with some 230 boats turning up for the Finn World Masters Championships. This is one for the experienced, and flexible, sailor!

Finn Gold Cup

Vallensbæk, Denmark   3 - 11 July 2009

Ninety eight sailors from thirty countries competed in the Finn Gold Cup, for the class World Championships, held in Denmark. The event was part of a year of celebration for this most durable of classes, having been designed sixty years ago, and still competing and developing at the very highest level.

Despite the absence of Ben Ainslie, the reigning champion, Team GBR were well represented with six boats including, amongst others, the on-form Ed Wright, and Giles Scott.

The event started in difficult conditions with little stable breeze to be be found, and many of the fancied runners collecting discards! First race winner was Bryan Boyd who then followed up with a thirtieth, whilst New Zealander Dan Slater rounded off Day One with a win, following on from a mid-thirties result in the first heat! Of the leading GB boats, Ed Wright collected a forty sixth and fourth, Giles Scott a sixteenth and sixth and Andrew Mills an impressive seventh and fifth.

Steadier breezes greeted the second day of racing. American Zach Railey (who we all will remember from his efforts against Ben Ainslie in the medal race at Beijing) found the conditions to suit him and, with a brace of sixth spots, took the lead overall.

Picture courtesy of Photo Zambra

2009 Finn Gold Cup winner Jonas Høgh-Christensen

Giles Scott took the winning gun in the first race of the day in eight to ten knots of wind. With slightly more wind for Race Four, Dane Jonas Høgh-Christensen found his form and won the race, ahead of Ivan Gaspic of Croatia. However, with four races down, there were three Brits in contention, and the best known names gravitating towards the top of the fleet.

Day Three dawned with fairly light conditions again, and ended with yet another new leader, this time in the form of Dan Slater who found himself level on thirty two points with Zach Railey at the end of the day, with Ed Wright in third position, and Giles Scott in fourth with fellow Brits Mark Andrews and Andrew Mills also in the top ten; showing the UK's strength in the fleet at the moment. However, the fourth day's racing was even better from a UK point of view with Scott and Wright both putting in excellent, consistent performances to see the day end with Wright first overall on forty four points, and Scott second overall on fifty one points; jointly with Ivan Gaspic of Croatia. A win in the first of the day's races cemented Wrights position, but a dogged fight back in the second, getting up to fourth was even more instrumental, whilst a fifth and second for Scott were great results in a difficult day.

The penultimate day saw much of Wright's hard work wasted as he was black flagged in one of the two races, and therefore had to carry a forty sixth place result in his scores. By contrast, Scott added another win to a thirteenth, and went into the medal race with everything to play for, behind American Zach Railey, and Dane Jonas Høgh-Christensen. A win in the double scoring event was enough to give the title to the popular Dane, with Railey in Silver medal position once more, following a third place final. Top Brit overall was Scott in fourth position, whilst Wright finished in sixth overall, and Andrew Mills in tenth, with a good second position in the medal heat.

P	Nat	Helm	R1	R2	R3	R4	R5	R6	R7	R8	R9	R10	Med	Pts
1	DEN	Jonas Høgh-Christensen	20	35	17	1	5	7	4	1	2	6	2	65
2	USA	Zach Railey	10	6	6	6	29	4	7	13	1	7	6	66
3	CRO	Ivan Kljakovic Gaspic	31	3	21	2	6	13	3	3	12	4	10	77
4	GBR	Giles Scott	6	16	1	13	20	8	5	2	13	1	16	81
5	SWE	Daniel Birgmark	17	2	13	20	8	5	20	12	3	3	12	95
6	GBR	Edward Wright	46	4	2	9	18	6	1	4	BFD	2	8	100
7	NZL	Dan Slater	33	1	3	5	3	20	12	14	15	8	MDNF	103
8	ESP	Rafael Trujillo	22	19	16	4	4	31	2	6	7	11	14	105
9	CRO	Marin Misura	3	21	10	11	21	1	6	10	10	16	18	106
10	GBR	Andrew Mills	7	5	32	16	2	16	13	16	22	10	4	111
P	Nat	Helm	R1	R2	R3	R4	R5	R6	R7	R8	R9	R10	R11	Pts
11	GBR	Mark Andrews	16	52	4	8	13	21	8	31	8	12	4	125
36	GBR	Henry Bagnall	53	43	70	39	32	46	35	25	44	23	21	36
86	GBR	Richard Hart	80	81	DNF	DNC	80	78	DNC	DNC	DNC	DNC	DNC	847

Finn European Championships

Varna, Bulgaria   24 - 29 August 2009

A fleet of seventy eight Finns from twenty three countries attended the Finn Europeans at the end of August with three days of registration and measurement, before the first race, and a contingent of five GB boats taking part. The event opened with a perfect day with a consistent breeze, sunshine and a good swell. Croatia's Ivan Kljakovic Gaspic and the UK's Giles Scott each took a win during the day, and led overall at the end of the day with Ed Wright in third position overall. The first race was held in eight knots, and this increased to fourteen knots by the second heat, and the Committee raised the Oscar flag to allow free pumping, and some great surfing in the rollers. On the second day, only one race was possible, and this was won by the UK's Andrew Mills. Ivan Kljakovic Gaspic retained the overall lead with a fourth place in the ten knot breeze. Mills' race win lifted him to third place overall, behind Tapio Nirkko from Finland.

Three races were sailed on the third day of the Championships, with Ivan Gaspic continuing his good form to lead at the end of the day. Race winners for the day were GB's Ed Wright, Jakub Pasik (Poland) and Pieter-Jan Postma (Netherlands), but the most consistent sailor of the day was Marin Misura with a fifth and two thirds. On day four the committee ran two races in eight to ten knot breezes, and it was the day that Gaspic really stamped his authority and intention on the meeting, by taking two victories, and leaving himself with a twenty one point lead, although only five points separated the next five boats, with Giles Scott and Ed Wright level in second position.

Racing in fickle and difficult winds, the penultimate day could have been a disaster for any of the main competitors, but Gaspic actually made the most of conditions, and scored a second and a sixth, to give him the title without the need to go to the medal race. One of the day's race winners, Tapio Nirkko, was one point ahead of Ed Wright as they went into the double scoring final heat. The other race winner on the penultimate day was Mark Andrews (GB). With the medal race cancelled on the final day through lack of breeze, the results remained unchanged, and Gaspic was pronounced the deserved European Champion, to cap what had been a successful year for him.

Nat	Helm	R1	R2	R3	R4	R5	R6	R7	R8	R9	R10	Tot	Nett
CRO	Ivan Gaspic	1	3	4	8	13	2	1	1	6	2	41	28
FIN	Tapio Nirkko	9	2	2	4	19	14	5	6	1	14	76	57
GBR	Edward Wright	2	4	OCS	11	1	4	9	10	9	8	134	58
CRO	Marin Misura	4	20	19	5	3	3	3	8	12	3	80	60
GBR	Giles Scott	5	1	14	12	2	17	2	5	15	36	109	73
NED	Pieter-Jan Postma	3	8	16	34	9	1	7	2	14	13	107	73
EST	Deniss Karpak	6	7	8	3	2	16	10	4	3	20	103	77
GBR	Andrew Mills	10	5	1	17	5	11	4	17	48	11	129	81
NOR	Peer Moberg	11	24	3	DNF	6	15	17	9	4	6	171	95
POL	Rafal Szukiel	13	21	10	18	7	BFD	18	3	8	4	178	102

Finn National Championships

Castle Cove Sailing Club   24 - 26 July 2009

Forty four Finns competed in the 2009 National Championships, held at Castle Cove in Weymouth. The fleet was augmented by a small scattering of international competitors, but was lacking some of the top GB sailors for whom the event was outside their schedules. First overall was taken by one of these international visitors, Daniel Birgmark from Sweden. Counting four wins, two seconds and discarding a third position, his record in this good-sized field was excellent. However, Largs' Mark Andrews also found an excellent streak of form, gaining a win, two second places, two thirds and a fourth in his counting results to pip Andrew Mills of Queen Mary SC by just one point in the overall margins, and to take the UK National Title. The Finnish entry, Tapio Nirkko, rounded off the top four. From this point onwards, the strength of the Finn dinghy as a club racer nowadays is emphasised, with excellent support from the fleets of such clubs as Mengham Rythe, Christchurch, and Thorpe Bay. It is this club level support that has done much to swell the boat's popularity in the UK, and also worldwide where it has a secondary, "non-Olympic" circuit that is second to none.

P	Nat	Helm	R1	R2	R3	R4	R5	R6	R7	Pts
1	SWE	Daniel Birgmark	3	2	1	1	2	1	1	8
2	GBR	Mark Andrews	2	1	4	2	3	3	5	15
3	GBR	Andrew Mills	1	4	2	3	4	2	7	16
4	FIN	Tapio Nirkko	4	5	3	4	1	5	2	19
5	GBR	Henry Bagnall	5	3	5	6	5	4	3	25
6	GBR	John Tremlett	7	6	6	5	6	7	4	34

Photo courtesy of BFA

Mark Andrews, top GBR sailor at the Finn Nationals

International Canoe

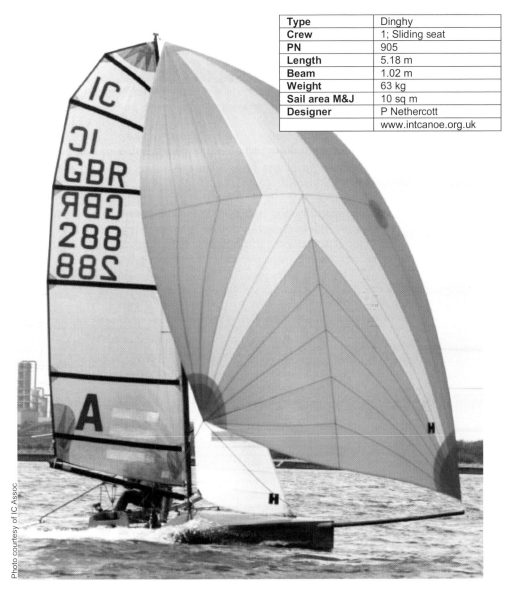

Type	Dinghy
Crew	1; Sliding seat
PN	905
Length	5.18 m
Beam	1.02 m
Weight	63 kg
Sail area M&J	10 sq m
Designer	P Nethercott
	www.intcanoe.org.uk

Photo courtesy of IC Assoc

The IC is simply one of the fastest single-handed boats afloat. This derives from its unique design, adopting the narrow hull form inherited from its ancient canoe origins, together with the famous sliding seat. Coupled with the latest asymmetric rig (the 'AC'), the canoe presents plenty of challenges. As with all things in life, the greater the challenge, the greater the reward. Once the canoe is mastered, you will experience one of the most exhilarating thrills that sailing can offer.

International Canoe National Championships

Stone Sailing Club   20 - 23 June 2009

Twenty two International Canoes competed in their National Championships at Stone SC with the fleet divided into the standard boats (without the asymmetric spinnaker and equipment) and the Asymmetrics, which were slightly more popular with thirteen entries.

With nine races held in each division, the IC title went to Phil Robin with a string of top three results, winning by some eight points from Alistair Warren, with Simon Allen in third and Mark Goodchild in fourth overall.

Colin Brown won a more closely fought battle in the Asymmetric fleet from Tony Robertshaw, whilst sailmaker Steve Goacher finished in third position; the points spread between second and sixth was only three points, with three boats all on twenty seven points!

Standard Fleet

P	No	Helm	Club	R1	R2	R3	R4	R5	R6	R7	R8	R9	Tot
1	311	P Robin	HISC	5	2	1	2	1	1	1	3	1	9
2	308	A Warren	BCU	1	3	5	5	2	3	3	2	3	17
3	278	S Allen	HISC	DNC	1	2	3	3	2	4	5	4	19
4	265	M Goodchild	WSC	3	4	4	4	4	4	2	1	2	20
5	292	J Ellis	SDSC	2	5	3	1	5	5	5	4	6	25
6	295	C Newman	DWSC	4	6	7	6	6	7	6	7	DNF	42

Asymmetric Fleet

P	No	Helm	Club	R1	R2	R3	R4	R5	R6	R7	R8	R9	Tot
1	299	C Brown	USC	1	9	3	2	4	1	5	6	3	19
2	306	T Robertshaw	WSC	3	4	4	7	5	3	2	4	5	25
3	286	S Goacher	RWYC	6	2	7	DNF	6	5	3	2	2	26
4	303	D Timson	LSC	4	7	8	9	2	2	1	7	4	27
5	283	J Robson	USC	2	10	5	4	7	4	4	1	7	27
6	298	R Bell	EPSC	9	3	1	3	3	6	6	5	6	27

Laser Pico

Type	Dinghy	Beam	1.43 m
Crew	1 or 2; Sit out	Weight	55 kg
PN	1258	Sail area M&J	5.9 sq m
Length	3.5 m	Designer	Jo Richards, 1994
			www.pico.lasersailing.com

Photo courtesy of Laser Centre

The Pico is a fun, durable, confidence-inspiring, rotomoulded boat that can be sailed by everyone. It's ideal for entry-level sailors and is equipped with a removable jib and reefing main sail for easy rigging. It is also available as the Pico Race, which is an upgraded version with a larger Mylar mainsail, a vang with 4:1 purchase and upgraded blocks.

Laser Pico Nationals

Thorpe Bay Yacht Club   4 - 5 July 2009

A fleet of fifty six entries turned up at Thorpe Bay YC for the Laser Pico Nationals in early July, with light conditions greeting the varied fleet (with helmsmen aged from nine to fifty nine).

Saturday racing was delayed initially as the sea breeze was awaited, and the fleet set sail with three scheduled races; the first starting in five knots of breeze. The winner's gun was taken by Alex Farrall from the host club, ahead of early leader Robbie Southwell, and Chris Clark in third. In the second race, another Thorne Bay man, Bob Binnedijk, led from the start to win, with Farrall taking a second to add to his impressive sail! With water running out, the Race Officer was very alert to the disappearing tide, and took every precaution to get the race completed in time. This time it was Southwell who took the gun from Alex Hadley, followed by Alex Warrington and Teddy Elmore in third. The fleet then made for home in time to enjoy the BBQ.

With cyclonic light winds on the second day, the Race Officer must have wished he had enjoyed the previous evening's social more! In Race Four Ben Green returned to the front of the fleet. The clear leader at the end was Alex Farrall, to take a second race victory in the event, and to leave him tied on points with Robbie Southwell.

Race Five was impossible to set and eventually abandoned, whilst the final heat was sailed in light but manageable winds with Chris Clarke taking an early lead ahead of Farrall, Sharland and Green. The results meant that the National Championship title, as well as the under fifteen's title, went deservedly to Alex Farrall.

P	Helm	Crew	Club	R1	R2	R3	R4	R6	Pts
1	Alex Farrall	-	TBYC	1	2	4	1	2	6
2	Robbie Southwell	-	Gurnard	2	3	1	2	31	8
3	Chris Clarke	Maddie Shields	TBYC	3	5.5	7	3	1	12.5
4	Bob Binnedijk	-	TBYC	8	1	8	4	42	21
5	Bruce Spratt	Peter Snow	TBYC	6	19	9	7	6	28
6	Jonathon Snow	-	TBYC	7	9	5	9	7	28

Laser Radial

Type	Dinghy
Crew	1; Sit out
PN	1078
Length	4.23 m
Beam	1.37 m
Weight	59 kg
Sail area M	5.7 sq m
Designer	Bruce Kirby, 1971
	www.laser.org.uk

The single-handed Laser dinghy is also available in a slightly de-powered version – the Laser Radial. The hull, fittings and foils are all identical; to use the boat as a Radial it is only necessary to purchase a different mast section, and a smaller sail, and away you go. The Radial is used extensively as a women's boat (at the Olympics and ISAF events) as well as for much youth racing. With the smaller, lighter rig, the boat is just a little more manageable for the smaller, lighter sailor!

Laser Radial European Championships

Charlottenlund, Denmark   9 - 16 July 2009

After something of a "Radialfest" at the beginning of July, in which both the Under Seventeen, and Youth European Championships were decided, the two adult sectors of the championships took place over 9 - 16 July with a total entry of one hundred and sixty six boats, ninety six women and seventy men.

Women's Championship

After four days of racing (the last of which was lost due to wind conditions), positions at the top of the Championship table were very tight, with the expected names appearing in place! Paige Railey, who has been one of the front runners throughout the ISAF World Cup this year, was one point clear of Sarah Steyaert, the reigning World Champion, with our own Charlotte Dobson in an excellent third position. The first day of Gold fleet sailing saw huge changes on the leader board, although Railey continued her assault on the title, despite one poor result which she could disgard, previous front runners Dobson and Steyaert both suffered two bad races. Railey ended the day seventeen and a half points in the lead from Tina Mihelic of Croatia who won her third race of the week, followed by Norway's Cathrine Gjerpen, having led by just one point at the beginning of the day.

With continuing tricky conditions, the outcome of the Women's European title hung in the balance to the very end, but it was Railey who added the Open European title to her record. As she did not qualify for the European title, this went to event runner-up, Tina Mihelic of Croatia after a very competitive and tense battle through the Gold fleet finals, in which the fleet swapped end for end with huge shifts and new breezes appearing. The first beat of the final race saw the left hand side prospering early on, then the right, before it died completely just short of the mark, and then once again the right hand group caught the breeze, including Railey, which enabled her to hold position to the race end, and to the title. Railey was of course delighted to have won, and Mihelic was left to ponder the consequences of a ten point penalty for not signing off early in the week!

P	Nat	Helm	Q1	Q2	Q3	Q4	Q5	Q6	F1	F2	F3	F4	Tot	Nett
1	USA	Paige Railey	6	4	3	3	2	10	45	3	20	1	97	42
2	CRO	Tina Mihelic	17	DPI	1	10	1	9	1	9	7	18	90	55
3	FRA	Sarah Steyaert	2	1	1	6	21	9	OCS	24	1	14	128	58
4	DEN	Alberte Lindberg	9	11	7	20	18	8	11	1	10	2	97	59
5	FIN	Sari Multala	1	4	16	2	4	24	17	13	3	22	106	60
6	NED	Marit Bouwmeester	5	3	16	1	25	5	6	38	2	24	125	62
7	NOR	Cathrine Gjerpen	1	17	10	11	3	10	3	17	14	10	96	62
8	BEL	Evi Van Acker	11	1	17	3	4	27	28	2	8	17	118	63
9	SWE	Josefin Olsson	11	17	2	15	5	43	5	5	5	23	131	65
10	GBR	Charlotte Dobson	3	2	6	4	11	4	30	34	18	3	115	70

Men's Championship

There were seven GB entries in the men's section of the Radial Europeans, and the Championship was similarly taking shape, with the early pace being set by Wojciech Zemke who won four of the first five races. Paying close attention to Zemke after four days was fellow Pole, Michael Gryglewski, just two points behind in second overall whilst GB's Jon Emmett lay in third position, with two race wins in the first six races, and only a four point deficit to the leader. Wojciech Zemke of Poland won the first two races of the finals, to put himself in a strong leading position, ahead of Aristeidis Michail of Greece, with top Brit, Jon Emmett, in fifth position after a disappointing start to the final heats (with a fifteenth and twenty-eighth position).

Despite having led all week to the final Gold fleet racing, leader Zemke Wojciech's wheels fell off at the last, with scores of twentieth and twenty-sixth to finish the regatta. This opened the door to Greek Michail Aristeidis to take the Men's European championship, with Ben Koppelaar of Holland in third and Jon Emmett in fourth.

P	Nat	Helm	Q1	Q2	Q3	Q4	Q5	Q6	F1	F2	F3	F4	Nett
1	GRE	Michail Aristeidis	1	2	2	2	17	8	2	3	4	DNF	24
2	POL	Wojciech Zemke	1	3	1	1	1	5	1	1	20	25	29
3	NED	Ben Koppelaar	2	3	17	3	4	3	3	8	7	OCS	33
4	GBR	Jon Emmett	3	8	1	4	2	1	14	27	3	10	38
5	SLO	Nik Pletikos	5	5	10	1	5	9	7	6	25	2	40
6	FRA	Nathan Babonneau	6	4	3	11	5	22	27	7	2	4	42
7	POL	Micha Gryglewski	2	2	2	3	1	2	DNF	15	19	11	54
8	FRA	Louis Moysan	4	15	4	RAF	2	7	8	21	1	21	62
9	POL	Filip Kobielski	17	5	16	10	14	1	4	2	17	DPI	69
10	ITA	Marco Baruzzi	5	6	14	2	11	12	5	14	15	24	70

Laser Radial Nationals

Paignton Sailing Club   26 - 31 July 2009

Ninety seven Radials attended the National Championships at Paignton, with racing divided into three different flights to ensure that fleet-size wasn't too much of an issue. After two days of racing, the leader board had a familiar "ring" to it, with Steve Cockerill counting four first places from his heats. Jack Wetherell, in second overall, had three wins and a third place to count, whilst Jon Emmett had three seconds and a win.

The third day saw two more heats, and Cockerill carrying on his steadfast progress with two more race wins, as did Jack Wetherell, the only difference between these two being in their discards, which left the advantage with Cockerill. Third overall at this stage was Britain's Jon Emmett, level on points with Royal Victoria's Richard Talbot. As Thursday closed, Cockerill remained in control of the event, with straight wins all the way through the week until the final race when conditions played against most of the leaders, and he had returned a discard in the form of a sixteenth position! Emmett made the most of the race with a fourth, but with virtually all the other leaders picking up poor results, the alterations to the overall tables were not too significant. This all left Cockerill on eight points, with Emmett on fifteen, Talbot on nineteen and fourth placed Wetherell on twenty points.

As Cockerill awoke on Friday, he couldn't have been aware that his luck had abandoned him and, whilst Emmett made the most of the final two races with two wins, Steve could do no better than a seventh and a fifth, to see a title that looked fairly secure, slip away from him. Third overall was Richard Keates with John Currie in fourth and Jack Wetherell in fifth.

P	Helm	Pts	R1	R2	R3	R4	R5	R6	R7	R9	R10	R11	R12
1	Jon Emmett	13	2	2	2	1	BFD	1	1	2	4	1	1
2	Stephen Cockerill	19	1	1	1	1	1	1	1	1	16	7	5
4	Richard Keates	36	10	3	5	1	1	2	2	12	17	8	2
5	John Currie	37	3	5	2	6	4	5	DNF	5	3	4	13
6	Jack Wetherell	39	1	1	1	3	1	1	1	11	25	15	7
7	Richard Cumpsty	50	5	10	7	2	3	3	7	16	12	5	6
8	Robbie Urwin	52	2	2	3	3	3	6	8	6	31	12	15
9	Christian Townrow	53	13	13	4	4	2	7	13	7	1	3	12
10	Roger Stabbins	65	5	10	9	8	5	7	4	8	9	10	BFD

Laser Standard

Type	Dinghy
Crew	1; Sit out
PN	1078
Length	4.23 m
Beam	1.37 m
Weight	59 kg
Sail area M	7.06 sq m
Designer	Bruce Kirby, 1971
	www.laser.org.uk

The single-handed Laser dinghy is one of the great successes in the dinghy world, sailed as an Olympic Class, or as a beach fun boat. With nearly 200,000 boats afloat, it has a worldwide following, and with the option to switch rigs between the Standard, Radial, and 4.7 versions, it offers a boat that can be sailed by all members of the family. The Laser is a strict one-design, and offers a range of events including World, European, and National Championships.

Laser World Championships

Halifax, Nova Scotia   20 - 26 August 2009

Racing in St Margaret's Bay on the opening day gave some idea of how perfect it could be with twenty knots of wind in warm conditions with two to three foot waves. The one hundred and sixty nine boat fleet, with entries from fifty one countries, were subjected to a number of recalls before finally getting underway, but at the end of the day the Croatian Tonci Stipanovic led from GB's Nick Thompson, with Clayton Johnson of the USA in third. Day Two was a mistier affair, with a number of recalls again hampering progress. The Committee held just one race instead of the three anticipated, and twenty boats were black flagged for line infringements, ending their days prematurely.

Day Three saw excellent conditions once again, with Nick Thompson moving to the top of the leader board ahead of Stipanovic, and Paul Goodison moving up to third in the course of the day. The fleet then prepared for an enforced lay day on Sunday, as the residue of Hurricane Bill was forecast to pass by. Having sheltered nearly two hundred boats inside buildings to protect them from the effects of the storm, the fleet was back afloat again a day later to recommence sailing, but with no wind to help, unfortunately a second day of sailing was lost, with the need to make up lost races later in the event. Things returned to normal on Tuesday however, with breeze ranging from nine to sixteen knots. Our Olympic Champion, Paul Goodison, finished the day in the lead, having scored two wins and a third in the day, ahead of New Zealander Michael Bullot.

On the final day, Goodison cemented his position at the top of the Championships with two steady results: a seventh and a twentieth (which would prove to be one of his two discards). A second and third in the final two races secured Bronze medal position for Thompson who had added a good Worlds result to what has already been a very good season. Bullot retained second position with a sixth and eighth in the final two heats.

P	Nat	Helm	R1	R2	R3	R4	R5	R6	R7	R8	R9	R10	Pts
1	GBR	Paul Goodison	5	2	5	5	2	3	1	1	7	20	24.5
2	NZL	Michael Bullot	1	OCS	1	18	7	1	3	4	6	8	31
3	GBR	Nick Thompson	2	2	1	1	4	14	10	19	3	2	35
4	ARG	Julio Alsogaray	7	9	BFD	1	1	7	8	14	4	1	38
5	CRO	Tonci Stipanovic	3	1	2	4	32	12	2	17	11	BFD	52
6	CAN	David Wright	4	17	10	3	15	2	12	7	43	6	59
7	CRO	Milan Vujasinovic	4	13	2	4	11	6	17	20	10	35	74
8	ESP	Javier Hernandez	11	4	16	6	3	10	5	24	49	19	82
9	AUT	Andreas Geritzer	2	6	3	13	23	32	19	3	34	14	92
10	CAN	Michael Leigh	8	7	7	2	5	21	20	23	8	23	93
11	NZL	Joshua Junior	4	14	4	6	8	47	4	27	16	24	93
12	SWE	Emil Cedergardh	15	1	16	4	16	36	15	22	9	15	97
13	CHI	Matias Del Solar	18	5	BFD	2	1	41	18	9	38	7	98
14	SWE	Johan Wigforss	8	7	6	6	18	4	26	41	2	BFD	100
15	BRA	Bruno Fontes	1	5	9	24	4	DNS	11	36	22	13	101

Paul Goodison: Olympic, World and European Champion

Laser European Championships

Borstahusens, Sweden   1 - 8 August 2009

One hundred and twenty two boats competed in the Laser Europeans Championships, which were held as part of Nordic Week at Borstabusens.

Paul Goodison, GB's Olympic Champion from Beijing finished the Championships as the European Champion, for the fifth consecutive time. Despite starting the event with a flag, he managed to keep any other poor results off of his scorecard, with all of his counting scores actually being impressively in the top eight. Event runner up and former World Champion Tom Slingby, by comparison, finished some twenty one points in arrears.

Having rested after his successful Olympic campaign, Goodison kicked his new campaign into gear in time to prepare for the 2009 World Championships in Canada in late August. His preparation for the event was all pretty comfortable, and this deter-mined European defence must have allowed him to travel to Canada with a healthy confidence.

Of the other British boats, UK number two, Nick Thompson, again performed well, finishing in fifth position, while Robert Holmes, a RYA Volvo National Youth Squad sailor, won the Under 19 European Championships, with Alex Mills-Barton in second position.

P	Nat	Helm	Q1	Q2	Q3	Q4	Q5	Q6	Q7	F1	F2	F3	Tot	Pts
1	GBR	Paul Goodison	BFD	8	1	1	2	2	1	4	3	20	104	22
2	AUS	Tom Slingsby	5	1	20	5	24	1	2	13	13	3	87	43
3	ESP	Javier Hernandez	12	3	4	3	13	11	4	7	16	2	75	46
4	CYP	Pavlos Kontides	10	40	2	24	1	2	8	1	6	55	149	54
5	CRO	Tonci Stipanovic	17	9	7	12	6	1	1	43	4	21	121	61
6	GBR	Nick Thompson	15	2	BFD	6	8	7	2	15	10	36	163	65
7	NED	Marc de Haas	21	12	BFD	19	11	3	6	6	8	1	149	66
8	NZL	Michael Bullot	27	1	29	16	3	14	BFD	12	2	9	175	84
9	ITA	Michele Regolo	13	19	2	12	8	13	21	25	15	4	132	86
10	CRO	Daniel Mihelic	6	6	13	4	9	22	DSQ	3	23	31	179	86

Laser Nationals

Paignton Sailing Club   26 - 31 July 2009

A surprisingly small entry of forty boats joined the Radial and 4.7 Laser Fleets for the National Championships at Paignton Sailing Club, with many of the more familiar class names absent in training for squad duties.

The first name to show at the front of the fleet was Daniel Holman, who won the inaugural race on Day One, and then followed up with a first and second on Day Two. Second after forty eight hours was Rob Spencer from Mudeford, who started with a sixth position, and added a second and fourth to leave him level on six points with James Green of Beer SC who had two excellent third place results to count, as well as a thirteenth in Race Two.

Holman's excellent progress came across a hiccup in Race Five when he was disqualified at the start, but his second place in the first race of the day, and the fact that with five races completed the first discard came in to play, left him leading overall at the end of the day, with James Green up to second, adding a race win and a second position to his tally. The penultimate day saw Daniel Holman's efforts continue unabated and, with another race win and a fifth, his position in the Championship was fairly assured with the Friday racing still to be completed. James Green still held second position, with Matt Reid third, four points behind. Holman finally emerged as the 2009 National Laser Champion with thirteen points, a score-line counting nothing worse than a third position, and having never been headed throughout the week. Similarly comfortable at the end of the week was James Green, eight points clear of third overall Rob Spencer and finishing with an excellent third-second-second set of results to fend off any problems that final race winner Spencer might have provided.

P	SN	Helm	R1	R2	R3	R4	R5	R6	R7	R8	R9	R10	Pts
1	189596	Daniel Holman	1	2	1	2	BFD	2	1	5	1	3	13
2	160521	James Green	3	13	3	3	1	10	8	3	2	2	25
3	187518	Rob Spencer	2	4	18	1	9	3	12	7	6	1	33
4	193651	Matt Reid	5	12	2	4	7	1	21	4	3	8	34
5	163426	Paul Proctor	4	6	9	13	2	5	19	2	14	16	55
6	188781	Ian Morgan	8	3	DNC	5	14	DNC	9	1	8	12	60
7	187491	James Spencer	BFD	5	5	7	6	9	BFD	11	13	7	63
8	189201	Louis McVeigh	16	14	8	11	5	7	5	29	12	10	72
9	194877	Stephen Beckett	19	8	12	16	16	11	7	14	5	4	77
10	192532	Simon Barrington	10	19	6	10	3	6	27	26	21	5	80

Lightning 368

Length	3.68 m
Beam	1.38 m
Weight	54.4 kg
Sail area M	7.05 sq m
Designer	Mark Giles, 1977
	www.lightning368.org.uk

Photos courtesy of Adrian Hollier, www.photoboxgallery.com/adrianhollier

The Lightning 368 is a single-handed dinghy designed in 1977 by Mark Giles. It is a one-design dinghy, which can be sailed by helmsmen of different weights, by adjusting the rig to suit. The boat has a self-draining cockpit and an easily driven hull, with a fine bow. The mast is unstayed, so the boat is quick to rig, and simple to use, even by inexperienced sailors.

The Dinghy & Smallcraft Review
2009~2010

Lightning 368 National Championships

Northampton Sailing Club   29 - 30 August 2009

The Lightning 368 Nationals were hosted at Northampton Sailing Club over two days in early September, with seventeen entries. The Lightning is unusual in having these National Championships, in addition to a Sea Championships, which were run earlier in the year in Plymouth, with boat-builder John Claridge coming out on top.

The first day was extremely windy, and competitors found the three races fairly hard work. Robert Claridge found the conditions to his liking however, and took the winning gun in all three. However, the tussle for second, third and fourth was very tight, with Paul White finishing the day with two seconds and a fourth, against John Claridge's two thirds and a second, whilst Hugh Spencer scored two fourths and a second to stay in contention.

Whilst conditions on the second day were slightly lighter, the same four boats dominated the final two races. Robert Claridge won the first race of the day to seal the title with four firsts, scoring a fourth in the final race, which was to be his discard. White added a second and third to his tally to confirm the runners-up position ahead of John Claridge, who also finished the event with a second and third on the final day. Final race winner, Hugh Spencer, added this result to a string of top thirds and fourths to confirm his fourth position overall after a very consistent regatta. In fact, none of the top four ever dropped beyond fourth in any race, suggesting that at the moment the rest of the fleet need to improve their game slightly to close the gap.

P	Helm	Club	R1	R2	R3	R4	R5	Tot	Nett
1	Robert Claridge	RLYC	1	1	1	1	4	8	4
2	Paul White	TBYC	2	4	2	2	3	13	9
3	John Claridge	RLYC	3	2	3	3	2	13	10
4	Hugh Spencer	RPCYC	4	3	4	4	1	16	12
5	Adam Styles	ESC	5	6	5	5	5	26	20
6	Caroline Key	WOSC	6	5	6	6	6	29	23
7	S Styles	ESC	9	7	7	7	7	37	28
8	Sue Thomas	OSC	8	10	8	8	10	44	34
9	Robin Stubbs	HSC	7	8	DNC	11	13	57	39
10	Bob Haynes	HSC	11	9	DNC	12	8	58	40

International Moth

Type	Dinghy	Beam	2.26 m
Crew	1; On racks	Weight	94 kg
PN	1447	Sail area M	6.25 sq m
Length	3.36 m	Designer	Various
			www.int-moth.org.uk

The International Moth is a single-handed development class that has always been at the cutting edge of dinghy sailing, and continues to lead the way, now on hydrofoils! These lightweight boats are incredibly fast and bring an element of flying to the sport of sailing. The hulls are now often built in carbon fibre to provide a structure that is strong enough to withstand the loads applied by moving the boundaries as the Moths have done. Whilst much attention has been given to the hydrofoils, the rest of this boat continues to develop apace; what on Earth will they do next?

International Moth World Championships

Cascade Locks, Oregon   10 - 15 August 2009

Fifty of the latest flying machines, from ten different countries, landed in Oregon for the Moth World Championships in August, with strong contingents from Great Britain, Singapore, Australia, Belgium, Canada, Japan, New Zealand, Switzerland, United Arab Emirates and, of course, the USA. There was much anticipation of the event, with the reappearance of Rohan Veal (previous multi World Champion coming back from retirement), together with 49er World Champion Nathan Outteridge, who had also shown his paces in the Moth during the winter and our own ex World Champion Simon Payne in the Mach 2 design to name just a few!

After the US Nationals, which were the "warmer" for the Worlds, Nathan Outterridge had promoted himself to favourite with a win, ahead of American Bora Gulari and fellow Aussie Scott Babbage. This continued after the first day of points racing when the fleet got four races under their belts, again led by Outteridge, with Gulari in hot pursuit. America's Dalton Bergan was third at this stage with Payne the top European in fourth overall.

Three more races were completed on the second day of the Worlds, in flat water with shifty breezes and slightly less wind. Outteridge still led at the end of the day, but saw his lead pruned back slightly by Gulari, whilst Arnaud Psarofaghis from Switzerland (the recently crowned European Champion) had pulled up to third overall, just ahead of Payne.

With forecasts of strong breezes for the third day, another three races were scheduled, and whilst the first race saw up to twenty five knot winds, the breeze reduced to the level of the previous days for Races Two and Three. It was a day of attrition at the front of the fleet, however. Outteridge retired from Race Nine for repairs, whilst Si Payne retired from Race Ten with a "damaged" knee, and Babbage, who had won the first race of the day, broke some gear between races and was unable to repair it afloat, which left him with two DNFs. When the air had cleared, American Bora Gulari was left at the top of the overall scoring tables, with Outteridge two points behind in second position, and Psarofaghis in third.

Day Four was cold, cloudy and had shifty breezes in the fifteen to eighteen knot range initially, but creeping up later which was an excellent prospect! Three races were held, and by the end of the day the scene was set for a final day show down. Bora Gulari of USA held a decisive seven point advantage from Australia's Nathan Outteridge, with Switzerland's Arnaud Psarofaghis five points further back.

The Dinghy & Smallcraft Review
2009~2010   **207**

On the final day, thirty three year old Gulari found the light conditions suited him, and underlined his abilities by talking two race wins to become the first American to win the title in more than three decades. In the overall stakes, Outteridge finished in runner up position ahead of Arnaud Psarofaghis of Switzerland, with American Dalton Bergan in fourth, our own Si Payne in fifth, and Moth legend Rohan Veal coming back from retirement in sixth.

P	Nat	Helm	R1	R2	R3	R4	R5	R6	R7	R8	R9	R10	R11	R12	R13	R14	R15	Tot	Nett
1	USA	B Gulari	6	2	1	3	11	1	1	2	1	4	1	5	1	1	1	41	24
2	AUS	N Outteridge	3	1	3	1	4	2	2	6	DNF	1	3	6	3	5	2	84	36
3	SUI	A Psarofaghis	4	4	6	4	3	3	3	4	3	2	2	2	4	3	3	50	40
4	USA	D Bergan	1	3	7	2	6	7	4	5	2	6	4	4	5	2	5	63	49
5	GBR	S Payne	2	5	2	7	1	6	6	10	11	DNF	7	1	8	7	4	116	66
6	AUS	R Veal	5	6	4	6	9	4	5	8	5	7	8	9	6	DNC	DNC	182	82
7	AUS	S Babbage	7	DNF	5	5	2	5	7	1	DNC	DNC	9	3	2	4	6	200	100
8	USA	B Funk	22	12	8	10	14	8	8	3	39	5	5	7	9	8	8	166	105
9	AUS	R Gough	12	10	11	8	10	13	12	9	4	3	6	10	7	9	9	133	108
10	NZL	K Hall	8	7	9	9	13	14	11	7	DNF	16	12	19	20	6	10	203	141

2009 World Champion Bora Gulari of the USA

International Moth Europeans

Horsens, Denmark   24 - 28 June 2009

The fast expanding International Moth fleet travelled to Horsens, in Denmark, for the European Championships, with an entry of forty two boats from ten countries. Whilst the Moth had reached a stable platform (in that the bulk of the fleet were sailing the Bladerider which is an off the shelf package) this season saw some alternatives coming to the fore, and the Mach Two design has been making inroads into the market, particularly in the hands of past World Champion, Simon Payne. After the first day's racing, with three heats completed, Payne led overall the current European Champion, Arnaud Psarofaghis, carrying a DNS after a gear failure on his Mach Two.

With stronger winds for Day Two, Psarofaghis led around the windward mark, and held on to win the race by half a second from Payne, who pulled into contention. With no more races possible, Psarofaghis and Payne were level in the lead with two firsts and a second each.

Four more races on the final day did nothing to separate this leading pairing, as they both scored a two wins and two seconds in the final four races, and thus finished on the same points. They also had the same numbers of firsts, and the same seconds! Eventually they could only be separated on the last race win, which went to the defending champion Psarofaghis, who became European champion for the second year. Third place overall went to Eelco Boers from Holland, with sail-maker Mike Lennon from GBR in fourth, and Mike Cooke in fifth. There were three Mach Two hulls in the first five overall, together with a Bladerider and a Ninja, to show more of a spread of equipment than has been seen for a while.

P	Helm	Nat	R1	R2	R3	R4	R5	R6	R7	R8	Pts	Nett
1	A Psarofaghis	SUI	DNC	2	1	1	1	2	2	1	53	8
2	S Payne	GBR	1	1	2	2	2	1	1	2	12	8
3	E Boers	NED	2	3	DNC	4	4	4	4	3	67	20
4	M Lennon	GBR	3	3	DNC	5	5	11	5	5	87	27
5	M Cooke	GBR	4	8	5	7	7	5	6	4	46	31
6	R Harris	GBR	5	6	4	6	6	8	7	7	49	34
7	M Gravare	SWE	7	11	7	8	9	6	8	10	66	45
8	R Matthias	SUI	11	7	3	19	15	10	10	8	83	49
9	P Anrefors	SWE	8	9	DNC	16	8	9	9	21	123	59
10	JP Ziegert	SUI	DNC	DNC	DNC	3	3	3	3	6	147	61

International Moth Nationals

Saundersfoot Sailing Club   10 - 14 July 2009

The 2009 Moth UK Nationals and Open Championship was held at Saundersfoot SC, with a fleet of thirty seven entries, entirely of the foil-borne variety, who used the testing to refine their controls and technique.

Racing started in a ten to fifteen knot breeze and, whilst the fleet coped admirably upwind, the learning curve downwind was fairly steep with foil setup offering one widespread area of improvement. After a close tussle, Mike Cooke took the winning gun in his Aardvark Ninja design, putting down his marker for the regatta. The programme for three races on the first day was cut short by a battering rain storm that reduced visibility for the remainder of the day.

Three races were held on a challenging second day, which saw large wind shifts, and huge gusts and waves. After a suitable delay, another race was started, and this time Si Payne, the reigning Champion, led for the first lap, having had to miss the first day owing to prior commitments. Payne suffered a minor gear failure which meant he was left with no option but he was forced to retire, which effectively ended his challenge. This left Mike Lennon in the driver's seat in this race, ahead of multi-class Champion, Geoff Carveth. On a tight course, Mike Cooke finally took control of the race to take the winning gun, ahead of Rob Harris and Ricky Tagg with Lennon in fourth. The next race was won by May, from Lennon, Tagg, Harris and Carveth, and Carveth took another step forward in his Moth career in the next race, winning his first class race ahead of Harris, Lennon, May and Cooke.

With Day Three blown off, the final two races on Tuesday would decide the winner, with the biggest waves of the event and fifteen knots. In the first race Lennon, Cooke and May all arrived at the windward mark together, with Lennon and May both pitch-poling before the gybe. This allowed Harris and Cooke to pull away, although the latter soon had his own problems downwind, dropping him to fourth. The winner finally was Paul Hignett, ahead of Rob Harris with Mike Lennon in third, the latter pair tied for the lead going into the last race! At the first mark, Lennon was in the driving seat, but a pitch-pole put paid to his options, allowing Harris, Cooke and Hignett through. Cooke pulled clear to take the win and as the calculators buzzed, it became apparent that the new National Champion was Mike Cooke.

P	Helm	R1	R4	R5	R6	R10	R11	Pts	Nett
1	Mike Cooke	1	1	9	5	4	1	21	12
2	Rod Harris	4	2	4	2	2	3	17	13
3	Michael Lennon	2	4	2	3	3	5	19	14
4	Paul Hignet	16	6	8	6	1	2	39	23
5	Ricky Tagg	38	3	3	7	8	4	63	25
6	Geoff Carveth	10	7	5	1	7	6	36	26
7	Adam May	3	5	1	4	17	15	45	28
8	Paul Hayden	8	8	6	8	15	9	54	39
9	Andrew Friend	5	9	15	9	11	11	60	45
10	Dougie Imrie	18	11	11	14	5	7	66	48

Musto Skiff

Type	Dinghy	Weight	80 kg
Crew	1; On trapeze	Sail area M	11.5 sq m
PN	875	Spi type	Asymmetric
Length	4.55 m	Spi area	15.5 sq m
Beam	1.35 m	Designer	Dr J Harpprecht
			www.mustoskiff.com

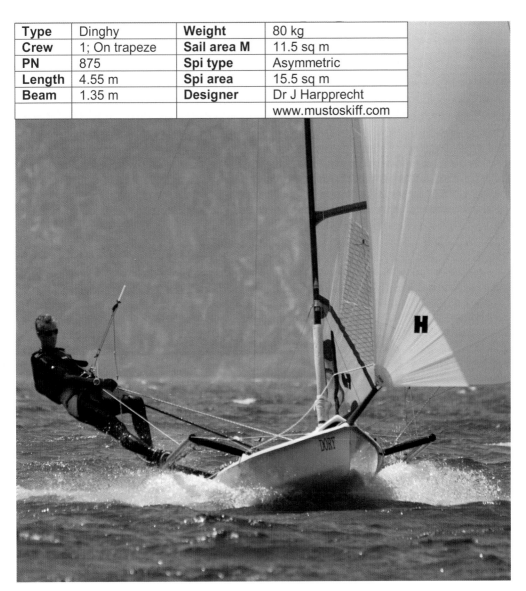

The Musto Performance Skiff is a very fast, single-handed boat, with the helmsman using both a trapeze and a gennaker to make life more exciting! When Dr Joachim Harpprecht designed the Musto Performance Skiff, it was with the design concept "to produce an elegant yet simple dinghy, with blistering performance that is highly enjoyable to sail." If you ask any MPS owner, they will confirm that the design brief has been achieved. The boat has become an international success, with fleets around the world, and Championships from National up to World level.

Musto Skiff European Championships

Lake Garda   30 August - 3 September 2009

Lake Garda was at its best to welcome a fleet of seventy four Musto Skiffs, representing ten countries, for their European Championships in early September.

The event was won by World Champion Richard Stenhouse, who dominated most of the week, winning a total of seven races, and taking the title without needing to sail the final two races (although he won them for good measure!). With winds between eight and eighteen knots for most of the week, the racing was excellent, and whilst for most of the week they were fairly consistent, the first day had some interesting shifts and bends to contend with. However, on the whole, the conditions were excellent, and a perfect demonstration of why so many championships go to Garda each year.

Stenhouse was comfortably in the driving seat; competition behind him was more intense, with the battle for second between Andy Peake and Russ Clark going to the final race, when Peake got the better of the fight in both races to push himself clear. In addition to Stenhouse's wins, other race victories were taken by Clark, Graeme Oliver, Ian Renilson, and Australian Marcus Hamilton, who had a fairly varied week, being over the line three times, disqualified once, and then strung some good results together to indicate that the Australians will be a force when the 2011 World Championships are held in Melbourne.

The first non-British boat in the event was Frenchman George Richards in seventh place with the second being Australian Tim Hill in twelfth.

P	Nat	Helm	R1	R2	R3	R4	R5	R6	R7	R8	R9	R10	R11	R12	Pts
1	GBR	R Stenhouse	3	3	6	1	1	1	8	1	1	3	1	1	16
2	GBR	A Peake	4	5	4	3	24	29	9	2	2	8	4	3	44
3	GBR	R Clark	2	1	9	4	10	3	10	3	15	9	6	6	53
4	GBR	G Oliver	8	6	1	35	3	2	4	OCS	18	15	2	9	68
5	GBR	I Renilson	9	19	8	13	2	5	1	4	4	10	23	34	75
6	GBR	B Keen	6	17	18	OCS	5	DNF	7	9	3	4	13	2	80.5
7	FRA	G Richards	14	13	12	2	6	23	3	19	10	12	12	16	100
8	GBR	J Reekie	1	7	3	9	4	DSQ	16	24	13	30	20	4	101
9	GBR	G Tanner	5	2	7	5	44	19	17	7	12	18	18	DNS	110
10	GBR	D Vincent	11	14	22	3	11	6	19	10	14	11	11	5	112

Musto Skiff Nationals

East Lothian Yacht Club   18 - 21 June 2009

The start of the National Championships weekend at East Lothian YC saw the fifty one strong Musto Skiff fleet under some pressure as the winds threatened to spoil their much anticipated Championships. Racing on the Thursday was adjourned as the Race Officer left the harbour to be greeted by winds often over forty knots. In order to get some competition in, events were delayed until five pm, and then a series of small group qualifying races were run at the local go kart track, which produced a series of largely confusing results as far as the sailing was concerned! With Friday similarly breezy, and winds never dropping below thirty mph, racing was again shelved in favour of a social day, hopefully in readiness for a very busy sailing weekend, wind permitting!

At last Saturday dawned with an eight knot breeze and a chance to catch up on the schedule, with five races held in the course of the day. Most results were up and down throughout the fleet but, at the end of the day, the leading three were Daniel Henderson, Iver Ahlmann, and current World Champion Richard Stenhouse. However, after two more races, the first discard would come in to play which would reorganise the score sheet significantly.

It was disappointing to wake to Sunday's light, unstable breezes. However,after allowing things to settle, proceedings commenced in eight knots of wind. The first heat of the day was beset with black flags, but it was still possible to fit in a second race, which at least ensured that the first discard came in to play. By taking a victory in the final race, Richard Stenhouse just pushed himself clear of the pack to take the National Championships, pipping Daniel Henderson at the last gasp, with Andrew Peake in third, and top Scotsman Ian Renilson in fourth overall.

P	Helm	Club	R1	R2	R3	R4	R5	R6	R7	Pts
1	Richard Stenhouse	RSC	1	4	15	7	8	4	1	25
2	Daniel Henderson	TBYC	2	5	12	1	9	2	8	27
3	Andrew Peake	WYC	32	1	6	14	4	3	2	30
4	Ian Renilson	DBSC	11	6	5	2	19	1	7	32
5	Tom Wright	RSC	10	9	18	5	3	5	3	35
6	Iver Ahlmann	DRSC	6	10	7	8	1	6	22	38
7	John Reekie	-	12	3	2	16	12	9	16	54
8	Rick Perkins	WYC	4	2	9	6	16	DSQ	18	55
9	Martin Boatman	-	24	12	1	12	2	DSQ	6	57
10	Tom Offer	CVLSC	7	23	11	4	10	DSQ	12	67
11	Nick Hollis	RSC	5	15	14	10	13	16	35	73
12	Paul Clements	CVLSC	3	29	4	3	20	21	26	77

OK

Type	Dinghy	Weight	72 kg
Crew	1; Sit out	Sail area M	8.5 sq m
PN	1111	Spi type	None
Length	4 m	Designer	Knud Olsen, 1960
Beam	1.25 m		www.okdinghy.co.uk

Photo courtesy of Jan Waller

The OK is an international design, with an unstayed mast and powerful mainsail. The boat was designed for ease of manufacture, and can be built by any home builder, although of course there are a number of professionals keen to produce boats. The class has World Championships, and is sailed keenly in Europe, and also in the southern hemisphere; in fact, there are some 15,000 boats sailed worldwide, and over 2,000 of these are UK-based.

International OK Worlds

Kalmar, Sweden   23 - 30 July 2009

Although some of the National entries were slightly down on previous years, the 2009 OK Worlds were almost fully subscribed with eighty entries from ten nations, including six former World Champions. Defending Champion Karl Purdie was one of three Kiwis to have made the massive trek. Britain's Nick Craig, a frequent previous winner, had not sailed the OK much since the previous Worlds owing to other commitments; not least the arrival of twins in May, but with a competitive boat, he was always going to be a force in the event.

The first points race eventually started under black flag after a series of false starts with the bulk of the fleet going to the starboard side of the course. Thomas Hansson-Mild (SWE) and 64 year old ex-Olympian Jørgen Lindhardtsen (DEN) led at the windward mark, and pulled out a large lead on the following pack. The second race also started following a general recall, with the black flag being brought in promptly once again. The moderate breeze created a short chop which suited Nick Craig who was first to the windward mark, with reigning champion Karl Purdie in pursuit. Craig sailed downwind quite conservatively, having fallen foul of the jury in the first race, which lost him some ground, particularly to Purdie who surfed past and off into the distance. Andre Blasse (AUS) and Jørgen Lindhardtsen also got past Craig before the end of the race.

Race Three was held in sunshine with a light breeze, but clouds soon rolled in with an increasing wind. The port side of the course paid dividends, and Purdie built an impressive lead on the two reaches ahead of Hansson-Mild and Lindhardtsen. Hansson-Mild showed impressive speed downwind to pass Purdie, who just slipped back through before the finish. The second race of the day saw an even fresher breeze, and this time it was the starboard side that paid dividends, with Hansson-Mild first to the windward mark in company with Lindhardtsen, Purdie and Nick Craig, and these positions were largely held to the finish of a race that experienced the best of OK sailing conditions!

With flatter water and lighter breeze on Day Three, some new faces appeared at the fore. Nick Craig, and retiring Class Chairman Greg Wilcox were clear at the first mark with Wilcox getting water and taking the lead at the wing mark; sailing off to win from Hansson-Mild, whilst Poland's Antoni Pawlowski took third. After some delay waiting for the wind to settle, Heat Six eventually started in a shifting breeze, under the black flag which caught out eight boats. As the conditions settled, Karl Purdie appeared once again in the driving seat, with Jørgen Lindhardtsen in second, and the Class's new Chairman, Andre Blasse picking up from seventh to third at the finish.

With two days to go, the title battle was tight between Purdie and Hansson-Mild, each level on points and both discarding an OCS from earlier in the week. With storm clouds gathering over the racecourse, and the sea building, Race Seven started on time in a light breeze. By the windward mark, the Swede had built up a good lead which he held to win from Purdie, who felt that whilst he had increased his downwind speed and was catching Hansson-Mild on the reaches, he had lost his upwind edge to the Swede! With two races left in the series, top Brit was Nick Craig in ninth overall, with two Swedes, two Danes, two New Zealanders, two Poles and an Australian filling the top ten positions in this international group!

The final day brought a steady breeze across the course and, after one attempt at a start, the black flag was introduced. The early leader was Jørgen Lindhardtsen, closely followed by Oliver Gronholz (GER) and Hannsson-Mild, with Purdie on his transom. Lindhardtsen increased his lead up the next beat and held it on the run to the leeward gate. Hansson-Mild had climbed to second place, with Purdie and Andre Blasse a short distance behind. Lindhardtsen was first to finish, closely followed by Hansson-Mild, but Blasse forced Purdie into fourth position, to introduce a little separation in the overall scores prior to the final heat.

The final race, Heat Ten saw the conclusion of the scheduled programme, and a great tussle for the title. Once again the black flag had to be introduced quite promptly, and Blasse was first to the windward mark from Zimmermann (GER). Purdie and Hansson-Mild were joined in fifth and sixth positions. As the race progressed, Purdie picked up to third position ahead of Hansson-Mild (in fourth) and Blasse held out to take the race win, whilst Purdie picked up a spot to second, only to see Hansson-Mild gain into third, sufficient to take the title by the narrowest of margins.

P	Nat	Helm	R1	R2	R3	R4	R5	R6	R7	R8	R9	R10	Tot	Nett
1	SWE	Thomas Hansson-Mild	1	5	2	1	2	BFD	1	1	2	3	98	18
2	NZL	Karl Purdie	4	1	1	2	OCS	1	2	2	4	2	99	19
3	DEN	Jørgen Lindhardtsen	2	3	3	3	30	2	6	4	1	7	61	31
4	AUS	Andre Blasse	7	2	4	5	25	3	3	3	3	1	56	31
5	NZL	Greg Wilcox	9	6	5	6	1	BFD	4	7	6	9	133	53
6	GBR	Nick Craig	6	4	12	4	4	6	9	6	11	DNS	142	62
7	GBR	Terry Curtis	3	7	8	9	5	22	13	10	8	8	93	71
8	POL	Pawel Pawlaczyk	5	8	15	19	16	18	5	5	12	6	100	82
9	GER	Martin Zimmermann	17	15	13	12	9	4	11	11	7	4	103	86
10	GER	Gunter Arndt	13	17	6	8	19	19	15	8	9	5	119	100

OK National Championships

Dabchicks Sailing Club   28 - 31 August 2009

Thirty five OK dinghies enjoyed exciting racing at the 2009 National Championships at Dabchicks Sailing Club in Essex. The regular competitors were joined by one or two visitors hoping to give the fleet a run for their money; not least two times Phantom National Champion, Andy Crouch who was to pit his abilities against reigning champion Terry Curtis from Upper Thames SC.

Strong winds caused the cancellation of racing on Friday, but perfect weather gave ideal sailing on Saturday, and Curtis took first blood, with Crouch coming to terms with the boat in second. In the next race, Jon Fish led throughout to take the win, to add to his third in the first encounter, with Curtis sailing through the fleet to gain second. Local sailor Robert Deaves was handily placed at the end of the first day with two fourths.

Andy Crouch made the most of the windy conditions on Sunday to take both race wins and the overall lead. Curtis could only manage a seventh and second leaving him second overall whilst Fish added a second and fourth to be third overall as the Championships entered the final day.

In the first race on the final day, Curtis pulled ahead of the fleet to open up a lead and emphasise his claim for the title. Behind him, Martin Evans took second position, with the major title pretenders out of the frame. The second race was subjected to two general recalls before the black flag came out. First around the first mark was Crouch, with Curtis in hot pursuit, and they finished in that order with Fish in third. This was sufficient to give the consistent Curtis the title for the second year running, with Crouch in a commendable second position overall, and Fish in third.

P	Helm	Club	R1	R2	R3	R4	R5	R6	Pts
1	Terry Curtis	UTSC	1	2	7	2	1	2	8
2	Andy Crouch	BSC	2	7	1	1	5	1	10
3	Jon Fish	WSC	3	1	2	4	4	3	13
4	Robert Deaves	WSC	4	4	5	7	6	4	23
5	Martin Evans	DSC	12	6	36	3	2	6	29
6	Dan Ager	WSC	10	3	4	8	36	10	35
7	Andy Turner	OSSC	13	5	6	9	9	8	37
8	Mike Edwards	SSSC	9	8	14	6	7	7	37
9	Julian Burnham	UTSC	8	9	9	5	11	9	40
10	Andy Davies	CSC	7	12	20	12	8	5	44

Phantom

Type	Dinghy	Beam	1.64 m
Crew	1; Sit out	Weight	61 kg
PN	1045	Sail area M&J	9.75 sq m
Length	4.42 m	Designer	P Wright / B Taylor, 1971
			www.phantomclass.org.uk

The Phantom was designed as a single-hander that was exciting to sail, manageable and at the same time affordable to build. As there were already boats on the market for the lighter helms, it was aimed as a boat that was both comfortable and fast for larger sailors. A Phantom sailor shouldn't weigh less than 10 stone, and it is most suitable for those in the weight range of 12 - 18 stone (76 - 115 kg). One major advantage with the Phantom is that both the class association and the designers view the development of the class in a proactive manner, always providing care is taken not to outclass older boats. Latterly, the design has been modified to incorporate self-draining cockpits and carbon spars.

Phantom National Championships

Llandudno Sailing Club   11 - 13 September 2009

An excellent entry of sixty four boats appeared at the Phantom Nationals in Llandudno, which was fifty per cent higher than last year, and underlines the fact that the class is currently going from strength to strength. The event was held over a series of seven points races with two discards, and close racing was enjoyed by competitors throughout the fleet.

This year the Class has made a strong impact on the various single race events around the country, winning the Bloody Mary, the Grafham Grand Prix, and also the Steve Nicholson Trophy, and the Championships have attracted some of the UK's best sailors. Not least of these is Charlie Cumley, ex-Finn star, and more recently Solo National Champion in both 2008 and 2009. Additionally, Nick Craig, one of the countries most versatile dinghy sailors, with recent championship wins in the OK, RS 400, B14, Enterprise etc, was also trying his hand in the Phantom.

These two, together with the previous year's championship runner-up, Andy Crouch, dominated the weekend, with Cumley finally taking the Championship by just one point from Crouch, with Nick Craig two points back in third. Cumley won three races, but more importantly he never dropped below third position in any race, whilst Crouch had a race win and four second positions to count. By the end of the weekend Craig was certainly getting his hand in, winning the final two races to take his tally to three victories in the event. Fourth position went to class stalwart and this year's Albacore National Champion, Will Gulliver.

P	Helm	Club	R1	R2	R3	R4	R5	R6	R7	Tot	Nett
1	C Cumley	TCYC	1	3	1	1	2	3	3	14	8
2	A Crouch	BSC	6	2	2	2	1	4	2	19	9
3	N Craig	FPSC	4	1	8	5	4	1	1	24	11
4	W Gulliver	NSC	3	6	10	6	12	6	6	49	27
5	P Evans	N&BSC	13	7	7	27	3	OCS	7	129	37
6	G Young	CSC	9	10	13	3	6	35	21	97	41
7	S Hawkes	WSC	57	11	4	7	28	7	12	126	41
8	R Parkin	HSC	8	5	16	12	5	17	DNC	128	46
9	L Crispin	SSC	7	BFD	3	10	31	25	4	145	49
10	A Davies	CSC	10	16	9	11	21	10	14	91	54

RS 300

Photo courtesy of Fotoboat

Type	Dinghy	Beam	2 m
Crew	1; Sit out	Weight	75 kg
PN	1000	Sail area M	9.25 or 9.94 sq m
Length	4.24 m	Designer	Clive Everest
			www.rs-association.com

The Clive Everest-designed RS 300 offers radical design, with cutting edge technology. Looking somewhat like a "stealth" dinghy, the boat has an epoxy sandwich hull, carbon spars, hi-tech sails, and a clever weight equalization system, using two sail sizes, to offer the best and fairest possible performance. This system aims to ensure that everyone is racing on level terms. The RS 300 is an ideal boat for people who sail in waters too restricted for trapeze dinghies, or who just prefer to sit-out!

RS 300 National Championships

Royal Torbay Yacht Club   3 - 6 September 2009

An entry of thirty three RS 300s made their way to Royal Torbay YC for their Championships in early September. This represented a good increase over the 2008 turnout, and was partly accounted for by the contingent from Thorney Island SC where their new and blossoming fleet had four members present.

The event opened with Force four to five winds which were made variable by the landscape around the bay, and therefore more difficult to read. Conditions on the second day were even more robust, with twenty knot winds and bigger gusts, and the event was a challenge for these radical-looking dinghies.

The eventual winner of the event was Steve Bolland who retained the title that he won last year in Wales. With a set of results that only wavered once from the top three, his victory on points was fairly decisive but he was made to fight for the title by those in pursuit including David Acres, who included two race wins in his tally of results, and finished second overall counting a string of top three results, whilst Steve Fisher of Draycote Water also finished in the top three results, with one race win, and a string of single figure results. However, Bolland's continued mastery of this little boat is unchallenged overall and, despite a few inevitable capsizes given the conditions, his performance never really left the end result in any doubt.

P	Helm	Club	R1	R2	R3	R4	R5	R6	R7	R8	R9	R10	Pts
1	Steve Bolland	BCYC	1	3	1	2	1	1	10	1	2	34	12
2	Dave Acres	TISC	2	10	34	3	2	34	1	2	4	1	25
3	Steve Fisher	DWSC	4	1	2	7	10	4	8	4	9	10	39
4	Richard Kennedy	TISC	6	6	10	14	5	2	6	6	17	6	47
5	Ben Yeats	CSC	11	12	3	25	7	34	15	3	1	3	55
6	Neil Beveridge	PSC	9	7	11	19	9	11	4	9	5	4	58
7	Luke South	BSC	7	19	8	8	8	9	3	5	12	34	60
8	Richard LeMare	DWSC	3	4	5	12	17	10	26	18	8	2	61
9	James Phare	RTYC	5	8	9	5	13	34	14	8	6	9	63
10	Tim Keen	SVSC	21	16	34	4	4	6	2	14	15	5	66

RS 600 & RS 600FF

Type	Dinghy	Beam	1.93 - 2.23 m
Crew	1; On trapeze	Weight	76 kg
PN	920	Sail area M	12.14 sq m
Length	4.47 m	Designer	C Everest / N Peters
			www.rs-association.com

The RS 600 is a light, responsive, single-handed dinghy, with the helmsman supported o.
a trapeze. The boat has a significantly adjustable rig, and a reefable mainsail, whic.
ensures that the boat can be sailed by a wide range of weights and abilities. The RS 600 i
built in vacuum-bagged epoxy for maximum strength, giving a hull weight of just 52 kg, s
she is very easy to move ashore.The RS 600 features a weight equalization system tha
ensures that the boat can be sailed on level terms by a wide range of shapes and sizes.

RS 600FF National Championships

Weymouth & Portland Sailing Academy   6 - 7 June 2009

The foil-borne RS 600FF fleet arrived in Weymouth to find that there was the potential for some breeze, but twenty knots was at the upper end of most people's comfort zone, encouraging the reduced rig to be used for all but the reigning Champion, Sam Pascoe. As the wind continued to increase, the gun eventually set the fleet off into a twenty seven knot breeze. Pascoe took the early lead, but made the decision to switch rigs, leaving Simon Hiscocks, Alex Torbutt and Alex Knight battling to finish in that order.

As the second race started Pascoe was still short of the line, and it was the same top three making the pace until Knight's mainsail became damaged and he couldn't continue, leaving Steve Birbeck in third. However, despite his tardy start, Pascoe managed make up ground through the race to finish with a third behind Alex Torbutt and Simon Hiscocks with Steve Birbeck in fouth. Race Three got under way with Sam Pascoe and Simon Hiscocks having a close tussle at the front whilst behind them Steve Birbeck, Alex Torbutt, Gareth Davies and Stuart Appleby all switched places. Final results were Simon Hiscocks first, Sam Pascoe second, Gareth Davies third, Alex Torbutt fourth. After Day One the overall results showed Simon Hiscocks in first, with Alex Torbutt second, and Sam Pascoe third. In the Master's Series Steve Birbeck was leading from Dave Smith-White while Graham Simmonds was in third. With less wind for Day Two and the fleet back to full rigs it was not even clear foiling would be possible. However Pascoe, Hislop and Alex Knight revelled in the conditions to finish in that order. After a delay to allow the breeze to build and change direction a few times Race Two got underway in a light but foiling breeze, and this allowed for some close racing with Pascoe leading from the start with Knight and Hiscocks giving chase. The breeze became unpleasantly light as the race finished with Sam ahead of Alex Knight with Simon Hiscocks in third.

Going into the last race Sam Pascoe or Simon Hiscocks could both still win the Championship but it was going to be close. At the beginning of the race Gareth Davies, Alex Knight and Simon Hiscocks all headed off on port tack on the foils, whilst the rest of the fleet could only watch. However, with a dying breeze, when they tacked there was no wind and they got headed and rounded in the middle of the fleet, effectively handing the title to Pascoe after a keenly fought regatta.

P	Sail No	Helm	R1	R2	R3	R4	R5	R6	Nett
1	1000	Sam Pascoe	8	3	2	1	1	1	8
2	7	Simon Hiscocks	1	2	1	2	3	DNC	9
3	5	Alex Torbutt	2	1	4	DNC	5	10	22
4	1002	Alex Knight	3	DNC	DNC	3	2	2	23
5	24	Gareth Davies	4	5	3	7	4	9	23
6	812	Steve Birbeck	6	4	5	8	8	5	28

RS 600 National Championships

Hayling Island Sailing Club   12 - 15 September 2009

Twenty two RS 600s attended their Nationals at Hayling Island in mid September, held in conjunction with the RS K6 Nationals.

The first day was raced in a force three, and saw Royal Torbay's Steve Birbeck lead at the first mark, and extended his lead to win the race from David Annan (Grafham Water SC). Birbeck then did the same again in the second race (this time beating Dan Jackson into second) to put down his marker for a Championships that he did not contest in 2008. Second after the first day was Dan Jackson of Tenby SC with a fifth and second, and with three further races on Day Two, this order remained the same as Birbeck took a first, second and third in the next three races, exactly matching Jackson to leave him just three points adrift at the halfway mark.

Only one race was held on the third day of the event, and this was won by Jackson, ahead of Birbeck, which reduced the deficit to two points with one day to go, but thirty knot winds caused the cancellation of the racing on the final day, and thus assured Birbeck of a title in yet another class to add to his impressive list of achievements. Jackson finished second, with Andy Heissig from Lymington Town SC in third place with a consistent scoreline counting four fourth places and a race win.

Birbeck also took the award for the first Master, in addition to the National Championship title.

It should be pointed out that the RS 600 of course is a different animal from the RS 600FF, being the original personification of this design, without the added foils. You will see from the report of the RS 600FF Nationals that Birbeck was in attendance there, but was not quite as dominant, finishing in sixth position.

Pos	SN	Helm	Club	R1	R2	R3	R4	R5	R6	Pts
1st	957	Steve Birbeck	RTSC	1	1	2	1	3	2	7
2nd	913	Dan Jackson	TSC	5	2	1	3	2	1	9
3rd	984	Andrew Heissig	LTSC	4	4	4	11	1	4	17
4th	827	James Sainsbury	GWSC	3	6	6	2	4	8	21
5th	702	John Charles	LoSSC	6	3	7	6	11	3	25
6th	740	Giles Chipperfeild	LTSC	14	5	5	5	10	DNC	39
7th	815	David Annan	GWSC	2	7	3	DNF	DNC	6	41
8th	983	Jon Bradbury	MBC	15	15	9	4	5	10	43
9th	811	James Nuttall	BCSC	16	9	8	10	7	9	43
10th	954	Jon Powell	PSC	12	11	11	9	6	7	44

RS 700

Type	Dinghy	Weight	94 kg
Crew	1; On trapeze	Sail area M	12.8 sq m
PN	857	Spi type	Asymmetric
Length	4.68 m	Spi area	16 sq m
Beam	1.92 m	Designer	N Peters / A Southon
			www.rs-association.com

The RS 700 takes single-handed sailing just one step further; with a large mainsail and an asymmetric spinnaker, this boat is a bit of a handful. However, the boat is designed with a sufficiently wide hull to offer some stability, especially for the inexperienced RS 700 sailor! The RS 700 benefits from a lively class association, with a well-supported racing circuit, National Championships, and events around Europe.

RS 700 European Championship

Yacht Club de Carnac   27 - 31 July 2009

Carnac was a fitting venue for the RS 700 Europeans, offering beautiful weather and conditions, cool evenings, and a relaxed atmosphere.

In the course of the week, there were five different race winners, and some closely matched competition. With Day One sailed in a Force three, the first race was taken by Richard Allen, whilst the second went to Dave Gorringe. The first race on Day Two saw Jon Heissig benefit from the gun, with Richard Allen again making the best of his navigational skills to take the fourth race of the series. Wednesday was an altogether more breezy affair, with many cowering in the dunes. In the first race of the day, Ian Nolan led from start to finish to gain his first win of the week, whilst Dave Gorringe added another victory to his collection in the second race.

Jon Heissig came to the fore on Thursday, and took both victories which, combined with his previous results, was sufficient to give him the overall win in the regatta, but the runner-up position was still very much in the melting pot, with four other boats in contention. With extremely light conditions on the final day, it became something of a lottery, and a group of boats finally spotted some wind, to allow Pete Shaw to take the win with Richard Allen picking up the second position.

P	Nat	Helm	R1	R2	R3	R4	R5	R6	R7	R8	R9	Pts
1	GBR	J Heissig	2	D+D	1	3	2	2	1	1	3	11
2	GBR	R Allen	1	DNF	7	1	4	4	8	4	2	23
3	GBR	M Pollington	4	8	5	2	DNF	DNF	3	3	6	31
4	FRA	C Fraboulet	5	3	3	6	3	7	5	D+D	9	31
5	GBR	E Gatehouse	7	6	2	5	5	6	9	8	4	35
6	GBR	P Shaw	11	7	8	4	DNF	DNF	6	5	1	42
7	GBR	I Nolan	8	5	9	OCS	1	3	13	10	8	44
8	GBR	D Gorringe	6	1	13	9	6	1	12	DNF	11	46
9	GBR	I Swann	10	DNF	11	8	8	5	2	6	10	49
10	GBR	G Peeters	DNF	DNF	6	7	7	8	7	9	7	51

RS 700 National Championship

Royal Torbay Yacht Club   26 - 29 September 2009

Thirty four RS 700 dinghies competed for their championships at the end of September at the Royal Torbay Yacht Club, a number that was slightly down on the previous year, when the Championship was held at Hayling Island, which of course is the spiritual home of the class!

The event started in very light winds, with two races completed on the first day. Despite the difficulty of the conditions, the competition was close, and at the end of the first day, the lead had been taken by Michael Dencher from Chew Valley, who had gained a second and fifth, and Richard Allen of Carsington, who had identical points after a third and fourth. Many of the class favourites struggled, ending the first day with at least one poor result which they hoped they would later be able to discard!

The second day was slightly better, with a further three races completed with one discard in force. Tim Johnson led overnight at the end of the day having won two of the races, with a gaggle of boats in close company behind, led by Jon Heissig and Ed Reeves. In what was another quite testing day, only two boats gained top ten positions in all three races, and former leader, Michael Dencher had two awful results.

With better conditions on Day Three, Heissig found his form, and by the end of the day he had taken the lead overall after the second discard was introduced. With a win and two seconds for the day, he was two points clear of Johnson as the fleet entered the final day, and Michael Dencher, having been able to discard both of his poor races from the previous day, added a first, second and fourth to lift himself back to third overall. The third race winner of the day was Michael Barnes, who was having something of an up and down regatta, having won two races as well as a fourth, but added a selection of slightly more random results for the balance of the meeting to this point. Two final races were held on the last day, and with the advantage of a first and third (which was the best score of the day) Tim Johnson managed to overcome Heissig's advantage and take the title. A steady sixth and third places were enough to ensure Heissig finished second overall, fourteen points clear of Michael Dencher, who added a race win to a tenth on the final day.

P	Helm	Club	R1	R2	R3	R4	R5	R6	R7	R8	R9	R10	Pts
1	Tim Johnson		4	7	10	1	4	1	3	6	3	1	23
2	Jon Heissig	GY&GYC	7	20	3	2	2	9	1	2	6	3	26
3	Michael Dencher	CVLSC	2	5	35	35	1	15	2	4	1	10	40
4	Nick Miller	MSClub	5	6	7	6	7	14	15	3	10	5	49
5	Richard Allen	CSC	3	4	9	7	11	8	8	21	2	12	52
6	Ed Reeves	RLYC	12	2	2	26	10	5	13	20	5	15	64
7	Chris Aston	WSC	22	8	22	8	6	7	17	12	4	2	64
8	Tony Dencher	NSC	6	3	11	13	3	10	9	19	15	17	70
9	Michael Barnes		21	1	24	15	20	4	18	1	7	11	77
10	Mark Nicholson	HISC	18	25	18	3	23	2	5	9	8	14	77

RS Vareo

Type	Dinghy
Crew	1; Sit out
PN	1035
Length	4.25 m
Beam	1.57 m
Weight	93 kg
Sail area M	8.8 sq m
Spi type	Asymmetric
Spi area	10 sq m
Designer	Phil Morrison
	www.rs-association.com

The RS Vareo is manufactured in GRP, and is unusual in offering asymmetric spinnaker sailing on a single-handed sit-out boat. The Vareo is also multifunctional, with a roomy cockpit which provides sufficient space to sail with some of the family, or in which to teach someone the rudiments of sailing. The Vareo class host an annual Championship, and a series of open meetings throughout the UK.

RS Vareo National Championships

Netley Sailing Club   11 - 13 September 2009

The 2009 RS Vareo National Championships were held as a three day event from Netley Sailing Club, in Southampton Waters, with thirty eight boats in attendance including the previous year's Champion Chris Larr, back to defend his title. Conditions were excellent throughout the weekend, with sunshine and moderate winds, although these were very shifty on all three days.

With winds on the first day ranging between eight and eighteen knots, Andy Temple started the event well to lead at the end of the first day with a win and two second places, just one point ahead of Matt Yallop, who earned a first, second and third. Chris Larr had a sound start with a win and two fourths, leaving him in third position overall at the end of the first day, with a further seven races scheduled to decide the destination of the title. This tended to be the trend throughout the weekend with these three boats battling in most races and filling the top three slots overall with a comfortable margin before fourth overall, which was Stevie Wilson.

The title went to Matt Yallop from the well represented Middle Nene SC. In fact he won less races than second placed Temple (with three victories) and third placed Larr (who took the winner's gun on four occasions, but Yallop's final counting score included nothing lower than third places whilst Temple had a string of firsts and seconds but had to count a fourth and a sixth as well, and Larr had to include four fourth places with his four race wins.

P	Helm	Club	R1	R2	R3	R4	R5	R6	R7	R8	R9	R10	Pts
1	Matt Yallop	MNSC	1	2	3	1	6	3	2	5	2	3	17
2	Andy Temple	BSC	2	1	2	2	1	6	1	DSQ	7	4	19
3	Chris Larr	NSC	4	4	1	4	4	1	7	1	10	1	20
4	Stevie Wilson	RYA	13	9	6	3	2	4	12	9	4	2	39
5	Jonathan Nuttall	PYC	6	7	4	19	8	2	3	6	28	17	53
6	Richard Willows	NSC	8	5	17	8	3	12	8	2	15	7	53
7	Andrew Wilson	DWSC	7	14	5	5	7	9	5	11	18	6	55
8	Matthew Moore	MNSC	9	8	8	6	5	8	9	12	3	10	56
9	Anthony Payne	BSC	3	12	15	21	9	5	15	8	16	12	79
10	Nicholas Crickmore	W&OBSC	16	10	21	12	14	11	6	7	11	8	79

Rooster 8.1

Type	Dinghy
Crew	1; Sit out
PN	1051
Length	4.23 m
Beam	1.37 m
Weight	59 kg
Sail area M	8.1 sq m
Designer	Bruce Kirby, 1971
	www.rooster8point1.com

Aimed at the heavier sailor, and those wishing for a little extra power, the Rooster 8.1 features a new rig mated with the standard Laser® hull, yet delivering an amazing performance that would suit anyone over 90 kg. The rig provides a steady power delivery upwind, and its downwind performance is amazing once you are past the beam, with planing being easy in most conditions. Rudder loads are reduced too! Whilst a new class, it is provided with a great boost in that there are nearly 200,000 hulls out there which will take the rig and provide a great, up-rated boat for little additional cost. The class offers open meeting and a National Championship.

Rooster 8.1 Nationals

Weston Sailing Club   18 - 19 October 2008

A seventeen boat fleet of Rooster 8.1s turned up at Weston for the 2008 National Championships, held in very varied mid October conditions.

A six race series saw Steve Cockerill take the National title after struggling slightly (by his standards) for the first part of the weekend, but coming good with three straight victories at the end of the event. Second overall was Simon Barrington of Weir Wood. His progression went in a similar way to Steve's; having taken two races to find his form, he then rounded the weekend off with results of three seconds and a third, to lift his score above Stokes Bay's Ian Morgan, who had had one of the best starts over the first three races, trailing just Greg Carey of Royal Lymington who started the event with two victories and a third and was right in the mix in Race Four until his boom gave up the fight, and left him ashore for the rest of the weekend.

Rounding off the top four overall was Andy Gordon, from Cockerill's home club, Stokes Bay, who sailed consistently throughout the event, whilst the award for first lady went to Kerry Tucker, who once again showed the versatility of this rig, finishing sixth overall and never placing outside the top nine.

P	Helm	Club	R1	R2	R3	R4	R5	R6	Tot	Pts
1	Steve Cockerill	SBSC	2	2	9	1	1	1	16	7
2	Simon Barrington	WWSC	4	10	2	3	2	2	23	13
3	Ian Morgan	SBSC	3	1	4	2	4	18	32	14
4	Andy Gordon	SBSC	6	4	10	4	3	4	31	21
5	Neil Peters	WWSC	7	5	7	5	18	3	45	27
6	Kerry Tucker	WSC	9	7	5	6	7	18	52	34
7	Alistair Glen	LSC	10	9	3	9	5	18	54	36
8	Greg Carey	RLYC	1	3	1	18	18	18	59	41
9	Chris Fyans	WWSC	11	17	14	8	6	5	61	44
10	Jenn Botterill	SBSC	14	14	11	10	9	6	64	50

Solo

Type	Dinghy	Beam	1.55 m
Crew	1; Sit out	Weight	70 kg
PN	1155	Sail area M	8.36 sq m
Length	3.79 m	Designer	Jack Holt, 1955
			www.solosailing.org.uk

Photo courtesy of Solo Class Assoc

The Solo is an exhilarating one-design single-hander with a strong following throughout the UK, and also in Europe. The class attracts sailors of all ages and a wide range of weights, as the rig can be made to accommodate significant variations. The Solo is raced successfully at many clubs inland and on the sea, and each year a National Championships week takes place, attracting some of the best dinghy sailors in the UK.

Solo National Champs

East Lothian Yacht Club   1 - 7 August 2009

Seventy boats tentatively ventured out from East Lothian at the start of the Solo National Championships, with a Force five (gusting to seven) breeze taking some of the effect of the sunshine away! With two races scheduled for Day One, the first race was taken by reigning National Champion, Charlie Cumbley having led for much of the race. Competition behind was hard fought, with Robbie Wilson of Wormit SC finally taking second ahead of Steve Cockerill in third. For the next race Andy Davis, took an early lead but allowed Jim Hunt to slip through on the second beat; a position he then held to the finish. Davis then successfully defend his second position from Cumbley who picked his way up the fleet to third after a slightly disappointing start.

The weather settled well in time for Race Five, and a slightly choppy sea was matched to a Force two to three. First boat around the windward mark was Alister Morley with Cumbley in hot pursuit, gaining an overlap by the third mark and then sailing off to a confirmation victory. A large front drifted through the area, making conditions quite difficult for the start, and a number of recalls followed, eventually causing this race to be cancelled for the day.

In Race Three, Davis took an early lead, and proceeded to win by a huge margin. Both Cumbley and Jim Hunt were black flagged in this race, leaving Robbie Wilson to take second place, and Ian Pinnell third in a brief 'sortie' into the class. Cumbley made up for his error in the fourth race and led from start to finish despite a tight battle for second and third behind him. Redress was sought for a minor collision between the two chasing boats, and Robbie Wilson and Andrew Bonsey were both given a shared second place (with two and a half pts) ahead of Jim Hunt in the fourth.

Race Five for the Mountifield Cup was held in a Force two to three with a slightly choppy sea, and conditions that once again seemed to suit Cumbley, who passed Alister Morley at the third mark and was not seriously challenged again. The wind became more variable for Race Six as a front moved through the area, and conditions meant that even starting was a nightmare. After five recalls, everyone called it a day!

The Portlemouth Trophy (Race Seven) was held in a solid Force four to five with a short chop, and the race got away without incident. Once again Cumbley prevailed to win the race, with Andy Davis in second and Robbie Wilson in third. The next race followed along similar lines, in like-conditions, but this time Wilson held out for the win ahead of Cumbley, with Jim Hunt in third position.

As the final day dawned the overall positions were not crystal clear, but there was certainly some evidence that Charlie Cumbley had made the most of his opportunities to lay down a definite claim to take the Championship for the second year. Apart from discarding the black flag disqualification, his worst result was a third place, and everything else were either wins or seconds. Robbie Wilson was in good shape; discarding his retirement in Race One, he had a sequence of top three results whilst Andy Davis had nothing outside of the top seven as they entered the final day. In the event, Cumbley used the final two races to underline his position, gaining two second places and finishing on just eleven points. Jim Hunt had a fifth and seventh on the final day to pull him through to second overall by one point from Robbie Wilson whose first place finish in Race Ten was matched to a discard. Most surprising was Andy Davis who finished an exemplary week with two disappointing races (tenth and twenty fifth) to drop him back down to fourth overall.

P	Helm	R1	R2	R3	R4	R5	R7	R8	R9	R10	R11	Total	Nett
1	Charlie Cumbley	1	3	DSQ	1	1	1	2	1	2	2	85	11
2	Jim Hunt	4	1	DSQ	3	4	4	3	12	5	7	114	31
3	Robbie Wilson	2	DNF	2	2 R	11	3	1	10	1	42	145	32
4	Andy Davis	9	2	1	4	6	2	7	4	10	25	70	35
5	Stephen Cockerill	3	8	6	6	9	20	4	5	6	9	76	47
6	Chris Brown	7	DNF	10	7	8	9	6	2	9	4	133	52
7	Ian Pinnell	13	15	3	17	7	5	14	3	4	6	87	55
8	Lee Sydenham	5	7	7	9	5	25	15	8	7	20	108	63
9	Alister Morley	6	5	13	15	3	13	13	18	3	DSQ	160	71
10	Ian MacLean	27	10	23	14	2	42	8	9	15	1	151	82

Solution

Type	Dinghy	Beam	1.75 m
Crew	1; Sit out	Weight	57 kg
PN	1070	Sail Area M	8.5 sq m
Length	3.92 m	Designer	K Clark & A Elliott
			www.solutionclass.org

The Solution is a hiking single-hander, designed to provide exciting but manageable sailing for sailors in the 65 - 85 kg weight range. The light epoxy hull, modern high-aspect rig, semi-battened 8.5 sq m sail, and full complement of dual controls make the Solution a well-designed dinghy, catering for both aspiring and experienced helms alike. The class has a circuit of open meetings, and also hosts a National Championship each year, which has an enthusiastic following.

Solution National Championships

Gunfleet Sailing Club   15 - 16 August 2009

The third Solution National Championships were sailed from Gunfleet Sailing Club, and based at Clacton on Sea with fifteen enjoying sunshine and good winds, with a testing seaway to add excitement!

The five race series was dominated by Kevin Clark from Seafarers SC, who won three of the first four races, and placed second in the other. This left him clear of second place overall without the need to participate in the final race. Simon Clarke from the host club tailed namesake Kevin for the whole event, and winning the one race here Kevin allowed his grip to slip slightly! Counting a first and three second places, this left him five points clear of third placed Tony King, who scored third place in every race of the weekend, whilst fourth went to the final race winner, Paul Davis from Gunfleet SC. The first lady was Kathryn Hayfield from Delph SC, who finished in fifth overall.

At the prizegiving, generous support from the club and sponsors ensured that prizes were presented throughout the fleet at the end of a very enjoyable event.

Pos	Sail No	Helm	Club	R1	R2	R3	R4	R5
1	435	Kevin Clark	Seafarers	1	1	2	1	DNS
2	418	Simon Clarke	Gunfleet	2	2	1	2	2
3	429	Tony King	Blackwater	3	3	3	3	3
4	397	Paul Davis	Gunfleet	7	5	RTD	4	1
5	411	Kathryn Hayfield	Delph	8	4	5	7	5
6	438	Colin Newman	Draycote Water	4	8	6	8	7
7	427	Wendy Pickstock	Rudyard	10	7	4	6	9
8	421	Phil Manning	Delph	6	6	RTD	RTD	4

Splash

Type	Dinghy	Beam	1.3 m
Crew	1	Weight	49 kg
PN	1184	Sail area M	5.5 sq m
Length	3.55 m	Designer	Jac de Ridder, 1990
			www.splashes.org.uk

The Splash is a modern, lively single-hander, offering the excitement of fast planing performance to a wide range of crew ages, with optimum crew weight being 50 - 70 kg. This boat is the ideal next step from the Optimist, presenting the chance for international racing for 13 - 18 year-olds. The boat's strict one-design keeps the cost down and the fun up! With specially-designed Proctor-extruded spars, this is an ISAF-recognised international class. The boat is car-toppable for ease of transport.

Splash World Championships

Pwllheli Sailing Club   8 - 14 August 2009

One hundred and eleven Splash dinghies from eight countries assembled at the World Championships in Pwllheli in mid August. In this junior class, which is restricted to competitors between the ages of fourteen and eighteen years, competition for the overall trophy was quite tight, although New Zealander Declan Burn appeared to have the beating of the fleet, leading throughout much of the week, and finally finishing with a margin of seventeen points ahead of the second placed Dutchman, Hansebas Meijer. The UK was represented by a small number of competitors, joined for the week by RYA Squad sailor Bleddyn Mon, who started the week with a race win but trailed off in mid week, only to finish with an excellent second and third to lift his overall result right back into the reckoning, in third place.

By contrast, Burn reeled off a set of top eight positions throughout the week until the final day when he needed do no better than gain a twenty first and a seventeenth. In fact, he entered the final day with a thirty five point margin and had only to sail safely to win overall. The twenty first position gave him the title with a race in hand, and sailing the final heat was really just for the fun of it!

Burn was a member of the New Zealand team that competed for the Championship in 2008 in Portugal, when he finished in sixteenth position overall. As in 2008, New Zealand again won the Team Trophy for the week; and the 2010 World Championships are due to be hosted off Takapuna in Auckland next year.

P	Nat	Helm	R1	R2	R3	R4	R5	R6	R7	R8	R9	R10	R11	R12	R13	Pts
1	NZL	D Burn	3	4	3	1	1	1	2	8	2	3	7	21	17	44
2	NED	H Meijer	BFD	4	5	9	4	9	2	2	9	12	37	3	2	61
3	GBR	B Mon	1	10	2	1	2	5	17	19	15	5	26	1	3	62
4	AHO	A Vanholt	6	6	9	5	3	14	5	10	25	6	2	12	10	74
5	NZL	S Fyfe	20	16	2	2	4	1	1	4	6	17	18	25	11	82
6	NED	T Tanis	11	1	13	9	15	2	8	3	3	4	13	22	39	89
7	NZL	J Edmonds	7	23	3	2	8	4	7	3	4	25	DSQ	13	13	89
8	NED	M de By	5	2	4	4	3	28	20	14	38	9	17	4	8	90
9	NZL	J Little	2	8	1	8	2	6	18	33	13	15	11	14	14	94
10	NED	S Hart	2	11	13	25	16	2	1	1	24	1	5	31	37	107

Streaker

Type	Dinghy
Crew	1; Sit out
PN	1162
Length	3.89 m
Beam	1.37 m
Weight	48 kg
Sail area	6.5 sq m
Designer	Jack Holt, 1975
	www.streaker-class.org.uk

The Streaker exhibits kindly sailing characteristics, with its stayed, uni-rig sail plan. It is an easy boat to handle, no matter how inexperienced the helm might be, yet offers extremely lively racing performance in a very broad range of conditions. She will accept a wide range of crew weights and sizes, without seriously affecting either comfort or performance. Recently, this versatility has been further enhanced by the addition of an optional 'cut-down' mainsail to the class regulations, making the Streaker even easier to handle for both novice and/or lightweight helms, even in the most trying of conditions.

Streaker Nationals

Lancing Sailing Club   18 -19 July 2009

Thirty eight Streaker sailors arrived at Lancing SC for their National Championships, to be greeted by force five to six winds on the first morning. With discretion playing the better part of valour, only twenty four went afloat for a triangular course which was dominated by Steve Cockerill who sailed on to win from Ian Jones, Alan Gillard, Chris Catt, Tom Gillard and Nick Lovell.

Between races the fleet returned to shore and with the aid of six shore-helpers per boat, a depleted fleet made its way out for Race Two. Cockerill again made the most of his experience and left the nine boat fleet in his wake to take a second gun ahead of Alan Gillard, Ian Jones, Chris Catt and Tom Gillard.

The fleet then called it a day for Saturday, and headed off to enjoy the hospitality of the club. On their return on Sunday morning, the wind had increased and the forecast was pretty appalling; in view of this, and the six bent and broken masts from Saturday, the second day's racing was cancelled, leaving Cockerill to add another title to his collection.

P	Helm	Club	R1	R2	Pts
1	Steve Cockerill	Stokes Bay	1	1	2
2	Alan Gillard	Sheffield Viking	3	2	5
3	Ian Jones	Dovestone	2	3	5
4	Chris Catt	Downs	4	4	8
5	Tom Gillard	Sheffield Viking	5	5	10
6	Nick Lovell	Ouse Amateur	8	7	15
7	Sarah Kennedy	Stokes Bay	12	6	18
8	Jonathan Shuster	Sheffield Viking	6	DNC	44
9	Ian Bradley	Ouse Amateur	7	DNF	45
10	Steven Garrett	Bough Beech	9	DNC	47

Supernova

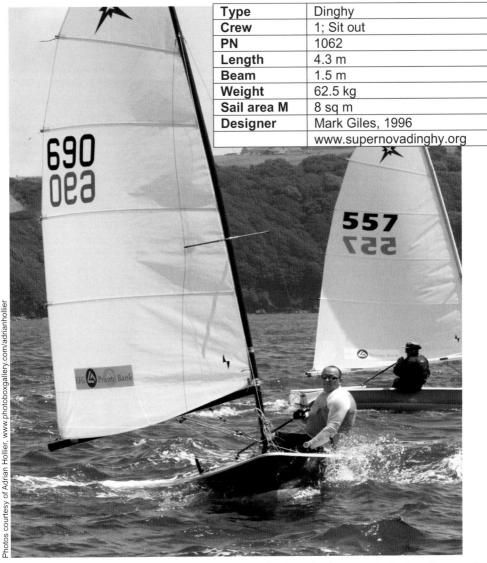

Type	Dinghy
Crew	1; Sit out
PN	1062
Length	4.3 m
Beam	1.5 m
Weight	62.5 kg
Sail area M	8 sq m
Designer	Mark Giles, 1996
	www.supernovadinghy.org

Photos courtesy of Adrian Hollier, www.photoboxgallery.com/adrianhollier

The Supernova is designed to take a stayed, foredeck-mounted, bendy mast, supporting an 8 sq m fully-battened Mylar sail. This provides an easily adjustable rig that can be de-powered, and thus is ideal for a weight range 60 - 90 kg. The hull is quite stable, giving safe and predictable sailing characteristics. With in excess of 300 boats sailing, the class offers an excellent open meeting and Championship programme. It is an easy boat to sail, and is a strict one-design, although there is some scope for freedom in fittings layout. Whilst possible to capsize, the Supernova is simple to right, and comes up virtually dry.

Supernova National Championships

Mayflower Sailing Club, Plymouth   3 - 5 July 2009

Thirty six entries arrived in Plymouth for the National Supernova Championships at the start of July. This was a welcome return to Mayflower SC after an enjoyable visit for the Nationals two years ago. Racing was held inside the breakwater on the first day but, because of the presence of some power boats racing in the flat water in the harbour, the fleet was sent beyond the breakwater for the subsequent two days. The winds ranged from light to boisterous over the course of the event, so if offered something for everyone!

The Championships were won by a comfortable margin by boat-builder Mark Hartley, who won five races during the event, whilst second position went to Rickard Pakes who had improved from fifth in 2008. Third position was earned by the reigning Champion, Mike Gibson, whilst 2008 runner up Bruce Howett could do no better than fifth this year. Hartley's performance, after an 'out-of-character' twenty-second in the first race, was very consistent, and this result betters his previous peak within the class, when he was runner- up in 2006.

Going into the final day, Hartley's position looked relatively assured, barring any debacles, but it was not to be an easy day with line squalls and, at times, very testing conditions. Third in the first race of the day, behind Bruce Howett and Jonathan Pakes, still left the door ajar, but a good win in the second race of the day pretty well sewed the title up, and his final race fourth merely secured a very good result for the class builder in a race that he had no real need to enter.

P	Helm	R1	R2	R3	R4	R5	R6	R7	R8	R9	R10	Total	Nett
1	Mark Hartley	22	1	3	5	1	1	1	3	1	4	42	15
2	Richard Pakes	1	9	4	2	2	5	4	8	4	2	41	24
3	Mike Gibson	3	7	5	1	4	3	2	9	2	8	44	27
4	Norman Halstead	4	2	2	4	RAF	2	5	7	6	5	74	30
5	Bruce Howett	2	5	8	7	22	18	9	1	3	1	76	36
6	Tony Critchley	6	3	7	15	18	7	11	5	5	3	80	47
7	Paul Earnshaw	5	11	6	3	5	11	10	12	DNS	DNS	137	63
8	Paul Undrell	7	6	11	13	8	10	3	DNS	7	16	118	65
9	Steve Hawley	12	15	1	9	6	9	16	14	10	7	99	68
10	Geoff Richards	9	14	14	14	7	4	15	4	9	10	100	71

Topper Taz

Type	Dinghy
Crew	1 or 2
PN	1500
Length	2.95 m
Beam	1.2 m
Weight	40 kg
Sail area	5.39 sq m
Spi type	None
Designer	I Howlett
	www.toppersailboats.com

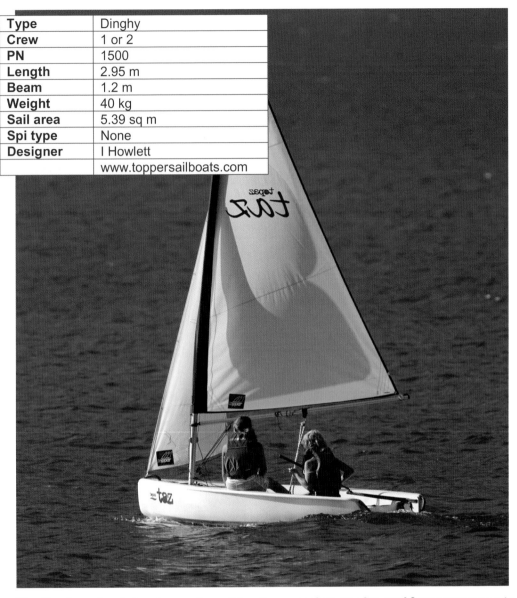

The Taz is a simple boat, easy to sail for the complete novice and for newcomers to sailing. At 40 kg she is light to handle, and can be easily transported on the roof of a car. The boat is designed with a roomy, self-draining cockpit, so you don't have to sail alone unless you choose to. The material used to produce the Taz offers a very strong moulding, yet one that requires hardly any maintenance, so it does give the opportunity to spend more time sailing, and less maintaining!

Topper

Type	Dinghy	Weight	40 kg
Crew	1 or 2	Sail area	5.39 sq m
PN	1500	Spi type	None
Length	2.95 m	Designer	I Proctor
Beam	1.2 m		www.gbrtopper.co.uk

Photo courtesy of Annie Porter

This Ian Proctor design is really the forerunner of all the new generation of roto-moulded dinghies. Originally produced in GRP, the Topper design was altered to suit the injection-moulding process, and has been a huge success ever since. Ideal as a racing, training, or pottering dinghy, or for beach sailing, this durable single-hander covers all of the bases, and continues to sell well. The class holds regular National and World Championship events, and the one-design nature of the class ensures that the racing is equal and fair.

Topper World Championships

Ebensee, Austria   19 - 25 July 2009

Ebensee is a small, typically Austrian village set on the south banks of the Traunsee amidst spectacular wooded and craggy mountains, and a fleet of ninety four Toppers converged to enjoy what everyone hoped would be a memorable Championships. However, there were a variety of the more memorable elements that would perhaps better be forgotten. The first day's sailing was lost through lack of wind, and so a very early start was scheduled for Day Two, with four qualification races to be held. However, amongst a backdrop of agitation, the result of Race Three was thrown out after video evidence from one of the the coaching boats that a large proportion of the fleet were over the line, and that this had been ignored. In addition, two of the remaining races were also suspect, and the Protest Committee and race organization had their hands full at the end of Day Two trying to get the Championships back on track without losing face. Another early morning start was called for Day Three!

With part of the qualifying series completed, there was much unrest, and no easy way forward. Two options were considered, one involving disregarding the qualifying series, but this failed to gain unanimous agreement, and so the racing proceeded, with many protests still to be heard and resolved.

After a long day, three Championship races were successfully completed, with the benefits of much improved race management and tight results in both the Gold and Silver fleets. In the Gold Fleet, Felicity Foulds led with twelve points, ahead of Finn Lynch (twenty four points) with Michael Beckett in third on thirty two points. In the Silver fleet: Helen Armstrong had the edge from Jamie Purcell and James O'Hare. Another early morning start was scheduled for the Thursday, so the socials were inevitably slightly subdued!

Four more Championship races were completed on Thursday, and Felicity Foulds' position at the front of the fleet was closed down slightly by the consistent Andrew Bridgman and Finn Lynch in the top Irish boat, but it did appear that the destination of the trophy was likely to be amongst these three youngsters. Two final races were held on the Friday and, with a first and a third, Bridgman got the best of the day, and took the title from Finn Lynch, who scored two second positions. Felicity Foulds was again on her back foot in the conditions, and sixteenth and seventh positions were enough to keep her in the top three overall, but not able to retain the promise that she had shown throughout the week.

P	Helm	Q1	Q2	Q4	F1	F2	F3	F4	F5	F6	F7	F8	F9	Pts
1	Andrew Bridgman	3	5	33	14	33	1	3	2	2	4	3	1	24
2	Finn Lynch	11	1	1	2	22	9	19	1	7	3	2	2	28
3	Felicity Foulds	1	10	2	1	1	7	5	9	19	5	16	7	38
4	Michael Beckett	2	14	39	3	8	5	4	13	8	1	21	12	56
5	Christopher Eames	16	7	63	11	12	28	2	18	3	7	5	10	73
6	Andrew Green	13	4	4	19	11	2	20	28	11	10	7	15	77
7	George Meredith	22	3	5	13	3	19	11	25	30	16	13	3	86
8	Robbie Gilmore	17	54	26	7	16	6	DNS	5	1	2	28	11	91
9	Edward Jones	32	15	8	18	7	20	7	11	16	15	12	14	105
10	Andrew McGowan	7	48	18	12	15	BFD	10	8	10	12	29	13	105
11	Alexander Alcock	35	17	20	31	24	39	1	3	9	8	10	22	114
12	Stephen Duke	4	2	14	26	23	43	15	14	5	27	15	36	118
13	Henry Wetherell	8	16	45	35	13	23	39	12	6	9	17	21	125
14	Ian Payne	15	44	29	16	9	14	12	7	22	22	40	16	133
15	Tom Bucktrout	6	11	19	30	5	4	40	26	27	19	26	19	135

Topper World Championship Results 2009

Photo courtesy of Salzkammergut-Rundblick

Stunning scenery at the Topper Worlds

Topper National Championships

Pwllheli Sailing Club   2 - 6 August 2009

As the Mirrors left Pwllheli after their World Championships, three hundred and forty six boats rolled up for the Topper Nationals in 2009, an increase of nearly fifty entries over last year. This figure included many who had dashed back from the World Championships in Austria, which had finished just the week before.

A five race qualifying system was run, at the end of which the fleet was divided up into medal fleets, and the Championship racing opened to beautiful conditions. Racing within the Gold fleet was, to some degree, a rerun of the European Championship racing, with one or two omissions! Christopher Eames, who had finished in fifth position at the Europeans, led well after the qualifying racing and, despite a varied final series, he was able to hang on to win by five points from Oliver Wright, who had been absent in Austria. Felicity Foulds again finished third overall, despite collecting an OCS in the final heat, and Finn Lynch took fourth overall after a strong fourth, fifth and first place finish to the event, to follow up his runners-up position at the Europeans.

Topper Nationals Gold Fleet

P	Helm	Q1	Q2	Q3	Q4	Q5	F1	F2	F3	F4	F5	F6	F7	Tot	Nett
1	Christopher Eames	3	5	1	1	1	3	5	2	35	12	24	41	133	33
2	Oliver Wright	8	8	8	2	6	4	4	9	2	2	2	28	83	38
3	Felicity Foulds	6	10	3	5	2	2	11	7	4	1	10	OCS	163	40
4	Finn Lynch	6	3	4	8	12	1	BFD	31	OCS	4	5	1	279	44
5	Andrew Bridgman	10	3	6	2	5	BFD	BFD	33	19	6	1	2	291	54
6	Tom Sully	3	4	1	7	17	10	8	8	34	28	3	OCS	225	61
7	Alex Benbow	4	8	11	2	1	9	BFD	16	16	13	11	9	202	68
8	Stephen Duke	10	24	12	3	11	13	10	28	14	35	7	3	170	83
9	James Wilson	7	1	2	6	1	6	23	6	17	24	62	35	210	87
10	Henry Wetherell	5	28	8	1	6	11	14	4	OCS	30	32	10	251	87

Topper Nationals Silver Fleet

P	Helm	Q1	Q2	Q3	Q4	Q5	F1	F2	F3	F4	F5	F6	F7	Tot	Pts
1	Robbie Robinson	28	28	29	44	DNF	1	7	3	2	7	10	25	287	111
2	Christopher Berry	35	27	37	DNC	38	11	25	5	6	2	1	6	296	118
3	Hannah Chambers	47	31	DNC	46	23	13	11	20	7	5	3	7	316	120

Topper Nationals Bronze Fleet

P	Helm	Q1	Q2	Q3	Q4	Q5	F1	F2	F3	F4	F5	F6	F7	Tot	Pts
1	James Cunnison	66	79	88	47	76	2	8	12	5	17	11	21	432	189
2	Tom Methven	62	61	60	64	61	3	4	7	16	5	13	35	391	204
3	Ariana Nielsen-Timms	66	59	71	58	78	6	10	17	38	7	18	11	439	224

Vortex

Type	Tunnel-hull dinghy
Crew	1; On trapeze
PN	936
Length	4.2 m
Beam	1.53 m
Weight	65 kg
Sail area M	10.5 sq m
Spi type	Asymmetric
Spi area	15 sq m
Designer	Jo Richards, 2000
	www.sailvortex.org

Photo courtesy of Mark Bloomfield

The Vortex offers some unique characteristics not found in other dinghies or multihulls, which are the result of designer Jo Richards' thoughtful approach. The boat itself is one-design, set up for single-handed sailing, and assisted by a trapeze. Recent developments have also added an asymmetric spinnaker to the boat. There is a National Championship each year, together with a series of open meetings, and a lively class association.

Vortex National Championships

Paignton Sailing Club   21 - 26 August 2009

Combining their Nationals with Torbay Week proved successful for the Vortex class as they saw an increased turnout for this years Championships, with the entire fleet now sporting the asymmetric rig for the first time.

On the first day racing started in very light breezes which built up during the course of the day to provide good, testing racing, whilst Sunday followed a similar pattern. In the absence of the previous year's National Champion, Ian Escritt, his brother Keith was left to dominate proceedings this year, scoring four race wins in a row from the outset, and seeming to ease a little at the end, when he scored two second places. Local sailor Chris Tilbrook took the runner-up position at the end of the event after a close battle with Jonathon Lister, who is a member of Escritt's club, Yorkshire Dales SC. Tilbrook had led races on several occasions only to see the position disappear, and was doubtless rueing those reversals. These two won one of the last two races, but Tilbrook's fine finishing sequence of a win, two seconds and a fourth pulled him through to make up for a slightly disappointing start to the racing.

Fourth position overall was taken by the consistent Chris Cunningham from Paignton who counted only top five results in his score-line, to finish just two points ahead of yet another Yorkshire Dales member, Ben Rayner.

Rank	Sail No	Helm	Club	R1	R2	R3	R4	R5	R6	Pts
1	1183	Keith Escritt	YDSC	1	1	1	1	2	2	6
2	1203	Chris Tilbrook	PSC	5	11	2	2	1	4	14
3	1164	Jonathan Lister	YDSC	4	3	4	5	4	1	16
4	1208	Chris Cunningham	PSC	2	5	3	6	5	3	18
5	1136	Ben Rayner	YDSC	6	2	6	3	3	6	20
6	1181	Angus Winchester	CSSC	7	4	7	4	7	5	27
7	1178	Andy Maw	BSC	8	6	8	7	9	7	36
8	1152	Jim Trice	CSC	13	12	5	10	6	8	41
9	1066	Ed Corteen	PSC	9	8	9	9	10	13	45
10	1037	Nik Hodson	BCSC	10	14	13	8	8	9	48

MERSEA MULTICRAFT

A fully comprehensive **_A-Frame_** range of kit form trolleys and trailers that are versatile yet robust, whilst still providing the very best for your boat.
Contemporary design coupled with free delivery make this quality range unrivalled!

Rapide MULTICRAFT

This budget **_T-FRAME_** range of trolleys and trailers belies its price range with fantastic features and build quality.
Modular design, ease of 'break down' for storage and free delivery make this a highly attractive range.

MERSEA *Rapide* MULTIBOAT

The same high end attributes as featured with Mersea Rapide but when two or more boats require safe and practical transportation.
Whether it is a lowering double stacker, 2 Oppy and box or a 6 boat trailer, each comes with the ease of use and the attention to detail you, the end user, expects and demands!

MERSEA *Rapide*

The premium brand of dinghy trolley and trailers are fabricated and assembled for the discerning sailor.
Unsurpassed quality, innovative design and functionality make this range the choice of boat builders and dealers worldwide.

MERSEA TRAILERS
Commercial & Leisure
www.merseatrailers.com

Tel: 0870 9099887

2 Beautiful Locations
Poole Park & Poole Harbour

- RYA Sailing , Powerboating & Windsurfing
- Children's Parties & Holiday Camps
- Boat Hire & Tuition at Poole Park
- Youth Sailing Activity Weeks
- Kayaking & Dragon Boating
- School & Group Activities
- RYA Instructor Courses
- Multi-Hull Courses
- Corporate Events

Multihulls

The Dinghy & Smallcraft Review
2009~2010

A Class Catamaran

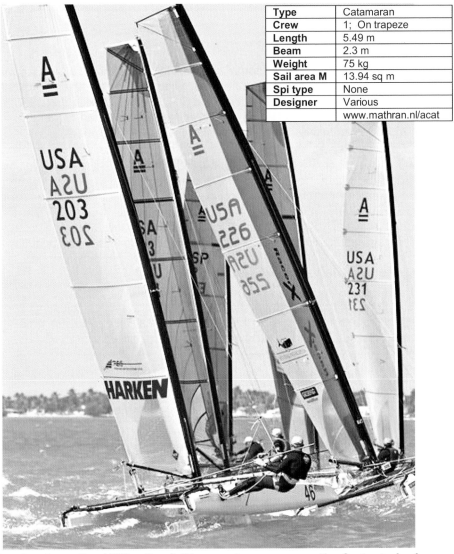

Type	Catamaran
Crew	1; On trapeze
Length	5.49 m
Beam	2.3 m
Weight	75 kg
Sail area M	13.94 sq m
Spi type	None
Designer	Various
	www.mathran.nl/acat

Originating from the 1950s, the A Class catamarans are the fastest single-handed racing boats in the world! The combination of the use of modern materials such as carbon and Kevlar in the mass production of both hulls and masts, as well as innovative sail craft design from some of the best designers in the world, the A Class catamaran has been able to push the boundaries to the point where it is considered Formula One amongst all sailing craft. Speeds exceeding 20 knots are possible, as is superb handling.

A Class World Championships

Lake Macquarie, Australia   2 - 9 January 2009

Ninety four A Class Cats joined for the 2009 World Championships at Lake Macquarie in Australia, headed by previous multi winner Glenn Ashby, in a fleet containing such sailing luminaries as Tom Slingsby (twice Laser World Champ), Andrew Landenberger (Tornado Olympic Bronze medalist), and 49er megastar Nathan Outteridge to race in what is widely described as the fasted single-handed racing boat.

In an impressive display of mastery, Ashby added what was to be his sixth World title to his collection, with a race in hand. His score of six wins, a second and a third gave him an impressive margin of eighteen points from second place Australian Steve Brewin, who similarly was not called on to finish the final heat. After that the results tightened considerably; Landemberger obviously found the transition to a one man boat fairly painless as he took third overall with the first overseas competitor, Manueal Calavia of Spain pipping Bob Baier of Germany for fourth spot ahead of another Australian 'legend', James Spithill in sixth spot.

Of the big-name visitors, Outteridge got the better of the battle in eleventh overall, with Slingsby in fourteenth place, but doubtless both really enjoyed the break from the continuous nature of Olympic sailing.

Two GBR boats made the long trek down for the event, Chris Field, who ended in twentieth position, and Nigel Lovett in forty eighth position.

P	Nat	Helm	R1	R2	R3	R4	R5	R6	R7	R8	R9	Pts
1	AUS	Glenn Ashby	3	1	1	1	1	2	1	1	DNS	8
2	AUS	Steve Brewin	1	8	5	4	3	6	2	5	DNS	26
3	AUS	Andrew Landenberger	13	7	6	3	10	21	3	2	4	35
4	ESP	Manuel Calavia	2	11	11	8	4	5	6	3	7	35
5	GER	Bob Baier	17	5	9	27	2	1	11	7	2	37
6	AUS	James Spithill	4	9	2	6	16	10	9	4	8	42
7	SUI	Luc Du Bois	8	2	7	23	9	4	8	8	5	42
8	AUS	Scott Anderson	23	6	3	2	5	9	5	17	15	45
9	AUS	Dave Brewer	6	10	4	10	6	3	32	11	9	48
10	AUS	Brad Collett	35	4	OCS	9	18	8	4	9	1	53

A Class European Championships

Yachtclub Rheindelta, Lake Constance   30 May - 7 June 09

A fleet of eighty A Class multihulls arrived at Lake Constance to compete in the 2009 European Championships, with boats from as far afield as Scandinavia and Australia. Initially lacking much wind strength, after the first two races Australian Steve Brewin (runner up in the 2009 World Championships) had the overall lead with a first and third place to count with four boats in close contention, and the result certainly not going to be a foregone conclusion.

However, conditions ensured that the event stayed close throughout and, by the end of the last day, Brewin was pipped to the title by one point by German Bob Baier, who had been fifth in the 2009 Worlds. In fact Brewin had been carrying a black flag disqualification through much of the week which he had been unable to discount until after the first race on Friday when at last they had achieved enough races to bring a discard into effect. Third place was taken by Sascha Wallmer whilst fourth went to GB's Chris Field of Mounts Bay SC, ahead of Andrew Landenberger of Australia, with World renown Mitch Booth, sailing for Netherlands in sixth spot overall.

Pos	Nat	Helm	R1	R2	R3	R4	R5	R6	R7	R8
1	GER	Bob Baier	8	2	1	1	5	1	4	14
2	AUS	Steven Brewin	3	1	2	BFD	3	3	1	15
3	SUI	Sascha Wallmer	1	3	5	6	2	7	8	24
4	GBR	Chris Field	18	15	22	3	9	6	7	58
5	AUS	Andrew Landenberger	38	7	9	BFD	6	2	3	65
6	NED	Mitch Booth	19	6	6	BFD	26	3	6	66

Photo courtesy of A Class Assoc

Action at the A Class European Championships

Dart 18

Type	Catamaran
Crew	2; 1 on trapeze
PN	798
Length	5.5 m
Beam	2.29 m
Weight	130 kg
Sail area M&J	16.08 sq m
Spi type	None
Designer	Rodney March, 1976
	www.dart18.com

The Dart 18 is a one-design international class, offering racing up to World Championship level. The hull features a built-in skeg, negating the need for a centreboard, and making the boat simpler to sail, and ideal for sailing from the beach. The fully-battened mainsail and jib make this a high-powered boat, that assures the sailor an exciting trip.

Dart 18 National Championships

Dee Sailing Club   20 - 23 August 2009

An impressive fifty seven boats, including entries from Holland, Italy and France, attended the Dart 18 Nationals at Dee SC. The initial schedule of eight races had to be reduced to six completed heats in the course of the event, with the first day marred by strong force six to eight gales. With the aid of the shelter from the Welsh hills, the first race got underway in twenty odd knots of wind with large gusts. First blood was taken by Jamie Lynch and Jamie Ferguson, with local sailor James Douglas, sailing with his thirteen year old son Alex, picking up a commendable second.

After this race, further activity was postponed for the day, and everyone was relieved to find the second day providing slightly more manageable conditions with ten knots of wind, which was stifled by a rain storm before the start of the racing, causing the fleet to return to shore and await developments. Racing finally commenced in fourteen knots of wind and the committee fitted two good races into the day. The first race was won by William Thompson and Zander Ozelton in what was something of an up and down event for them. Paul Wakelin and Ellie Draper finished second in this heat, whilst the next race of the day was won by defending Champions Dan Norman and Mel Rogers, with the local team of James and Alex Douglas gaining another second position.

Day Three was beautifully sunny, but with little or no breeze, and only time to fit in one race. Dave and Louise Roberts took the gun in this with Norman and Rogers in second position and Dave Lloyd and Janna Jones-Pearce in third. However, the final day showed more promise, and two races were held in about twenty knots of wind. Gareth Owen and Amanda Gadsby port tacked the fleet in the first, and held their advantage to the finishing gun, whilst Lloyd and Jones-Pierce added another second and the Roberts' posted a fourth to put them in the reckoning overall. However, whilst any one of five boats was still in the running as the fleet were led away by the Douglas team taking their turn to port tack the fleet, in reality they all suffered a poor race with two having gear failures, and the rest failing to get to grips with the very significant tides. Marco Manganelli and Rachel Foster won the race, ahead of Emmanuelle Dode, with Stuart Snell and Simon Farthing passing Douglas to take third before the finish, which left the Roberts team as National Champions, despite final race gear problems.

P	Helm	Crew	Club	R1	R2	R3	R4	R5	R6	Nett	Pts
1	D Roberts	L Roberts	SBSC	4	6	7	1	4	DNF	22	80
2	J Douglas	A Douglas	DSC	2	15	2	4	11	4	23	38
3	D Lloyd	J Jones-Pierce	SBSC	5	9	6	3	2	13	25	38
4	P Wakelin	E Draper	MSC	7	2	11	6	6	6	27	38
5	M Manganelli	R Foster	SBSC	5	4	17	11	9	1	30	47
6	D Norman	M Rogers	CCS	DNF	7	1	2	5	17	32	90
7	G Owen	A Gadsby	DSC	7	10	BFD	8	1	9	35	93
8	A Kelley	T Kelley	SBSC	DNF	8	4	5	8	18	43	101
9	J Lynch	J Ferguson	NSSC	1	37	9	26	7	16	59	96
10	M Exon	H Jones	RYYC	3	29	19	9	18	11	60	89

F18

Type	Catamaran	Sail area M&J	20.45 – 21.15 sq m
Crew	2; Both on trapeze	Spi type	Asymmetric
Length	5.52 m	Spi area	19 – 21 sq m
Beam	2.6 m	Designer	Various
Weight	130 kg		www.f18-international.org

Photo courtesy of Hobie Europe

*The Formula 18 Class is a development class for catamarans that allows deve
lopment of new designs within the measurement parameters that are laid down. I
order to offer a boat suitable for a wide range of weights, there is an equalizatio
system in force which, apart from anything else, provides a variation in total sa
area for the all up weight. The class offers National and World Championship
each year, and is sailed throughout the world.*

F18 World Championships

Royal Belgium Sailing Club   11 - 17 July 2009

A massive fleet of one hundred and seventy three F18 cats competed for the 2009 F18 World Championships at the Royal Belgium Sailing Club, with the racing divided into Gold and Silver fleets to provide slightly more manageable numbers. The fleet was made up from fifteen National teams, with a further nine 'Open' boats completing the fleet.

At the end of a somewhat confused series, given constantly difficult conditions, the reigning 2008 World Champion, Coen de Koning from Holland, sailing with Thijs Visser, retained his title ahead of stiff competition from the GB pairings of Rob Wilson and Marcus Lynch, and Hugh Styles and Ferdinand West. In fact, at the end of the event, both Wilson and de Koning were level on thirty seven points, with the title being split on count-back in the Dutchman's favour. During the week, racing was lost for both too much wind and, of course, for too little as well! However, despite all of the tribulations, the final race proved to be decisive. The Gold fleet started under a black flag led away by Mischa Heemskerk and Bastiaan Tentij, and Billy Besson and Arneaud Jarlegan. Besson led at the top mark but capsized, leaving Heemskerk ahead of De Koning, who then also capsized on the final run. As Heemskerk crossed the line, there was no finishing signal, leaving Mitch Booth to take the win as Heemskerk's worst fears were realized, and he had to count a black flag result.

P	Nat	Helm	Crew	R1	R2	R3	R4	R5	R6	R7	R8	R9	Pts
1	NED	C DeKoning	T Visser	1	4	12	1	2	3	2	11	13	37
2	GBR	R Wilson	M Lynch	16	3	6	1	12	2	4	6	3	37
3	GBR	H Styles	F West	2	BFD	2	13	19	6	10	4	2	58
4	AUS	G Ashby	W Howden	13	10	6	9	14	1	7	1	16	63
5	NED	G Larsen	S Dubbeldam	11	BFD	10	17	7	7	6	3	6	67
6	FRA	J Mourniac	A Guyader	5	2	3	3	27	18	3	22	14	70
7	FRA	M Vaireaux	R Petit	10	8	9	4	11	6	29	13	15	94
8	FRA	L Fequet	F Filippi	7	6	BFD	11	5	17	31	8	9	94
9	FRA	F Morvan	M Vandame	3	7	4	2	16	9	8	30	33	96
10	NED	A Macpherson	H Derckson	23	16	2	5	33	1	23	9	25	104
15	GBR	S Gummer	R Crawford	51	11	7	23	15	20	12	20	12	120

F18 National Championships

Parkstone Yacht Club   21 - 23 August 2009

Some thirty F18 cats turned up at Parkstone YC for the 2009 National Championships, to be welcomed by gusts of up to twenty six knots on the first day, with increasing waves. To get things underway, two races were held on the first day, with Adam Piggott winning the first from father Grant with Hugh Styles in third position, and Jon Worthing promoted to joint second on redress having stopped to assist a fellow sailor in trouble. In the second race, Grant Piggott had a gear failure after the start leaving Hugh Styles, sailing with Ferdinand Van West to take advantage to take a secure victory. Grant Piggott made good his problems and got back up to fifth position, one place behind son Adam.

Racing on Saturday enjoyed lighter winds with five to nine knots, and the race officer managed to fit in four good races. David White led the first race of the day from start to finish ahead of John Payne, with Hugh Styles coming in third. In the next race Styles led for much of the race, only to be passed by White downwind; a position that they then held to the finish with John Payne adding a third to his tally. By Race Three the wind had increased and Styles again found himself battling for the lead, with Toby Orpin this time. They battled throughout, with Orpin finally taking the gun, whilst Grant Piggott picked up a third place. Having vied for the lead for the first three races, Styles found his form in the fourth race and took the win, extending throughout the race ahead of Grant Piggott with Payne gaining another top-three result. Going into the last day this left Styles and Van West in first overall ahead of Grant Piggott and Andrew Sinclair, with Adam Piggott and Guy Filmore in third.

Similar conditions opened the final day, and Hugh Styles had obviously found 'the groove', leading from the first mark and pulling away all the way around the course, with Jon Worthington in second and David White in third. Styles did the same again in the second race of the day, this time taking the win from Stuart Gummer with David White again in third, and this result was enough to confirm Styles and Van West as the new National Champions with a race to spare. With these two retiring home for a beer, the final race took place with John Payne leading the fleet home ahead of Grant Piggott, with Toby Orbin rounding off his weekend with a third.

P	Helm	Crew	Club	R1	R2	R3	R4	R5	R6	R7	R8	R9	Nett	Pts
1	H Styles	F Van West	Downs SC	3	1	3	2	2	1	1	1	DNS	14	42
2	G Piggott	A Sinclair	Weston SC	2	5	5	4	4	2	6	8	2	30	38
3	S Gummer	E Forshaw	Stokes Bay SC	RTD	2	6	5	7	4	4	2	4	34	62
4	D White	J Sweet	Thorpe Bay YC	8	8	1	1	6	8	3	3	7	37	45
5	J Payne	M Hunt	Brightlingsea SC	13	RTD	2	3	3	3	13	4	1	42	70
6	J Worthington	S Greber	Eastbourne SC	2*	OCS	7	6	8	6	2	7	5	43	71

* Signifies redress

Hobie Dragoon

Type	Catamaran
Crew	2; On trapeze
Length	3.91 m
Beam	2.15 m
Weight	104 kg
Sail area M&J	11.06 sq m
Spi type	Asym
Designer	Hobie Cat
	www.hobiecat.org.uk

The Dragoon is a cat designed specifically for younger sailors, and offers a great introduction to multihull sailing. In addition to the standard boat, the Dragoon is also available in "Extreme" specification, with spinnaker included, and more power! Each year the class hosts a series of international events, including World and European Championships, and the class is supported by the might of the Hobie empire, which even offers Dragoon charter for people wishing to enter the class activities, without the need to initially commit to a new boat purchase.

Hobie Tiger

Type	Catamaran
Crew	2; Both on trapeze
Length	5.51 m
Beam	2.5 - 2.6 m
Weight	180 kg
Sail area M&J	21.15 sq m
Spi type	Asymmetric
Spi area	21 sq m
Designer	Hobie Cat Europe
	www.hobiecat.org.uk

The Hobie Tiger offers the best of the two modern performance cat worlds, Formula 18 racing, together with the ISAF-recognized Hobie Tiger international class. There are around 1,000 Hobie Tigers worldwide, and the class has an active fleet racing on four continents, with European and World Championships. With a twin trapeze, and a large gennaker, the performance of the Hobie Tiger goes without saying. Like all Hobie-produced boats, the quality and specification of the boats is excellent, and a tight set of rules ensures that racing anywhere around the world is on a level footing.

Hobie Europeans

Lake Como, Italy   1 - 8 August 2009

Hobie Europe hosted their customary joint European Championships at Como at the start of August with racing across seven different fleets, thirteen different championships being decided within the regatta and a total entry approaching three hundred boats! Of these events, some featured competitors and interest from the UK.

Hobie Dragoon

A fleet of 16 Hobie Dragoons competed for their European Championships, including five boats from the UK. After a five race series, a consistent Sebastien Samways and Daniel Channing took the overall title for GB, ahead of the Dutch pair of Teuntje van Es and Marloes Sprii. Patrick and Benedict Harrison, and Adam and Jack Murphy rounded off a successful team for the UK, finishing in fourth and fifth positions overall.

P	Helm	Crew	Nat	R1	R2	R3	R4	R5	Pts
1	Sebastien Samways	Daniel Channing	GBR	2	1	12	2	2	7
2	Teuntje van Es	Marloes Sprij	NED	8	5	3	1	1	10
3	Johan Neiras	Solune Robert	FRA	7	DNF	1	8	4	20
4	Patrick Harrison	Benedict Harrison	GBR	4	9	6	6	5	21
5	Adam Murphy	Jack Murphy	GBR	1	DNF	9	4	8	22

Hobie 16

Sixty four boats competed in the Hobie 16 Open European Championships, with just two UK based competitors. In a twelve race series, the event was dominated by the Swedish pairing of Tim Shuwalow and Cecilia Colling who, despite starting with a twenty fourth position, then proceeded to win six of the remaining races, and to open up a twenty two point lead over the runners-up in the class, Stefan Griesmeyer and Edward Capepa, with the podium being completed by the French team of Cedric Bader and Nathalie Souquet.

P	Helm	Crew	Nat	R1	R2	R3	R4	R5	R6	R7	R8	R9	R10	R11	R12	Pts
1	T Shuwalow	C Colling	SWE	24	1	3	3	1	10	1	1	1	3	1	6	21
2	S Rriesmeyer	E Canepa	ITA	20	7	1	1	2	1	7	4	4	1	BFD	15	43
3	C Bader	N Souquet	FRA	1	4	OCS	18	4	6	3	3	5	17	7	2	52
4	K Jansen	M Siebrecht	GER	6	8	4	5	7	50	18	14	13	2	2	11	72
5	T Booth	E Sturgeon	AUS	3	3	25	4	18	11	9	28	2	8	BFD	4	87

Hobie Tiger Europeans

Twenty five Tigers attended the European Championships in an event that also incorporated the Italian National Championships. Four entrants made the trip from the UK, but they could do nothing about the domination of Mischa Heemskerk and Tentij Bastiaan from Holland who won all of the thirteen races run, and consequently discarded two wins. Finishing twenty points in front of the Italians, Vittorio Bissaro and Lamberto Cesari, and thirty seven points clear of third placed Sebastien Dol and Yann Montoya of France, the results were never in doubt throughout the week. Darren Stower and Adam Beattie finished as top UK boat in seventh overall, with several second place finishes during the week, but were not quite able to maintain the consistency throughout.

P	Helm / Crew	Nat	R1	R2	R3	R4	R5	R6	R7	R8	R9	R10	R11	R12	R13	Pts
1	M Heemskerk B Tentij	NED	1	1	1	1	1	1	1	1	1	1	1	1	1	11
2	V Bissaro L Cesari	ITA	5	11	2	2	4	3	2	2	3	4	2	4	3	31
3	S Dol Y Montoya	FRA	3	5	3	5	2	11	5	5	10	2	5	3	11	48
7	D Stower A Beattie	GBR	13	14	8	6	11	2	18	10	2	11	4	11	2	80

Photo courtesy of Hobie Assoc/P.Contin

Action at the Hobie Europeans

Hurricane 5.9

Type	Catamaran	Weight	180.5 kg
Crew	2; Both on trapeze	Sail area M&J	23.4 sq m
Length	5.9 m	Spi type	None
Beam	2.43 m	Designer	Reg and Rob White
			www.hurricane59.com

The Hurricane 5.9 (and the associated 5.9 Sport and 5.9 SX) was developed to offer high-performance cat sailing at a sensible price. Based on the standard boat, the Sport and SX each offer a gennaker and other adjustments to add to the basic boat's performance. The boat is produced in foam sandwich carbon constructions, and can be raced satisfactorily by combined crew weights varying from 18 - 30 stone. The class has a racing circuit, and an annual National Championships, which attract a good turn-out.

Hurricane 5.9 SX Nationals

Stone Sailing Club   28 - 31 May 2009

A fleet of twenty Hurricane 5.9SXs arrived at Stone SC to take part in what was obviously going to be a keenly contested event with a number of previous winners being joined by boats from around the UK, including Scotland and Northern Ireland. Interest was to be further heightened by the introduction of the new square headed mainsail, with more than half of the fleet sporting these as yet untried sails.

Ten races were scheduled over four days, with races expected to run about fifty minutes for the leaders. For Day One, conditions dawned light and variable, and the first race got underway promptly, only to be abandoned as the wind fizzled out. As the wind filled in from another quarter, the race team again grabbed the opportunity to set things running, and again changes in direction and strength were prodigious. With everything up for grabs, the winner's gun went to Adrian Allen and Dave Anderson from Ballyhome YC, with Mark Thompson and Jack Tindale from the host club in second.

With no further racing possible on Day One, Day Two dawned with a need to catch up on the schedule and a light breeze with sunshine. The breeze continued to grow and provided excellent conditions, and the first race of the day was taken by Trevor Bawden and Tom Wass from the home club, whilst the defending Champions, Neil Connelly and Buster Tickner won Race Three after Ready was disqualified from first place. Similar conditions remained for the fourth race and once again, Connelly and Tickner made the most of things to finish with another victory.

As the breeze continued to grow above twenty knots for Race Five, the new mainsail began to show its worth. In the progressively harder conditions, John Ready and Alan Morgan got everything right, to win the race by the biggest margin to date, leaving Allen and Anderson in first overall, with Thompson and Tindale second and Connelly and Tickner in third.

Day Three saw more bright and breezy conditions, and the defending Champions, still sailing with the old style mainsail, showed their true form, winning the first two races of the day. Race Eight saw Ready and Morgan start well, and once again rush off into the distance, only to start struggling with a gear issue, allowing Allen through to take the win ahead of the consistent Connelly. This left Connelly two points clear at the top of the table going into the final day, with Allen the man to watch.

In the first race of the day, Connelly took the advantage to win, with Allen back in twelfth position, whilst again they played fairly safe in the final heat, but took the winning gun to finish the event an impressive eleven points clear after a great battle.

P	Helm	Crew	Club	R1	R2	R3	R4	R5	R6	R7	R8	R9	R10	Pts
1	Neil Connelly	Buster Tickner	SSC	5	DNF	1	1	4	1	1	2	1	1	12
2	Adrian Allen	Dave Anderson	BYC	1	2	4	2	7	2	4	1	12	11	23
3	Mark Thompson	Hack Tindale	SSC	2	3	2	4	3	4	10	4	2	5	24
4	Trevoir Bawden	Tom Wass	SSC	4	1	7	6	6	OCS	2	3	3	2	27
5	Richie Hanmore	Chris Hanmore	SSC	3	10	3	3	5	9	5	8	7	6	40
6	Kami Marshall	Helen Scott	SSSC	6	11	6	13	2	8	11	12	9	7	60
7	Kevin Bawden	Ben Cox	SSC	DNF	8	9	14	12	3	8	9	5	10	64
8	Nick Dorks	David Elias	SSC	DNF	7	8	DNF	9	5	9	7	11	8	64
9	Geoff Tindale	Clint Foreman	SSC	DNF	6	2	7	11	6	12	10	6	8	67
10	Paul Palmer	Robert Palmer	TBYC	DNF	5	11	11	14	7	6	11	4	DNF	6

Shadow

Type	Dinghy	Sail area M&J	12.95 sq m
Crew	1; On trapeze	Spi type	Asymmetric
Length	4.8 m	Spi area	10 sq m
Beam	2.4 m	Designer	Yves Loday & Reg White
Weight	99 kg		www.shadowsailing.org.uk

The Shadow is a high-performance single-handed catamaran with an asymmetric spinnaker. Thanks to its light weight and simple, powerful controls, it is an attainable challenge to sailors who may have never considered a single-handed asymmetric or a catamaran before. The performance on all points of sail is far beyond almost all other single-handed boats but you don't have to spend a lot of time swimming while you learn the skills.

Shearwater

Type	Catamaran	Weight	120 kg
Crew	2; 1 on trapeze	Sail area M&J	15.5 sq m
PN	839	Spi type	Symmetric
Length	5.05 m	Spi area	17.6 sq m
Beam	2.28 m	Designer	F & R Prout
			www.shearwater-asc.org.uk

The modern Shearwater catamaran has been refined and developed over a period of years to give a light-weight, strong, high-performance catamaran. Hulls are now manufactured in either glassfibre, wood or carbon fibre. The high-aspect sail plan, well-proven over many years, is complemented by a spinnaker, which has resulted in a race-winning combination in open meetings and Championships. There is now the option of the latest sail design and technology, with 'Fat Head' mainsails and Kevlar materials proving very successful. Unlike some classes, older Shearwaters still remain competitive with new boats. In fact, a five-year-old wooden boat has won the National Championships two years running. This maintains the resale value of the boat and protects your investment.

Shearwater National Championships

Stone Sailing Club   17 - 21 August 2009

This year the Shearwater Nationals were held on the Blackwater Estuary deep in the heart of Essex at Stone Sailing Club, and were run in conjunction with the annual Stone Regatta Week. This club is a favourite venue for the Shearwater fleet, and the event is held over five days. The Shearwater National title was scheduled to be fought out over eight races with six races to count.

The meeting started in very light winds for the first half of the week, but as the week pro-gressed the breezes increased and racing took place in Force fives towards the end of the event. The week finished with two races on the final day as the Thursday race was postponed, adding to the excitement at the end of the event!

The overall winners of the Championships were Ben Farnborough and Alex Flay. Despite a slow start, with a thirteenth in the first race and a seventh in the third heat, their subsequent results hovered in the top three all week, including two race wins. The ability to discard the two worst results left them with an enviable eleven points at the end of the week, ten points clear of both the second and third boats. Of these two, Alan Howland and Jenny Allen were awarded second overall on the basis of discards, with two race wins in their week's sailing, whilst Dion Allen and Sarah Connelly picked up third place overall.

This result of course means than Ben Farnborough and Alex Flay had retained the title that they won at Pevensey Bay in 2008, whilst Alan Howland and Jenny Allen and Dion Allen and Sarah Connelly had both managed to improve by one place this year at the expense of Nigel and Sarah Stuart.

P	Helm	Crew	R1	R2	R3	R4	R5	R6	R7	R8	Pts
1	Ben Farnborough	Alex Flay	13	2	7	3	1	2	2	1	11
2	Alan Howland	Jenny Allen	1	1	4	6	5	DNF	4	9	21
3	Dion Allen	Sarah Connelly	7	3	2	2	2	5	11	8	21
4	Nigel Stuart	Sarah Stuart	2	5	5	4	7	4	5	7	25
5	Derek Williams	Grace Williams	9	7	12	OCS	4	3	1	2	26
6	James Farnborough	Jenny Hart	4	9	1	5R	DNF	9	9	4	32
7	Claire Robinson	Shaun Allen	5	10	8	5	9	6	3	5	32
8	Roger Crooks	Georgia Stone	10	6	6	1	8	10	7	6	34
9	Daniel Stone	Will Ayre	8	4	3	7	3	DNF	10	DNC	35
10	Catherine Howland	Darren Tulley	3	11	14	8	6	7	12	DNF	47

Spitfire

Type	Catamaran
Crew	2; Twin trapeze
PN	714
Length	5 m
Beam	2.52 m
Weight	140 kg
Sail area M&J	20 sq m
Spi type	Asymmetric
Spi area	18 sq m
Designer	Reg White & Yves Loday, 2000
	www.spitfiresailing.org.uk

Photo courtesy of Spitfire Class Assoc

The Spitfire was designed by two Olympic gold medallists, Reg White and Yves Loday. The boat is a one design catamaran, with a crew of two, using twin trapeze, spinnaker and boards. The Spitfire provides the best of both worlds, combining dinghy like handling with the speed of a racing catamaran. It is a rapidly swelling fleet, with boats in the UK, France, Ireland and Belgium and as far afield as Dubai.

Sprint 15

Type	Catamaran	Weight	104 kg
Crew	1 or 2; Trapeze optional	Sail area M&J	12.29 sq m
PN	916 (883 Sport)	Spi type	None
Length	4.54 m	Designer	Rodney Marsh, 1978
Beam	2.13 m		www.sprint15.com

The Sprint 15 is a versatile catamaran which appeals to a variety of people. It can be sailed by one or two, and is ideal for a parent/youth combination. When sailed with the jib and trapeze, it is faster and more exciting (Sport format). Singlehanded, it is easy to sail, and easy to right after a capsize. The Sprint is a strict one-design that can be transported on the top of a car, sailed from the beach, or raced in three formats: single-handed una rig, two-up with jib, or single-handed with jib and trapeze (Sport).

Sprint 15 Sport Nationals

North Devon Yacht Club   30 May - 1 June 2009

Forty one competitors arrived at North Devon YC for the annual National Championships, in a healthy aura of sunshine and light winds, but with more breeze forecast to come through.

At the first mark, the fleet got away well with Kyle Stoneham leading Peter Ewing and Brian Phipps around the mark, and opening up a lead from the rest of the fleet. The wind promptly disappeared, and it was Phipps who made the most of the tidal conditions to win, ahead of Charles Watson and Erling Holmberg.

In very light winds, the second race set off straight after the conclusion of Heat One, and it was the experienced Phipps who again made best use of the conditions to win, from Stoneham with Annette Madison in third.

Sunday morning arrived without significantly more breeze. With all of the locals applying their knowledge and sticking to the Appledore side, it was nearly inevitable that first around the mark would be Martin Scott from the "visitor's" side! Scott sailed on to win; one of only eight finishers, ahead of Mark Aldridge and David Casale. The second Sunday race was slightly easier with the breeze having filled in a little. With a shortage of water now, a small course was set, and Martin Scott picked up another race win, ahead of Charles Watson, with Brian Phipps picking up a third.

After an enjoyable supper on Sunday evening, Monday at least dawned with a little more breeze, allowing Phipps to take the final two heats, and with it a deserved Championship title. Scott did enough in the final day to take second overall, with Stoneham in third, and the Carsington pairing of Erling Holmberg and Robert England in fifth and sixth respectively.

P	Helm	Club	R1	R2	R3	R4	R5	R6	Pts
1	Brian Phipps	RSC	1	1	42	3	1	1	4
2	Martin Scott	Gurnard	9	5	1	1	3	11	10
3	Kyle Stoneham	TBYC	4	2	7	4	9	6	16
4	Erling Holmberg	Shanklin	3	20	8	8	5	2	18
5	Robert England	Carsington	10	4	5	19	7	7	23
6	Robin Newbold	Carsington	7	8	6	9	14	3	24
7	Charles Watson	Halifax	2	12	42	2	16	12	28
8	Annette Maddison	NDYC	13	3	42	2	16	12	28
9	Steve Sawford	Rutland	13	3	42	12	2	13	30
10	Mark Aldridge	Grafham	8	18	2	11	17	10	31

Topper Topaz 14 CX

Type	Catamaran	Weight	110 kg
Crew	2 on trapeze	Sail area M&J	11.5 sq m
Length	4.25 m	Spi type	Asymmetric
Beam	2.05 m	Spi area	10 sq m
		Designer	Yves Loday and Rob White, 2007

Built to the same high principals as the Topaz 16, the 14 CX is also an unashamedly fast cat with exhilarating performance. Available in four different specifications, from basic up to "expert", the boat offers something for everyone and benefits from the kind of attention to detail that you would expect from designers with such experience.

Topper Topaz 16 CX

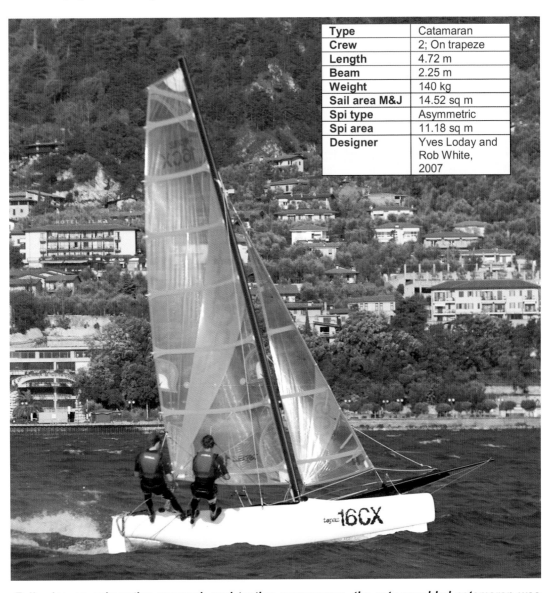

Type	Catamaran
Crew	2; On trapeze
Length	4.72 m
Beam	2.25 m
Weight	140 kg
Sail area M&J	14.52 sq m
Spi type	Asymmetric
Spi area	11.18 sq m
Designer	Yves Loday and Rob White, 2007

Following an exhaustive research and testing programme, the roto-moulded catamaran was launched in 2007 in three forms, from the S to the hi-tech CX. It provides exhilarating performance but she can easily be handled by inexperienced crew. The responsiveness resembles that of an Olympic racing machine, but is exceptionally stable and forgiving in any conditions. It can be quickly and easily rigged ashore, and even the controls for raising and lowering the sails and for coping with mainsheeting loads are set up to ensure that it can be rigged, even in a stiff breeze.

Tornado

Type	Catamaran
Crew	2; 2 on trapeze
Length	6.1 m
Beam	3 m
Weight	155 kg
Sail area M&J	21.64 sq m
Spi type	Asymmetric
Spi area	25.77 sq m
Designer	Rodney March, 1966
	www.tornadouk.com

Photo courtesy of Rolex /Dan Nerney

The Tornado was designed by Rodney March in 1966, and was promoted to Olympic status a few years later. Since then, the class has continued to develop, adding a second trapeze and a large gennaker to produce an extremely high-performance racing boat. The class offers World and European Championships, as well as a National event, and although it is not included in the list of Olympic classes for 2012, the class will continue to thrive worldwide.

Tornado National Championships

Whitstable Yacht Club   5 - 6 September 2009

Despite the disappointment about the announcement that the Tornado would not get a slot at the next Olympics, which was made only a week or so before the Nationals, a keen group of Tornado sailors competed in their National Championships at Whitstable over a two day meeting, with the second day dominated by a single long distance race following the first day's three points races. With no discard to count, every race was obviously vital. The event took place immediately after the World Championships on Lake Garda, and two or three boats, including two Australian entries, made their way overnight to Whitstable for the event.

The wind on Day One was blowing a steady fifteen to eighteen knots and first blood went to Kyle Stoneham, crewed by Ollie Herve from Thorpe Bay. Stoneham and Herve then finished second in the next race behind the Australian crew of Brett Burvill and Ryan Duffield, and the Australian team then added the third race to their results.

The wind on the second day was a bit lighter. The Championships taking in the Forts Race as their final, double scoring heat. The race started with a tight gennaker leg which caused a few capsizes towards the back of the fleet, and then they dropped the kites to two sail reach all the way out to the Forts, with another gennaker leg back to the wind farm and a beat home. Brett Burvill and Ryan Duffield built up a healthy lead, followed by Aaron Young and Robert Butterfield with Stoneham and Herve in third, and these positions remained until the finishing gun, giving the young team of Stoneham and Herve the title ahead of the Australians, Burvill and Duffield, with Peter Jary and Tim Roden in third.

P	Helm	Crew	Club	R1	R2	R3	R4	R5	Pts
1	Kyle Stoneham	Ollie Herve	TBYC	1	2	2	3	3	11
2	Brett Burvill	Ryan Duffield	NYC	16	1	1	1	1	20
3	Pete Jary	Tim Roden	WSC	4	6	4	4	4	22
4	Phil Marks	Dan Taylor	DWSC	2	5	10	5	5	27
5	Aaron Young	Robert Butterfield	DWSC	6	3	16	2	2	29
6	Mick Davidson	Grant Forward	WYC	10	8	6	7	7	38
7	Richard Lamb	David Figgis	WYC	9	7	7	9	9	41
8	Paul Mines	Stuart Smith	BSC	9	12	8	8	8	45
9	Kevin Turner	Lloyd Turner	IYC	3	16	16	6	6	47
10	Lee Harrison	Andrew Dowley	MSC	5	9	5	16	16	51

Unicorn

Type	Catamaran
Crew	1; On trapeze
PN	775
Length	5.49 m
Beam	2.29 m
Weight	94 kg
Sail Area M	13 sq m
	www.unicorn-cat.co.uk

The Unicorn is a single-handed catamaran, with the helmsman using a trapeze. It offers the best of cat performance, without any of the crew problems associated with two-man boats, yet it is easy to launch and recover. The long waterline means that the sailing characteristics are excellent, even in rough water. The boat has strict class rules, but these do permit some variation in hull shape and rig design.

Unicorn Nationals

Stone Sailing Club   3 - 7 August 2009

The 2009 Unicorn Nationals took place as part of Stone Week in early August, and the fleet enjoyed a highly mixed range of conditions with racing taking place around local marks as well as over full Olympic courses.

In very light winds, day one was raced around club marks, liberally interspersed with wind "voids". Sailing well in the difficult condition, Peter Toft took the lead early on in both heats and sailed comfortably to the win, despite being under pressure from Gary Piper and Bob Dorks in both races.

For the second day, the winds had certainly arrived and the two races were held over Olympic courses with gusts over thirty knots. This time it was reigning champion, Gary Piper's turn to excel, and return two wins for the day. Toft added a second and a fourth to his tally, whilst Dorks was second in Race Two, but had to retire, having missed the control gate in Race One.

Hot weather and light winds greeted Day Three, with Toft again showing his liking for the conditions by winning the first race. A tight battle ensued in the second race between John Wade, Toft and Piper, with Wade losing out when he found a patch of weed, allowing Toft through to yet another light airs gun. This left the final day as a somewhat tense affair! Piper needed to win both races to equal the score, whilst Toft just needed to win one to secure his first National Championship. The very light winds favoured Toft, but in the first race his form deserted a bit, with Wade taking the victory, just beating Piper at the finish, with Rogers in third and Toft down in fifth. The final race was less troublesome for Toft, however, gaining an early lead that he never lost and holding off Piper to the very end, to take the title by just three points.

P	Helm	Sail No	Club	Pts
1	Peter Toft	1074	Stone SC	7
2	Gary Piper	1098	Stone SC	10
3	John Wade	1092	Weston SC	20
4	Richard Taylor	1088	Stone SC	25
5	Iain Rogers	1084	Weston SC	26
6	Julius Mach	1091	Weston SC	28

windsport
INTERNATIONAL

- **Need a catamaran??**
  Talk with Windsport
- **Need some cat advice??**
  Talk with Windsport
- **Need replacement parts??**
  Talk with Windsport
- **Need coaching support??**
  Talk with Windsport
- **Need a hull repair??**
  Talk with Windsport

Just want to chat about cats!!
Talk to Windsport ....

Supplying you with parts, instruction and coaching
is only a small part of our job ....
Contact :- Windsport International
Tel:- 01326 376191   Fax:- 01326 376192
Email:- catparts@windsport.co.uk
Website:- www.catparts.windsport.co.uk
Home page:- www.windsport.co.uk

Keelboat Classes

Ajax 23

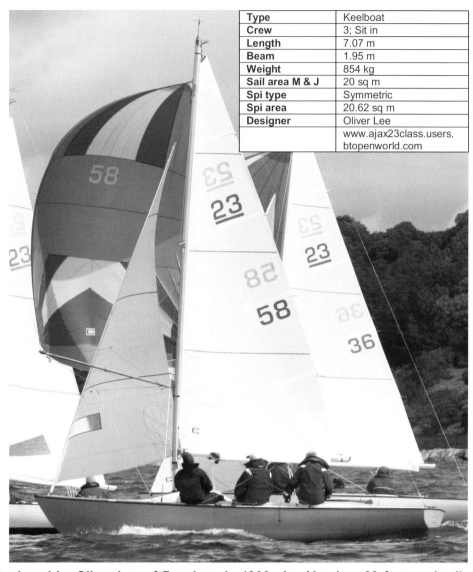

Type	Keelboat
Crew	3; Sit in
Length	7.07 m
Beam	1.95 m
Weight	854 kg
Sail area M & J	20 sq m
Spi type	Symmetric
Spi area	20.62 sq m
Designer	Oliver Lee
	www.ajax23class.users. btopenworld.com

Designed by Oliver Lee of Burnham in 1966, the Ajax is a 23 ft open keelboat. The majority of new boat growth within the class was at the hands of builders Halmatics, in 1968, with the odd boat being manufactured subsequently. As a result of the strict one design rules, the class enjoys excellent racing amongst a bunch of friendly and helpful owners, and there is a trend towards "syndicate-ownership" between 2 or 3 owners which ensures that the cost of racing is kept to a minimum, and the good turnouts are maintained.

Ajax Nationals

Royal Harwich Yacht Club   12 - 14 June 2009

Seventeen boats congregated at the Royal Harwich YC, including a large local contingent, for the 2009 National Championships for the Ajax class where they enjoyed good weather and largely light, variable breezes, with three days of racing in Dovercourt Bay.

With two races in a shifting westerly breeze on the opening Friday, place changing was the norm, but the first race was won by Chris Brown in *Mars*, after a long tussle, from David Mayne in *Guillemot* in second, with Tony James in *Sirius* third. In another slow-motion race, the second heat produced a reverse in fortunes for the leaders, with Mayne taking the winning gun, ahead of Brown in second.

A more promising Force three greeted the fleet on Saturday, and *Pegasus*, sailed by James Skellorn led around the first mark, only to be chased down by Brown, with Richard Chenery in *Avocet* taking second. Mayne made the mistake of going inshore on the first beat, and was never able to get back into contention. In the second race of the day, Brown again was amongst the leaders at the first mark and battled with Skellorn and John Williams's *Thunderer* with Brown eventually taking third spot, one ahead of *Guillemot*, which was just sufficient to ensure that *Mars* took the title with a race in hand.

In the final heat on Sunday, Chenery's *Avocet*, helmed by Cedric Thomas of St Mawes, took the advantage and held on for a good win, ahead of Brown who pulled through from a poor start. At the end of the race, *Guillemot* was left in second position overall, with *Pegasus* in third and *Avocet* fourth. Brown's victory is remarkable in that it maintains his record of winning an Ajax Championship in every decade since the boat was designed, in 1966!

P	Boat	Helm	Club	R1	R2	R3	R4	R5	Tot	Nett
1	Mars	C Brown	RHYC	1	2	1	3	2	9	6
2	Guillemot	D Mayne	RHYC	2	1	8	4	5	20	12
3	Pegasus	D Kerridge	RHYC	15	6	3	1	4	29	14
4	Avocet	D Sharps	RHYC	6	10	2	7	1	26	16
5	Thunderer	J Williams	RHYC	12	4	4	2	6	28	16
6	Artemis	M Mackley	RHYC	5	12	7	8	3	35	23
7	Goosander	P Richardson	RHYC	4	5	11	6	9	35	24
8	Teal	R Tate	RHYC	8	7	5	5	10	35	25

Dragon

Type	Keelboat
Crew	3; Sit in
PN	1447
Length	8.9 m
Beam	2.0 m
Weight	1700 kg
Sail area M&J	27.05 sq m
Spi type	Symmetric
Spi area	33.2 sq m
Designer	Johan Anker, 1927
	www.britishdragons.org

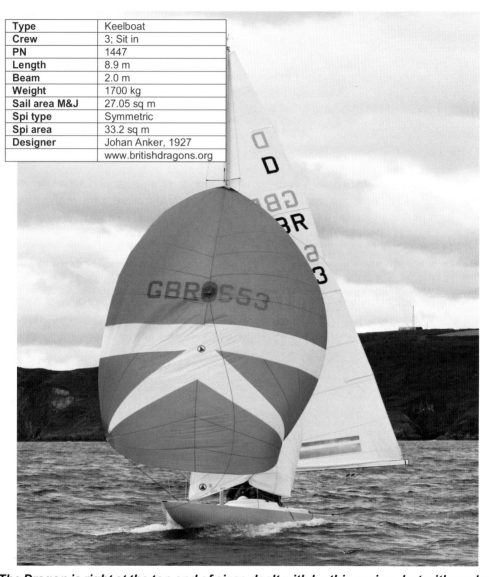

The Dragon is right at the top end of sizes dealt with by this review, but with such a lively racing scene, and being such an elegant boat, we felt that it should be included. The boat was raced as one of the Olympic classes from 1948 until 1972, but the transition back to a 'mere' international class has been painless, and in many ways popularity has increased because of it. Sailed by a crew of three, the boat has continued to be developed alongside technology, and a modern-day Dragon is as advanced as any new design, but offering the long, slender hull that is a Scandinavian design trademark.

Dragon World Championships

Medemblik, Holland   3 - 11 September 2009

An impressive fleet of sixty eight Dragons arrived at Medemblik in Holland for the Class World Championships, including reigning champion, Poul Ricard Hoj Jensen.

In a week where conditions were often trying, Hoj Jensen, sailing with Theis Palm and Lars Jensen,did not win any races, but had a string of results in the top half dozen, and this was sufficient to take him into the final day two points clear of his main rival, Ukranian Lars Hendriksen (sailing with Michael Hestbek and Sergei Pugatchev) and they sailed nearly all of the final race just three boat lengths apart, until the final beat when Hoj Jensen managed to squeeze away from him, to assure the British team of the title for the second year. The Danish team of Jorgen Schönherr, crewed by Axel Waltersdorph and Christian Videbaek, finished third overall, with five results in the top six during the week, but two in the tens which just pulled them out of contention. Dutchman Mark Neeleman was disqualified for early starting in the final heat. Otherwise his eventual seventh overall would certainly have been better, as the only person to have gained two race wins in the course of the regatta.

Of the other British boats, Gavia Wilkinson-Cox (crewed by Ron Rosenberg and John Mortimer) had an excellent week, to finish in tenth position, whilst Jamie Lea, sailing with owner Quentin Strauss and Nigel Young, had a fine finish to the week with three top five results, to improve to fifteenth from a sluggish start.

P	Helm	Crew	Nat	R1	R2	R3	R4	R5	R6	R7	R8	Pts
1	P Hoj Jensen	T Palm L Jensen	GBR	2	3	4	17	15	6	4	3	37
2	L Hendriksen	M Hestbek S Pugatchev	UKR	1	5	8	8	5	14	9	8	44
3	J Schönherr	A Waltersdorph C Videbæk	DEN	5	6	14	1	48	18	3	4	51
4	A Loginov	A Kirilyuk A Shalagin	RUS	4	16	47	9	2	5	16	2	54
5	T Müller	V Hoesch M Lipp	GER	16	1	6	45	17	12	12	6	70
6	F Berg	S Kaestel S Lassen	DEN	15	24	2	46	22	2	8	1	74
7	M Neeleman	P v Reeuwijk G vd Krogt	NED	14	15	18	5	25	1	1	BFD	79
8	U Libor	F Butzmann S Hellriegel	SUI	11	10	10	15	21	22	6	11	84
9	R Taran	R Sadchikov G Leonchuk	UKR	9	14	19	12	1	16	26	23	94
10	G Wilkinson-Cox	R Rosenberg J Mortimer	GBR	29	23	3	7	30	11	11	17	101
15	J Lea	Q Strauss N Young	GBR	21	37	21	56	32	3	2	5	121

Dragon Edinburgh Cup

Falmouth   5 - 11 July 2009

Dragon sailors from around Europe and as far afield as the USA gathered in Falmouth for the running of the Edinburgh Cup (the British Championships), which was run in early July following the South Western Championships "tune up" event, featuring racing until the Tuesday, then followed by the "main event".

Victorious in the South Western Championships, Quentin Strauss, sailing with Nigel Young, and Melges 24 World Champion, American Bill Hardesty were certainly amongst the favourites as the "main event got underway, but a very tricky first day, left the results in mid air, with Strauss in fourth, with a win and a ninth, behind the Irish leaders, Andrew Craig, Pedro Andrade and Brian Matthew with a win and a sixth, and third overall, Len Jones, Jamie Lea and Jeremy Jordan having accumulated a second and seventh.

Slightly easier conditions greeted the fleet on Day Two, and allowed the completion of two more races, with one final heat scheduled for Friday,and the very last race on Saturday. As the day closed, the new overall leaders were Rob Campbell, John Torrance and Matt Walker, whilst Strauss and his team pulled through to second by just one point, with Craig and his crew level on points with Strauss in third.

Friday's race saw a welcome win for Gavia Wilkinson-Cox, sailing with Mark Hart and Mark Daly, with second position lifting Andrew Craig's team into overall lead with Hardesty in second, following a fourth place finish.With several boats in the reckoning, the final race was inevitably a tense affair, and a first mark pile-up did much to complicate the matters. In the event, it was Hardesty, sailing with Quentin Strauss and Nigel Young, who claimed the victory ahead of overnight leader, Craig Andrew from Ireland, with a late spirited challenge from Gavia Wilkinson-Cox and crew.

P	Sail No	Helm	Crew	R1	R2	R3	R4	R5	R6	Pts
1	GBR 723	Bill Hardesty	Quentin Strauss Nigel Young	1	9	7	2	4	1	15
2	IRL 192	Andrew Craig	Pedro Andrade Brian Matthew	6	1	3	9	2	9	21
3	GBR 716	Gavia Wilkinson-Cox	Mark Hart Mark Daly	15	2	1	15	1	5	24
4	GBR 743	Rob Campbell	John Torrance Matt Walker	5	3	9	1	13	14	31
5	GBR 708	Len Jones	Jamie Lea Jeremy Jordan	2	7	8	10	5	DSQ	32
6	GBR 744	Tim Tavinor	Nicola Wilton Thomas Wilton	4	18	2	4	16	8	34
7	GBR 748	Thorkild Junker	Jochem Visser Tom Whitburn	12	8	11	5	18	3	39
8	GBR 720	Julia Bailey	Graham Bailey David Heritage	3	13	18	8	20	2	44

Etchells

Type	Keelboat	Weight	1508 kg
Crew	3 or 4; Sit out	Sail area M&J	28.5 sq m
PN	1447	Spi type	Symmetric
Length	9.3 m	Spi area	48 sq m
Beam	2.125 m		www.etchellsukfleet.co.uk

Photo courtesy of Audi/ Andrea Francolini

Designed some 30 years ago, the elegant Etchells keelboat has gained enth-
usiastic and loyal support around the world. The boat is a sleek, open racing
sloop that offers excellent performance, yet is fairly simple to sail, even in windy
conditions. The boat is a strict one-design, with an efficient class association
network, and is overseen by the ISAF, which ensures the quality and uniformity.
The boat attracts many of the world's leading sailors, particularly to the World
Championships, but racing within the UK is friendly and competitive.

Etchells World Championships

Royal Brighton Yacht Club, Melbourne   5 - 14 March 2009

The 2009 Audi Etchells World Championships were sailed from the Royal Brighton Yacht Club Melbourne and attracted eighty five entries, with twenty international entries including the best Etchells sailors in the world, joined by some of the biggest names in sailing with Olympic, America's Cup, and round the world sailors competing.

After wind delays, the first race eventually got underway and gave some indication of form. It was won by Australian Dave Clark, who was fresh from winning the pre-World event, with Chris Busch of USA in second, with the much hyped team of America's Cup helm John Bertrand, sailing with our own Ben Ainslie, and Olympian Andrew Palfrey in third, whilst GB's Stuart Childerley (the 2001 and 2002 World Champion), sailing with Robert Elliott and Sam Richmond, opened their account with a fourth.

Photo courtesy of Audi/ Andrea Francolini

Close racing during the 2009 Audi Etchells World Championships

Whilst this seemed a good indicator to form for the regatta, the second race turned everything on its head. This was won by Noel Brennan, Steve Jarvin and William McCarthy, ahead of fellow Australians, David Rose, Craig Ginnivan and Andrew Turton. John Bertrand, and his crew could manage no better than eleventh position, but this still left them in the overall lead, as first race winner Clarke was buried in forty eighth place, and Childerley could do no better than fifty ninth in the second race!

With ten knot breezes, the second day saw Bertrand, Ainslie and Palfrey lead throughout to reinforce their claims for the title, pulling away slowly to the end of the race. Second place went to Chris Busch, Chad Hough, Chuck Sinks and David Hughes from the USA, with Stuart Childerley, Robert Elliott, and Sam Richmond (UK) in third, and Jud Smith, Mark Johnson and Nik Burfoot (AUS) getting into the action in fourth position after their poor first day.

The 'Dream Team' of Bertrand, Ainslie and Palfrey, third overall

Race Four, in a steady ten knot breeze, saw an upset as Bertrand was disqualified for being over the start after the black flag rule was instigated. This left the way clear for two British boats to head the field, with the race being won by Rob Goddard, Anthony Thackray and Guy McGregor, ahead of Laurence Mead, sailing with Phil Lawrence and Andrew Yates, these boats having rounded the first mark in that order, and held station for the rest of the race. Race Five was won by Judd Smith who rounded the first mark in fifth position and sailed through to beat Australia's Brendan Garner, sailing with Michael Schilt and Tim Clark. Two top ten results during the day for Jason Muir left his team (of Matthew Chew, Paul Wyatt and Bucky Smith) at the top of the overnight leader-board, ahead of Jud Smith, with Gardner's team third overall. Bertrand, counting his eighty six points for the black flag, was down in the mid teens overall, but with the discard due to come into effect after the next race; his position was still strong, although he could not afford any more hiccups!

Day Four was a little breezier (starting in around sixteen knots with the strength building) and it bought new faces to the front of the fleet in the form of Australian Graeme Taylor, sailing with Ben Morrison-Jack and Grant Wharington. They led for much of the race, only being overtaken by Bertrand at the end of the penultimate leg, but in a nail-biting finish they edged back past to take the winning gun by half a boat length. Second place, with the discard now in operation, lifted Bertrand, Ainslie and Palfrey to the top of the overall leader board once more, whilst a third place for Stuart Childerley and his team took him up to third on the overall table, behind Jason Muir who added a fourth place to his excellent string of results. Laurence Mead lay in fourth overall after this sixth race, ensuring that two British boats entered the final throes of the event in contention for the podium.

Photo courtesy of Audi/ Andrea Francolini

And to the victor, the spoils! Champions Jason Muir, Matthew Chew, Paul Wyatt and Bucky Smith view the benefits of first class event sponsors!

With two days, and three races left to go, Bertrand started in pole position, but with his discard already used up, the results were still wide open, and the two races held on the penultimate day proved decisive. Racing was delayed through lack of wind initially, and it was always going to be a difficult day. All of the overall front-runners, found it testing; Bertrand could do no better than record a twelfth and a thirty second for the day - in essence finishing his chances of overall victory. The consistent Jason Muir managed to gain a ninth and eighth position which, as the fleet returned to port, proved to be sufficient for Muir to have taken the World Championship with a day in hand, much to his own amazement! Although they had won the 2008 Australian Nationals, the crew were not initially one of the event's pre-favourites, but they maintained their place in the top ten throughout the week when others were ranging up and down the results. The two race winners on the day were Graeme Taylor and the UK's Rob Goddard, both boats taking their second victories of the week. Taylor took his victory, having led from start to finish, whilst Goddard picked his way through to win after rounding the first mark in third position after a good first beat.

With just one race to go, Australian Damien King, with Simon Cunnington, James Ware and Andrew Butler was lying second, two points clear of Bertrand and his team, whilst American Chris Busch had risen to fourth overall ahead of Judd Smith and his team. Top Brit Stuart Childerley was back in seventh overall after results of twentieth and thirty fifth for the day.

The final day dawned with black skies and thirty knot breezes. Racing was postponed initially, but with no sign of improvement, the wait was abandoned, and the Championships came to a close, leaving positions as they had finished the previous day. Despite unusual wind conditions for the area, the fleet were united in their praise for the Race Committee and organization, and for the overall winners led by Jason Muir.

P	Crew	Nat	R1	R2	R3	R4	R5	R6	R7	R8	Tot
1	J Muir M Chew / P Wyatt/ B Smith	AUS	10	5	5	7	5	4	9	8	53
2	D King A Butler / S Cunningham / J Ware	AUS	15	3	23	38	3	8	7	4	101
3	J Bertrand A Palfrey / B Ainslie	AUS	3	11	1	BFD	4	2	12	32	151
4	C Busch C Hough / D Hughes	USA	2	60	2	6	32	7	6	18	133
5	J Smith M Johnson / N Burfoot	AUS	18	13	4	13	1	16	35	14	114
6	N Drennan S Jarvin / W McCarthy	AUS	21	1	20	5	24	23	11	9	114
7	S Childerley R Elliott / S Richmond	GBR	4	59	3	11	15	3	20	35	150
8	M Bulka S Young / J Ryssenbeek	AUS	14	29	19	24	7	13	24	6	136
9	L Mead A Yates / P Lawrence	GBR	7	53	9	2	12	14	52	12	161
10	I Johnson I Walker / T Ede	AUS	20	10	33	8	10	35	25	2	143
41	D Franks M Watson / G Sunderland	GBR	72	12	44	28	61	29	43	56	345
42	R Goddard A Thackray / G McGregor	GBR	48	72	12	1	64	77	1	80	355
61	G Gibbons W Mihns / D Moy / C O'Dell	GBR	38	62	77	22	42	72	47	61	421
77	A Cooper S Skeggs / D Richard	GBR	41	70	69	70	76	86	45	62	519
85	M Till J Coates / R MacIntosh	GBR	82	79	82	84	68	74	76	76	621

Overall results 2009 Audi Etchells World Championship

Etchells Europeans

Royal Mersea Yacht Club   23 - 25 May 2009

A fleet of twenty one boats from Ireland, Holland, Italy, and the UK took part in the Etchells European Championship organised and run by the Royal Mersey Yacht Club and the Holyhead Sailing over the late May bank holiday weekend.

The racing started in nineteen knots of wind, and stayed fairly brisk for the entire three races of Day One, which ended with the Irish contingent in control, with Jay Burke, David Cagney and Declan Macmanus scoring a first, second and fourth to leave them, ahead of David Burrows, Tom Hughes and Peter Coad who had two wins and an eighth position. Reigning European Champions, Ante Razmilovic, Chris Larson and Stuart Flinn had to return to harbour with gear breakage which left them without any counting results at the end of the day.

The second and third days dawned with bright sunshine and lighter winds. With his tiller repaired, Razmilovic and his team had the best of he second half of the meeting, winning two races and getting fifth in the other but, after the debacle of Day One, this left them back in twelfth overall. Overnight leaders Jay Burke and his team were over the line in one race, but the second and fourth positions that they earned were enough to hand them the title by five points ahead of David Burrows and crew, whilst third place went to Stephen Quinn, Peter Kingston and Stephen O'Flaherty, giving the Irish a clean sweep in this well contested event.

Pos	Nat	Helm	Crew 1	Crew 2	R1	R2	R3	R4	R5	R6	Pts
1	IRL	J Burke	D Cagney	D Macmanus	4	1	2	2	OCS	4	13
2	IRL	D Burrows	T Hughes	P Coad	1	8	1	5	9	3	18
3	IRL	S Quinn	P Kingston	S O'Flaherty	5	2	8	6	3	6	22
4	IRL	A Lacy	P Durham	R McGovern	8	11	9	3	2	5	27
5	GBC	S Carter	R Glen	T Owen	9	7	3	BFD	4	7	30
6	GBR	R Goddard	T Thackery	D Bedford	7	3	5	10	6	9	30
7	GBR	R Elliott	M Cartwright	S Richmond	10	6	4	4	8	11	32
8	GBR	T Alexander	P Kingston	C Windsor	6	4	6	7	10	OCS	33
9	GBR	G Gibbons	N Gibbons	H Draper/D Moy	11	5	7	8	7	8	35
10	IRL	D O'Grady	P Reilly	O Meade	2	9	DNS	BFD	1	2	36

Flying Fifteen

Type	Keelboat
Crew	2; Sit out
PN	1025
Length	6.1 m
Beam	1.54 m
Weight	329 kg
Sail area M&J	18.58 sq m
Spi type	Symmetric
Spi area	19.4 sq m
Designer	Uffa Fox, 1947
	www.flying15.org

The Flying Fifteen was designed by Uffa Fox in 1947 but, whilst the design has changed little over the years, there has been considerable development in the rig and in the materials that are used in the boat. The class meet for regular World Championships, and fleets continue to develop in additional areas. The boat is exciting yet manageable to sail, and offers the thrill of dinghy sailing, with the assurance of a small keelboat.

Flying Fifteen World Championships

Royal Yacht Club of Victoria, Melbourne   9 - 15 January 2009

One hundred and six Flying Fifteens opened 2009 by competing at the World Championships, held in Melbourne with an impressive nineteen boats making the trip from the UK, and a further five from Ireland.

Following the pre-World event, which was held in the form of the forty seventh Australian National Championships, New Zealand's Aaron Goodmanson and Alister Rowlands had laid down their marker by taking the title in the last race, ahead of Barry Parkin and Tim Hall, from the UK, with the Australian team of Grant Alderson and Dean Mcaullay in third, ahead of defending World title holders Steve Goacher and Phil Evans.

Following a respite between events, the World Championships started on ninth January. First day conditions started at eight knots but grew to an exhilarating twenty five knots by the end with somewhat lighter conditions on Day Two. At this stage, with three races completed, the battle for the title was already set, with Barry Parkin and Tim Hall leading overall ahead of Australians Grant Alderson and Dean Mcaullay, whilst former World Champion, Steve Goacher held third spot.

After Day Three, held in a force three, Goacher and Evans had managed to clamber to the top of the tables on equal points with Parkin, but the light winds of Day Four, together with extremely shifty conditions, reshuffled the pack yet again, with Alderson and Mcaullay taking the race win (in conditions not thought to be their favourite), lifting them to the top of the table, level with the consistent Parkin and Hall. Goacher dropped to third overall, but with just one race to go it looked as though the title was really between the two front-runners.

The final race excitement was drawn out to the full, with the scheduled race being delayed overnight, and, in the absence of any huge calamities, the winner of the race between Barry Parkin and Tim Hall and Grant Alderson with Dean Mcaullay would finish as the 2009 World Champions. In the event, the Australians took third position in the final heat, battling back from a poor start, just one place ahead of the British team, to add the World title to the Australian National title (as the first home boat in the pre-World Nationals). Steve Goacher and Phil Evans finished in third position overall whilst New Zealanders Aaron Goodmanson and Alister Rowlands finished in fourth, following their win in the previous week's event.

World Champions Grant Alderson and Dean Mcaullay

Barry Parkin and Tim Hall, runners up this time

The Dinghy & Smallcraft Review
2009~2010

295

Copyright Bernie Kaaks 2009 FFI Worlds RYC, Melbourne, Australia

World Champions 2009 Grant Alderson and Dean Mcaullay

P	Nat	Helm	Crew	R1	R2	R3	R4	R5	R6	R7	Tot
1	AUS	G Alderson	D Mcaullay	2	2	12	12	1	1	3	21
2	GBR	B Parkin	T Hall	6	1	5	3	4	5	4	22
3	GBR	S Goacher	P Evans	1	3	13	6	3	16	2	28
4	NZL	A Goodmanson	A Rowlands	5	6	11	7	6	8	1	33
5	GBR	D McKee	C Hewkin	9	18	8	8	5	11	6	47
6	GBR	M Hart	R Rigg	3	36	81	1	2	2	5	49
7	AUS	D Tucker	M Summers	15	5	1	5	11	33	13	50
8	NZL	M Gilbert	J Burgen	11	17	3	4	16	4	18	55
9	GBR	A Bax	B Masterman	8	4	40	2	9	23	10	56
10	GBR	C Apthorp	A Green	4	7	81	34	14	3	7	69
14	GBR	V Falat	B Falat	23	20	2	19	22	12	50	98
20	GBR	A Tattersall	T Smart	20	42	42	20	13	15	20	130
21	GBR	I Cleaver	G Wells	36	21	19	43	29	13	19	137
23	GBR	J Lavery	G Donceavy	38	11	9	24	81	61	9	152
24	IRL	A Martin	R Martin	22	31	15	47	27	30	33	158
34	GBR	G Bayliss	M Grady	13	35	29	54	42	39	21	179
35	GBR	I Linder	K Sweetman	19	38	51	32	32	20	55	192
38	GBR	S Douthawaite	P Averley	37	8	20	51	40	65	43	199
41	GBR	G Browning	S Weatherill	44	13	81	46	38	29	40	210
42	IRL	K Dumpleton	S Murray	32	32	32	81	55	28	38	217
43	GBR	H Green	J Bullen	26	33	81	33	20	64	45	221
47	GBR	C Harris	T Harris	51	43	25	45	67	42	26	232
48	GBR	A Goddard	M Hartland	46	24	81	9	81	49	35	244
55	IRL	T Murphy	N Kafer	39	62	59	57	39	53	42	289
61	GBR	P Hogg	P Rees	34	61	54	64	51	54	60	314
62	GBR	P Lawson	O Lawson	62	41	81	56	49	67	53	328
63	GBR	A King	T Bellis	57	59	60	35	60	69	64	335

Flying 15 Nationals

South Caernarvonshire Yacht Club   18 - 21 July 2009

An entry of fifty boats took part in the 2009 Flying Fifteen Nationals, held over a four day period. With a number of past Champions from the 15s in attendance, as well as some renowned guest helms from other classes, the racing was of the usual high standard, starting in a slightly murky Force four. After a close battle, sail-maker and past World Champion, Steve Goacher came through to take the victory on the last beat, with another past World Champion, Mike Hart, sailing with Richard Rigg in second position.

With lighter, and duller conditions for Day Two, Charles Apthorpe took an early lead, only to be passed by RS 800 National Champion Ben McGrane in his first Fifteen Championships. He held off the attention of Alan Bax, David McKee and Mike Hart. After a laborious wait for conditions to improve once again, a third race was started in a good force three. An early lead was taken by Justin Waples, who held it throughout to win the race, with David McKee and Chris Hewkin second. This, together with their previous consistency, left McKee in the overnight lead going to Day Three, which opened as a lovely sunny day with a fairly steady Force five breeze from the south west. The forecast for the following day, however, was for a strong easterly wind which would produce sizeable waves on the beach, making launching impossible. The Race Officer decided, therefore, to run three races on the third day because of the risk of losing the last day.

Race Four was led throughout by Steve Goacher, sailing with Phil Evans, who were never seriously challenged. Second place went to Henry Craven-Smith and Matt Alvarado with overall contenders McKee in fifth and Hart in seventh. For the next race Hart took an early lead to win the race whilst Alan Bax finished in second place, with Goacher third. Thus, going into the final race, the event was still wide open. The final race win was taken by Charles Apthorpe whilst Andy Davis and Andy Farmer took second, and the previous year's Champions, Greg Wells and Mark Darling in third. In a difficult race, the Championship front runners were spread around the fleet, with McKee in ninth, Goacher seventh, Hart sixth and Bax fourth leaving only four points separating the top five boats! Steve Goacher and Phil Evans had the same number of points as Mike Hart and Richard Rigg, but took the title by dint of the tie break.

P	Helm	Crew	Club	R1	R2	R3	R4	R5	R6	Pts
1	S Goacher	P Evans	RWYC	1	9	5	1	3	7	17
2	M Hart	R Rigg	PDYC	3	4	3	7	1	6	17
3	A Bax	B Masterman	HISC	8	2	6	4	2	4	18
4	D McKee	C Hewkin	DSC	2	3	2	5	7	9	10
5	G Wells	M Darling	HISC	7	22	4	3	4	3	21
6	B McGrane	J Stewart	HISC	9	1	22	6	5	12	33
7	J Davy	T Harper	HISC	13	6	26	10	6	5	40
8	A Davis	A Farmer	CSC	6	46	19	13	9	2	48
9	S Mettam	M Grady	HISC	4	12	11	24	11	10	48
10	B McKee	I Smyth	SLSC	18	11	12	8	8	11	50

J24

LOA	7.32 m	Spi type	Symmetric
Beam	2.71 m	Spi area	17.3 sq m
Weight	950 kg	Designer	Rod Johnstone
Sail area M&J	24.25 sq m		www.j24class.org

Photo courtesy of Fiona Brown

The J24 is a strict one-design which has attracted sailors the world over, with its combination of close, exciting performance, tight one-design rules, and well-run international and national class associations. The J24 is the world's most popular keelboat, with over 5,500 boats built, and over 50,000 people actively sailing in more than 100 fleets in 36 countries.

J24 World Championships

Annapolis Yacht Club, Maryland   30 April - 8 May 2009

The 2009 World Championship, hosted by Annapolis Yacht Club had an entry of eighty two boats from eighteen countries. The fleet included five former J24 World Champions together with five North American champions, a four-time European Champion, two South American and five US Midwinter Champions. Two boats made the trip from the UK, Nick McDonald and his crew in *Magpie*, and Chris McLaughlin's *Hedgehog*, sailed by Ian Southworth.

After the first day's racing in winds of ten to fifteen knots, Brazilian Mauricio Santa Cruz (the 2006 and 2007 World Champion) made his intent clear, counting sixth and first positions, two points ahead of 2005 World Champion, Anthony Kotoun from the US Virgin Islands with a seven, two score-line. Southworth had a win in the opening heat, but followed with a black flag (along with nineteen other boats) in the second.

The second day's two races were lost to the windless conditions, and the fleet set out on Day Three with the plan to hold three races. Again, with very fickle breezes, the racing was curtailed after just one heat, in which the breeze died at one stage but appeared to allow all the rest of the fleet to finish. With this, Tony Parker and his crew

Photo courtesy of Tim Wilkes

Some rare breeze at the J24 Worlds

from Washington moved into the lead with a sound second position, whilst Jorge Xavier Murireta moved into second overall, and Canadian Rossi Milev into third. The erst-while leaders fared less well, picking up a penalty, and dropping to fourteenth overall (as no discard was in force yet), whilst Southworth finished the day in seventh overall, despite an eighteenth position finish.

With the schedule under pressure, Day Four emerged yet again with light breezes, and only one race was completed, leaving the final day looking like a busy affair. In fact Race Four was won by Scott Weakley of Canada ahead of Chilean Raul del Castillo, and Al Constants from the USA in third. Overnight leader Parker had finished in twentieth position but picked up forty per cent in penalties, giving him an unfortunate fifty two points for the day! Second overall overnight, Murireta finished fiftieth in the up-and-down conditions as the leaders all floundered during the day.

Entering the final day of racing, the fleet had still not completed sufficient races to invoke a discard, so there was much opportunity for changes on the leader board. In the event the Race Committee managed to fit in three races, to give a final seven race series. As the event drew to a conclusion, Brazilian Mauricio Santa Cruz, the leader at the end of Day One, again had risen to the top of the leader board to take his third World Championships, six points clear of American Chris Larson in a fairly high scoring regatta. Matias Pereira of Argentina took the third spot on the podium with the best scoring on the final day (second, first and sixth). Ian Southworth had a disappointing final day, dropping him to nineteenth overall, despite having started the week so well!

P	Helm	Nat	R1	R2	R3	R4	R5	R6	R7	Pts
1	M Santa Cruz	BRA	6	1	63/20%	11	16	4	3	41
2	C Larson	USA	2	22/ZFP	43	6	3	3	11	47
3	M Pereira	ARG	8	14	17	29	2	1	6	48
4	R Milev	CAN	23	5	6	10	12	5	14	52
5	A Kotoun	USVI	7	2	80/RAF	32	11	7	2	61
6	W Welles	USA	14	7	22	26	7	25	10	85
7	P Levesque	USA	10	31	9	9	20	8	31	87
8	A Casale	ITA	21	9	8	5	44	40	18	101
9	A Parker	USA	5	22	2	52/40%	56	23	5	109
10	T Matsunaga	JAP	12	3	23	35	80/BFD	24	12	109
19	I Southworth	GBR	1	24/ZFP	18	24	50	46	29	142
73	N McDonald	GBR	72	41	80/20%	72/20%	80/20%	76	45	386

J24 UK Nationals

Royal Western Yacht Club   3 - 6 September 2009

Royal Western Yacht Club in Plymouth, hosted the J24 Nationals with an entry of twenty boats taking part in the ten race series. There were three days of close and exciting racing in varied conditions, at the end of which last year's National Champion Gavin Watson had just done enough to retain his title for another year, by just one point.

With racing in the sound on the first, second and last day conditions only permitted the fleet to venture out of the protected area on the third day but, regardless of this, the racing was still tight and fair. First to get his nose in front was Robert Turner in *Serco* who took three wins in the first four races, with Stuart Jardine in close pursuit with a first, two seconds and a third. However, the next phase of racing favoured Watson's *Reloaded* crew, and they collected three of the subsequent four race wins, to narrow the gap. By the last day, which had just a single race, Turner's *Serco* needed just a third, or a better result than *Stouche* and *Reloaded* to take the title. Jardine's *Stouche* needed a first and Watson's *Reloaded* a top three, with the others faltering. In the end *Reloaded* did what they had to, and gained a third, with *Stouche* in fifth, and *Serco* gaining one of their two discards with an eighth, leaving *Reloaded* just one point clear in first place, ahead of *Serco* and *Stouche*.

P	Boat	Helm	R1	R2	R3	R4	R5	R6	R7	R8	R9	R10	Pts
1	*Reloaded*	Gavin Watson	3	4	4	2	1	16	1	1	9	3	19
2	*Serco*	Robert Turner	1	1	3	1	3	10	3	6	2	8	20
3	*Stouche*	Stuart Jardine	2	2	1	3	5	1	9	5	10	5	24
4	*Madeline*	Duncan McCarthy	6	5	2	4	2	2	6	4	17	1	26
5	*Legal Alien*	Nick McDonald	4	8	5	7	5	4	11	11	1	4	38
6	*Writing Instruments*	Chris McLaughlin	8	3	21	21	4	5	17	2	3	2	44
7	*Joya*	Paul Toms	5	11	6	6	7	3	14	3	7	9	46
8	*St James*	David Cooper	10	9	9	9	6	8	5	14	19	10	66
9	*Ju Ju*	Rob Clark	14	12	8	16	13	12	2	18	4	7	72
10	*Jam Too*	Stig McDonald	9	15	12	18	11	9	8	7	11	17	82

www.fotoboat.com

sailing images by sailors, for sailors

for more information visit the website o
call Mike Rice on 07774 946930

The Dinghy & Smallcraft Review
2009~2010

Laser SB3

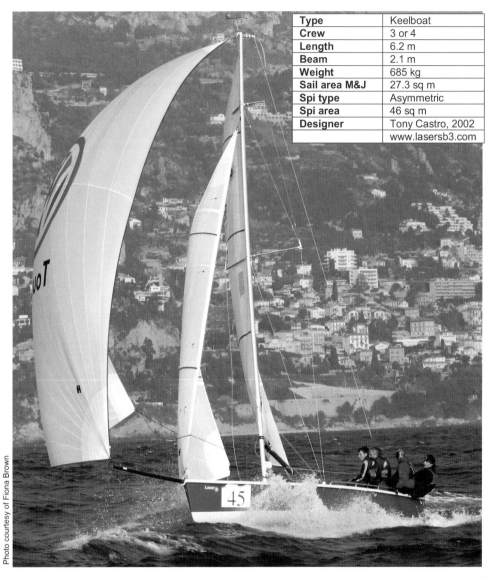

Type	Keelboat
Crew	3 or 4
Length	6.2 m
Beam	2.1 m
Weight	685 kg
Sail area M&J	27.3 sq m
Spi type	Asymmetric
Spi area	46 sq m
Designer	Tony Castro, 2002
	www.lasersb3.com

Photo courtesy of Fiona Brown

The Laser SB3 is undoubtedly one of the most successful of all the sports boats. She was designed to provide fun above all, together with competitive racing in large fleets, and the SB3 has achieved just that in the seven years since it was introduced. The Laser SB3 is now an international class, with the inaugural World Championships held in Ireland in 2008, and more than 500 boats now being sailed. The boat attracts many internationally renowned sailors, and the events are always assured of close competition.

Laser SB3 World Championships

Cascais, Portugal   31 August - 4 September 2009

Fifty six Laser SB3s arrived in Cascais, Portugal to take part in their second World Championships at the end of August, representing eight countries. With fourteen races scheduled for the event, and the forecast is for stable winds of about twenty knots: perfect!

Whilst the first day started with very light breezes, the wind strength built throughout the day, to see a good twenty five knots. The first race was won by Mike Budd and his crew on *Zimmer*, Roger Hudson followed Budd in the first race, but went one better in Race Two, taking the victory. Craig Burlton crept through the fleet to gain second place in the second race of the day. Despite poor starts Jerry Hill and crew on *Three Sad Old Blokes* sailed his way through to the lead in the final race of the day with Burlton again in second position leaving him, with crew Adam Healley and Stephen White in the overnight lead at the end of the day.

With a similar strength of wind on Day Two, Burlton got the first leg of the day badly wrong and rounded the mark in the bottom third of the fleet. Whilst they managed to gain positions throughout, they couldn't get beyond seventh at the end, whilst South African David Hudson in *City of Cape Town* took the win, ahead of Ian Sullivan and crew in *Cheeky Monkey*. Robert Gullan sailing *Sun Microsystems* build up a fine lead to take the second race of the day ahead of Burlton, and Roger Hudson, who then won the final race of the second day ahead of Mike Budd's team to leave him in second position overnight behind Burlton, with Gullan adding a fourth position to take third spot overnight.

Race winners on the third day were Roger Hudson, his father David Hudson, and Robert Gullan, but none of these were able to make a dent in Burlton's lead as he scored a consistent two second places and a fourth to leave himself at the top of the score-board overnight once again. Roger Hudson retained second position, whilst David Hudson crept up a spot to third, and Jerry Hill crept into fourth. Three more races were scheduled for the fourth day, and this would allow the second discard to come into play.

With winds in the mid-teens on Day Four, with rolling waves, conditions were set for a perfect day. South African David Hudson took his turn to get the winning gun, ahead of Mike Budd's team. However, Hudson's day went downhill from that point, with a collision in the second race pulling him down to twelfth and he was black-flagged in the final race of the day.

With the wind increasing through the day, the second race was won by Burlton and his crew, back on form after taking a penalty in the previous race. They pipped Roger Hudson and top Portuguese sailor Filipe Silva to get things back on track, whilst the final race of the day created something of a surprise, being won by John Pollard on board *Xcellent,* with Budd in second, and Burlton in third. At the end of the final day, this left Burlton in overall lead by two points from Roger Hudson, who was nineteen points ahead of the chasing pack, led by Jerry Hill and his crew.

The final day was scheduled for two races, and the first was recalled with a third of the fleet over the line. The black flag was then introduced and a clear start was made in 14 knots of breeze. Mike Budd rounded the first mark in the lead and held this to win the race ahead of John Pollard and Marshall King. The final race of the championships was started promptly in an eighteen knot wind, and the fleet were led by David Cummins in *Rumbeflurg* from David Hudson. Burlton rounded the mark in the mid twenties in desperate need to reduce the gap to the leaders! David Hudson took the race in the end, with Cummins in second and Sarah Allan in third. Burlton, with crew Adam Healley and Stephen White had made up to thirteenth, which was sufficient to ensure that the Championships were theirs. Roger Hudson,sailing with Taariq Jacobs, Ashton Sampson and Marlon Jones beat his father to second position overall, whilst David, in the company of Neil Malan, Wandisile Xayimpi and Jamie Waters took a deserved third place overall, with the valuable win in the final heat.

P	Nat	Helm	Crew	R1	R2	R3	R4	R5	R6	R7	R8	R9	R10	R11	R12	R13	R14	Pts
1	GBR	C Burlton	A Healley S White	8	2	2	7	2	5	2	2	4	8	1	3	2	13	40
2	RSA	R Hudson	T Jacobs A Sampson M Jones	2	1	55	13	3	1	1	6	3	9	2	4	6	7	45
3	RSA	D Hudson	N Malan W Xayimpi J Waters	3	6	7	1	12	17	3	9	1	1	14	55	4	1	62
4	GBR	M Budd	M Greaves S Gardner	1	5	12	55	8	2	12	10	5	16	6	2	1	4	68
5	GBR	J Hill	J Llewellyn P Kameen	9	12	1	3	4	15	9	3	2	4	4	17	12	10	73
6	GBR	R Gullan	B Ainsworth P Heyn M Stanley	7	7	6	17	1	4	13	1	12	3	17	7	9	5	75
7	POR	F Silva	J Moreira P Alemão	6	4	18	12	9	8	5	5	7	14	3	8	10	6	83
8	GBR	S Allan	CSavage M Gifford D Giles	4	9	11	20	5	3	10	20	8	10	24	18	18	3	119
9	GBR	D Cummins	I Schenkel C Cousins	14	10	9	15	20	14	6	11	9	6	55	26	7	2	123
10	GBR	GJackson	J Stromquist J Moore	55	3	35	18	7	9	7	7	33	12	10	5	11	8	130

Laser SB3 National Championships

Royal Cornwall Yacht Club, Falmouth   24 - 27 June 2009

Seventy three Laser SB3s joined forces to compete for their National title, hosted by the Royal Cornwall Yacht Club in Falmouth.

With a pleasant sixteen knot breeze for the first day's racing, the Race Officer managed to fit four races into the schedule, despite a little "line-madness" in the final heat of the day when it took four attempts to set the race off. At the end of the initial day, two boats sat on ten points, Mike Budd, and Geoff Carveth (the current World Champion), with a significant gap back to the third boat of Craig Burlton.

Day Two dawned with similar conditions and the fleet headed to sea for another full day's programme. As the fleet returned after a great day's racing, three more races had been completed, and Craig Burlton and Mike Budd had made themselves a little gap at the top of the leader-board, with Burlton taking two seconds and a fourth to win the day and climb ahead of Budd and Carveth, who started the day with a black flag.

With a forecast of no wind on Day Three, the worst was expected, but the reality was a ten knot breeze from the south that enabled three more races to take place. Overnight leader Burlton managed to extend his lead in the overall standings to eight points ahead of Mike Budd, whilst Carveth had a testing day but still sits in third overall, ahead of reigning National Champion, Jerry Hill on *Three Sad Old Blokes*!

After a hard competition, the final day saw Craig Burlton, Steve White and Adam Heeley crowned as National Champions with a race in hand, whilst Mike Budd and his crew had to be content with second overall ahead of reigning World Champion Geoff Carveth, with renowned dinghy sailor Mark Rushall (who pulled up with a good solid set of results at the end of the week) finishing in fourth place overall.

P	Helm	R1	R2	R3	R4	R5	R6	R7	R8	R9	R10	R11	R12	Tot	Nett
1	C Burlton	7	2	1	4	2	2	4	4	2	1	2	DNC	100	24
2	M Budd	1	4	2	2	9	5	2	1	26	11	1	BFD	133	38
3	G Carveth	2	1	4	3	BFD	8	3	8	9	4	7	14	132	49
4	M Rushall	4	21	8	8	3	17	18	2	3	7	3	5	99	60
5	A Oddie	10	5	5	14	4	12	6	13	13	9	5	4	100	73
6	G Jackson	3	10	13	5	10	1	5	9	38	41	12	8	155	76
7	J Hill	5	9	7	6	5	7	1	33	8	34	19	15	149	82
8	C Simonds	21	13	12	1	17	9	14	5	17	12	10	1	132	94
9	R Hudson	13	3	10	BFD	7	3	11	17	10	BFD	16	11	239	101
10	S Osgood	14	11	3	7	26	14	13	19	15	BFD	8	6	205	110

Melges 24

Type	Keelboat
Crew	4 or 5; Sit out
Length	7.56 m
Beam	2.49 m
Weight	822 kg
Sail area M&J	29.13 sq m
Spi type	Asymmetric
Spi area	54.2 sq m
Designer	Reichel & Pugh, 1992
	www.melges24.com

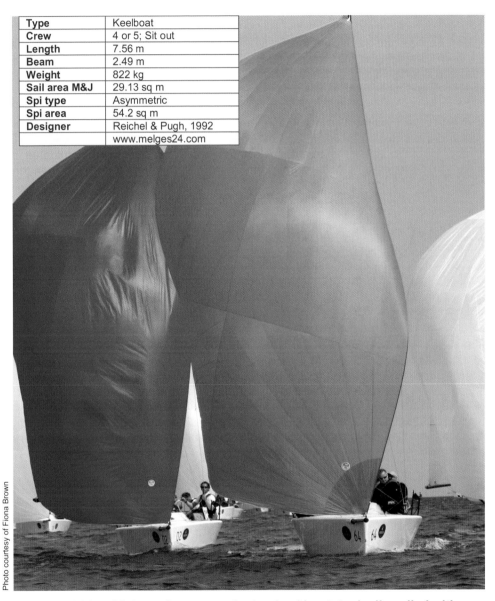

Photo courtesy of Fiona Brown

The Melges 24 is a high-performance planing keel boat, typically sailed with a crew of four. The large asymmetrical spinnaker combines with the lively hull characteristics, promoting rapid planing. The boat is very responsive with simple, comfortable ease of handling. The retractable keel enables the boat to be easily trailed and launched. Racing at Melges 24 events is close and tactically challenging, and the boat can be simply adapted to race in IRC fleets.

Melges 24 European Championships

Hyères, France   24 - 28 August 2009

A perfect day opened the racing for the Melges Europeans where a fleet of eighty six boats were competing in the waters off Hyères, in the South of France. Temperatures soared into the high thirty degrees, winds got up to eighteen knots, and the fleet got two races under their belts.

First overall after the first day was Italian Lorenzo Santini sailing *Ukauka Racing*, who scored a perfect two victories, ahead of *Alina*, sailed by Maurizio Abba, who had a third and fourth to open the event. In fact the entire top five were dominated by Italians, with Switzerland's Jean Marc Monnard in *Poizon Rouge* the first to break the domination. The second day also provided perfect weather conditions, with three races sailed in twelve to fifteen knots with a significant chop!

Maurizio Abba's *Alina* crew were impressively consistent on the second day and now top the leader board with five results in the top four, ahead of *Ukauka Racing* the previous leaders who scored a poor fourteenth in the morning, but added a third and a win to keep them in the hunt. Lanfranco Cirillo's *Fantastica*, sailed by Nico Celon also kept the pressure on, with results of second, and two fifths, leaving them level on points with *Ukauka Racing*.

Santini's crew made the most of the conditions on day three, finishing with a first and second to take a ten point lead in the event, and gaining places all the way around the course. In contrast, overnight leader *Alina* had a poor day when they had starting problems in the first race, but came back with a fifth in the subsequent race, leaving them in second overall, albeit ten points behind *Ukauka Racing*. *Fantastica* (Lanfranco Cirillo) was in third spot after getting a third in the final race of the day. However, with three races and two days remaining, and the forecast for light winds, the event was still wide open.

Lighter conditions on Day Four were expected to bring a change to the leader board, and indeed *Ukauka Racing* had their worst day with thirty first in race nine. Alina faired little better, finishing with a twelfth. Alberto Blozan in *Pilot Italia Hurricane*, won the first race of the day whilst Franco Rossini's *Blu Moon* won the second race of the day. This win was Rossini's third victory of the week, but his overall scoring had been sadly inconsistent, leaving him in seventh at this stage, but positions at the top of the table remain the same with *Ukauka Racing* still leading by seven points from *Alina*, with *Blu Moon* a further twelve points in arrears.

For the final showdown, it was evident from the start that three boats were paying tight attention to one another. *Alina* spent the pre start moments setting themselves up to dictate *Ukauka Racing's* race, but he forgot in the meantime that *Blu Moon* had a good

Action during the Melges 24 Europeans

reason to keep an eye on them. *Blu Moon* slotted onto *Alina* in a most effective way, and this allowed *Ukauka Racing* to sail their own race, and forced the troubled *Alina* to the unfavoured side of the course to lick wounds. Of course, to add to the situation, the unfavoured changed, and *Alina* found themselves in second position and ahead of the boats on the other side, including their opponents. With a cruel twist of fate, this all changed again, and as they finished, *Ukauka Racing* came in fourth position; easily enough to secure the European title to add to their World Championships. *Blu Moon* came in ninth, and then had to count the boats until Alina finally finished; in nineteenth position. This was just enough to secure runners-up position for *Alina*, with *Blu Moon* in third, while *Pilot Italia Hurricane* too the final race win; their fourth of the week, and enough to lift them to fifth spot overall.

P	Nat	Competitors	R1	R2	R3	R4	R5	R6	R7	R8	R9	R10	Nett	Pts
1	ITA	*UKAUKA RACING* L Santini L Bressani F Prina F Michetti B Branco	1	1	13	3	1	2	1	31	8	4	34	65
2	ITA	*ALINA* M Abba R De Paolil N Bianchi D Cassinari N Dal Ferro	3	4	3	2	2	ZFP	5	12	6	19	56	117
3	SUI	*BLU MOON* F Rissini N Favini S Rizzi F Valenti S Col	5	12	5	1	18	9	8	8	1	9	58	76
4	ITA	*JOE FLY* G Maspero A Felci G Zandona F Bruni A Sensini	18	15	6	4	ZFP	8	6	4	13	2	76	134
5	ITA	*PILOT ITALIA HURRICANE* A Bolzan M Paoletti S Ciampalini S Spangaro S Nicolettis	41	2	1	22	OCS	1	22	1	10	1	101	188
6	FRA	*BIG SHIP* M Paul E Garcin E Supiot M Milanese C Ponthieu	15	18	10	8	3	5	7	23	14	ZFP	103	156

Photo courtesy of Fiona Brown

Beautiful conditions at the Melges 24 European Championships

RS Elite

Type	Keelboat	Sail area M&J	23.5 sq m
Crew	3 – 4	Spi type	Symmetric
Length	7.4 m	Spi area	25 sq m
Beam	1.72 m	Designer	Phil Morrison
Weight	975 kg		www.rselite.org

Photo courtesy of Annie Porter

The RS Elite was conceived as a keelboat for those wishing to experience dinghy-like racing, but in a more forgiving craft. The boat requires minimum maintenance, and can be raced competitively by men and women of all ages, on an equal footing, and with a National Championships, and class racing at several major regattas, there is still something for those who wish to sail at different venues from time to time.

RS Elite Nationals

Royal North of Ireland Yacht Club   25 - 28 June 2009

A fleet of twenty one RS Elites competed for their National Championships. After three races on the first day, it was evident that racing would be tight, with three boats tied on five points each.

After the second day, the results became somewhat clearer, with Shaun Maclean sailing with sons Donald and Ian taking four more wins in *Elixir*, and now discarding a fourth place to give a perfect score of race wins, leaving him eight points clear of Simon Brien (a past Dragon champion), David Gomes and Qingdao Olympian Stephen Milne sailing *Sea Breezes*, with Brian Shaw in *Swallow* a further five points in arrears; these latter two being members at the host club. However, hopes of putting a stop to the dominance of Maclean and his crew were soon dashed, and he made a clean sweep of all of the remaining races, winning nine out of ten in total, and discarding a fourth; a worthy champion! Simon Brien and defending champion Jono Brown (with David and Lyn Brown) kept battling to the end, with Brien taking the second position overall, Brown third, and Brian Shaw of the home club fourth, one place ahead of Racing Sailboat's Martin Wadhams.

P	Helm	Club	R1	R2	R3	R4	R5	R6	R7	R8	R9	R10	Nett
1	Shaun Maclean	RFYC	1	4	1	1	1	1	1	1	1	1	8
2	Simon Brien	RNIYC	3	2	3	2	3	3	OCS	BFD	2.5	3	21.5
3	Jono Brown	RBYC	2	3	10	4	10	2	5	4	2.5	2	24.5
4	Brian Shaw	RNIYC	10	1	5	5	2	5	4	2	7	5	29
5	Martin Wadhams	RLYC	5	7	2	3	7	6	3	BFD	5	4	35
6	John Patterson	RNIYC	4	6	9	7	8	12	7	BFD	4	7	52
7	Mike Ennis	RNIYC	13	14	4	11	6	4	10	6	6	8	55
8	Steve Powell	RLYMYC	7	OCS	6	9	11	13	8	3	8	16	65
9	Mike Vaughan	RNIYC	8	8	16	6	4	7	6	BFD	14	15	68
10	Mike Tong	HISC	15	5	11	15	14	17	2	7	9	6	69

RS K6

Type	Keelboat
Crew	3 – 4
Length	5.8 m
Beam	1.82 m
Weight	280 kg
Sail area M&J	19.7 sq m
Spi type	Asymmetric
Spi area	26 sq m
Designer	Paul Handley
	www.rs-association.com

Photo courtesy of Annie Porter

RS K6 National Championships

Hayling Island Sailing Club   12 - 15 September 2009

A fleet of nineteen RS K6s met at Hayling Island for their National Championships, to be held over four days. The meeting was held in one of the sunnier periods of the summer, although the final day was blessed with rainy squalls, and very strong winds.

The previous year's National Champions, Dave Hitchcock and Ian Nicholson, started the event as they meant to carry on, winning both of the races on the first day in a perfect force three breeze in Hayling Bay. Ian Robson and Sandy Johnson from Aldeburgh YC, who had been runners-up last year, finished the first day in second position overall with a second and a fifth, looking as though they were unable to close the gap to Hitchcock. However, on the second day, Robson obviously had the extra Shredded Wheat at breakfast time, with three more races under their belts, Robson and Johnson ended the day with two wins and a second position to add to their tally, which lifted them closer to Hitchcock and Nicholson who had a win and two seconds for the day.

The third day was even more tense, with Robson and Johnson winning all three races against Hitchock and Nicholson with two second places and a third leaving both boats on level points overall, with Robson two points ahead taking discards into account. This left just one day to decide the destination of the title which could still go to either pairing. However, the conditions on the final day were too bad to race, and therefore the title was awarded to Aldeburgh's Ian Robson and Sandy Johnson, with David Hitchcock and Ian Nicholson suffering a very rare defeat. Robson's score of five wins and a second was exceptional, but it needed to be as, in most events, Hitchcock's score of three wins and three second places would have been easily enough to win the event.

Jonathan Calscione and Pyers Tucker from Queen Mary SC finished the event in third place overall with Bill Masterman and Ian Andrew in fourth place overall.

P	Helm	Crew	R1	R2	R3	R4	R5	R6	R7	R8	Total	Nett
1	I Robson	S Johnson	2	5	1	2	1	1	1	1	14	7
2	D Hitchcock	I Nicholson	1	1	2	1	2	3	2	2	14	9
3	J Calscione	P Tucker	5	8	5	3	4	2	8	3	38	22
4	B Masterman	I Andrew	3	4	3	11	DNC	7	3	7	58	27
5	R Richardson	C Cooper	12	3	6	8	OCS	4	4	5	62	30
6	T Crook	J Crook	6	7	DNF	DNC	6	5	6	4	74	34
7	M Woodworth	R Hayes	7	2	4	5	3	DNC	DNC	DNC	81	41
8	P Dann	D Stanislaus	4	10	7	9	8	8	12	9	67	45
9	C Hyde	M Ridgeon	11	6	9	12	9	11	5	6	69	46
10	D Darling	P Young	DNC	DNC	14	6	10	6	7	8	91	51

Boat Insurance

at the touch of a button

craftinsure.com

- Quick and easy online quotations and cover
- Internet cost savings – compare us!
- 24 hour claims help line and online tracking of claims
- Less paperwork – save time and trees!
- Monthly payments available for premiums over £100 at NO EXTRA COST!
- Thousands of satisfied customers – and recommended daily!

24 hours a day, seven days a week, for boats valued from £250 to £500,000

Quality cover at internet prices for a wide range of craft

www.craftinsure.com

Catch us on the web or telephone us on 08452 607888

The Dinghy & Smallcraft Review
2009~2010

Sandhopper

Type	Keelboat
Crew	2 or 3; Sit out
Length	5.79 m
Beam	1.87 m
Weight	700 kg
Sail area M&J	15.78 sq m
Spi type	Symmetric
Spi area	15.5 sq m
Designer	Oliver Lee
	www.sandhopper.org.uk

The Sandhopper is a popular bilge keeler that is raced largely in estuaries around the country by a crew of two or three. Inevitably, she is also popular as a day-sailing and pottering boat, with the bilge keels improving access to shallower grounds. There are two very popular centres for the boat: at Maylandsea Bay on the Blackwater and Thorpe Bay on the Thames Estuary.

Sandhopper National Championships

Thorpe Bay Yacht Club   5 - 6 September 2009

Twenty nine Sandhoppers joined in the class's National Championships, held at Thorpe Bay YC in early September. The fleet enjoyed perfect sailing with twenty knot breezes and glorious sunshine for the weekend, with the event decided over four races, with three to count.

After the first day's racing *Sandstar* (sailed by Peter Thompson and Steve Hopper) led overall, from *Squiffy* (Martin Binnendijk and Gordon Saunders) whilst *Scruffy* (Nick Binnendijk and Paul Dell) held third place despite being relative newcomers to the class.

Following a great supper on Saturday night *Sandstorm,* sailed by Chris Clarke and Nick Barnes, took first place, to underline their disappointment when they had a rig failure before racing on Saturday after working hard in preparation of the boat in an effort for Clark to reclaim the title they had held in 2007. Second place in the final race, underlined just how much of a threat this pair would have been to the title, but with a non-finish counting, it unfortunately left them outside of the prizes. Thompson and Hooper were second in the first race of the day, which was sufficient to confirm that they were National Champions with a race in hand, whilst Martin Eyre and Alan Burrell in *Apollo* finished the race in third, to lift them up the results sheet.

Winds in the final race were much shiftier, and *Apollo* read the beat best to pop out well in front, with Clark and Barnes in second position, and *Phoenix* (Tony Padbury and Bruce Spratt) gaining a third place finish. This improved final day was enough to lift Eyre and Burrell, one of the pre-event favourites, up into second overall, whilst Martin Binnendijk and Gordon Saunders added a fourth and fifth on Sunday to give them third position in the final table.

P	Helm	Crew	R1	R2	R3	R4	Pts
1	Peter Thompson	Steve Hopper	2	1	2	8	5
2	Martin Eyre	Alan Burrell	13	4	3	1	8
3	Martin Binnendijk	Gordon Saunders	3	2	5	4	9
4	Phil Crawford	Margaret Kennedy	1	10	6	6	13
5	Richard Barnes	Mark Dell	4	5	9	9	19
6	Paul Clarke	Toby Speller	7	7	7	5	19
7	Nick Binnendijk	Paul Dell	6	3	11	12	20
8	Barry Duce	David Hopper	8	6	13	7	21
9	Sue Daley	Will Daley	5	9	9	10	21
10	John Evans	Sam Husk	11	9	4	19	24

Squib

Type	Keelboat	Sail area M&J	15 sq m
Crew	2; Sit out	Spi type	Symmetric
Length	5.79 m	Spi area	13.5 sq m
Beam	1.87 m	Designer	Oliver Lee
Weight	680 kg		www.squibs.co.uk

The Squib is a nationally recognized keelboat class, sailed by a crew of two. The class boasts well supported Championships each year, and is sailed by young and old, male and female alike. There are Squib fleets based in Northern and Southern Ireland, Scotland, Wales and around the coast of England.

Squib National Championships

Weymouth Sailing Club   27 June - 3 July 2009

With the maximum permitted entry of one hundred and eight boats being filled for the Squib Nationals, and the prospect of a very open Championship in hand, there was much anticipation for the 2009 Squib Nationals which were finally won by Chris and Mark Horgan.

The first four days were subjected to light and variable south-easterlies which left some inconsistencies within the results. However, after Wednesday's racing, with four races completed, there was a tight tussle for the lead between three boats; *Crossfire*, sailed by reigning champions Dave Best and Pete Richards, with two wins and a fourth (discarding thirteenth), led from *Cariad Bach* sailed by Alan Johnson and Dave Garlick, with a first, second and fourth (discarding a forty eighth), and Chris Hogan's *Rico'shea* sailing with Mark Hogan, who had scored a first, third and fifth score-line, with the very useful discard of a fifth position. The previous year's Championships runners-up, Owen Delaney and Tony Holman sailing *Firebird*, were not finding the conditions to their liking, lying thirty fifth after the fourth race and in desperate need of a change of fortune. The Thursday did not provide the anticipated weather and, in a largely windless day, no racing was completed, although twenty five boats picked up black flags in the course of the half dozen start-attempts that were made.

These penalties would carry forward to the final day, when Race Five was rerun as the first of two scheduled heats! With excellent first and second finishes, Chris and Mark Horgan found themselves as clear winners of the Championships. In what had been difficult conditions, even their discarded score of fifth underlined an excellent show of consistency. Best and Richards in *Crossfire*, found themselves on the wrong side of the black flag rule for Race Five, and even a second in the final race could not defend their position, finally dropping them into third overall behind Johnson and Garlick in *Cariad Bach*.

P	SN	Name	Helm	R1	R2	R3	R4	R5	R6	Pts
1	136	Rico'shea	Chris Hogan	3	5	1	5	2	1	12
2	132	Cariad Bach	Alan Johnson	2	4	48	1	6	4	17
3	797	Crossfire	Dave Best	1	1	4	13	109	2	21
4	65	Banshee	Nigel Harris	5	2	6	10	109	5	28
5	800	Alchemy	Gerard Dyson	109	6	5	2	1	15	29
6	758	Ghost Rider	Mike Fenwick	6	11	2	11	4	7	30
7	128	Pani Munta	Mike Probert	7	7	3	16	3	13	33
8	73	Brimstone	Bryan Riley	8	3	7	7	109	14	39
9	105	Helmut Shoing II	Nigel Grogan	109	20	21	3	5	3	52
10	869	Tears in Heaven	Peter Marchant	9	16	14	4	109	11	54
11	789	Dream On	Brian Holland	4	21	33	9	7	18	59
12	127	Misfire	Roger Harris	16	25	10	22	8	12	68
13	51	Battalion	Dick Batt	10	9	12	17	109	39	87
14	868	By The Lee	Nic Tolhurst	20	28	11	21	109	10	90
15	828	White Magic	David Wines	51	10	15	36	18	20	99

Star

Photo courtesy of Rolex /Daniel Forster

Type	Keelboat	Sail area M&J	30.7 sq m
Crew	2; Sit out	Spi type	None
Length	6.92 m	Designer	William Gardner, 1911
Beam	1.73 m		www.starclass.org
Weight	671 kg		

The Star is a unique keelboat; sailed by two people, and designed in 1911, she still offers the very best of sailing, with competition up to Olympic standard. Many of the world's best-known racing sailors have competed in the Star, and the entry at a major Championship is like a who's who of yachting. The Star's rig is simple enough for the novice, yet the large, powerful sail plan is enough to test the most technically adept. The boat is generally manufactured in GRP these days, and the design and rules are governed extremely carefully by the class association. This does much to ensure that older boats remain competitive, and that results are down to talent, more than purchasing power.

Star World Championships

Varberg, Sweden   2 - 9 August 2009

Three British competitors joined the ninety five boat fleet to compete for the World Star Championships, not including Iain Percy and Bart Simpson (who was quite busy getting married).

With six scheduled races, in a class renowned for offering the closest of racing, it was inevitable that the Championships would be a high scoring affair, and the 2009 World Championships were to be no exception, although the eventual victors kept their indiscretions to a minimum.

George Szabo, a sailmaker from San Diego, has been helming Stars since he was sixteen years old, and this was a reward that had been coming for a long time. Sailing with Rick Peters, the pair set off with a "game plan", including their route up the beats, at the start of the week, and didn't alter it. This is particularly brave when you see they had a fifty fourth in the first race! However, playing the odds obviously worked, and their tally of first, third, twentieth, third and third for the rest of the week was pretty impressive, finishing as the only boat in the fleet with four single figure results.

Runners-up, New Zealanders Hamish Pepper and Craig Monk, fell at the final hurdle. Having scored no worse that eleventh throughout the week, anything in the top seventeen would have handed them the title, but in the event they struggled with the final conditions to finish twenty fifth for second overall, whilst Lars Schmidt Grael and Ronald Seifert of Brazil pulled themselves into third overall by virtue of their last race win; finishing on level points with Germans Alex Schlonski and Frithjof Kleen. Past Champion Freddie Loof also saw his chances disappear with a horrible final day, whilst pre-event hopefuls, Robert Scheidt and Bruno Prada, didn't really find their form and only recorded one single figure result, for eleventh overall.

P	Nat	Helm	Crew	R1	R2	R3	R4	R5	R6	Tot
1	USA	George Szabo	Rick Peters	54	1	3	20	3	3	30
2	NZL	Hamish Pepper	Craig Monk	11	9	1	11	5	25	37
3	BRA	Lars Schmidt Grael	Ronald Seifert	30	6	14	14	12	1	47
4	GER	Alexander Schlonski	Frithjof Kleen	9	17	11	5	32	5	47
5	USA	Andrew Campbell	Magnus Liljedahl	14	14	4	8	8	37	48
6	SWE	Fredrik Loof	Johan Tillander	2	5	15	23	7	54	52
7	POL	Mat.Kusznierewicz	Dominik Zycki	1	12	50	18	6	21	58
8	SUI	Flavio Marazzi	Enrico De Maria	3	3	35	1	20	35	62
9	ARG	Alejo Rigoni	Juan Pablo Percossi	16	16	38	15	16	2	65
10	GER	Johannes Polgar	Tim Kroeger	31	22	7	4	2	31	66
11	BRA	Robert Scheidt	Bruno Prada	26	2	33	13	15	11	67
12	POR	Afonso Domingos	Frederico Melo	38	7	10	10	50	4	69
13	ITA	Diego Negri	Valerio Chinca	22	11	19	22	9	9	70
14	USA	Andrew Macdonald	Brian Fatih	17	13	64	17	10	13	70
15	USA	Mark Mendelblatt	Mark Strube	8	4	2	26	35	34	74
29	GBR	John Gimson	Ed Greig	19	27	12	21	70	62	141

Star European Championships

Rolex Baltic Week, Bay of Luebeck   4 - 11 July 2009

Ninety Stars lined up for their European Championships, with many of the biggest names in the fleet in attendance, including Britain's Olympic Champions, Iain Percy and Bart Simpson, who had, by their own admissions, done their utmost to avoid gyms during the interim months!

With such an impressive line-up, including eleven out of the top twelve ranked teams they must have been delighted by their form, after a successful warm-up at Kiel in June. They hovered at the front of the overall rankings throughout the event; behind Freddie Loof and Johan Tillander of Sweden after Day One, ahead after Day Two and Three, and battling with Robert Scheidt and Bruno Prada of Brazil as the week ended. They were really mixing with the very best, and in all other cases, teams who had been working at it for months already!

The week was finally won by Scheidt and Prada. Going into the final race with just one point clear, the World number one ranked team was initially buried in the pack, but managed to sail themselves clear to finally take the event. Percy and Simpson were disappointed with their final day's racing, but managed to retain second position on count-back from Loof and Tillander, and the fleet were now all moving off to the World Championships in Sweden, although Percy and Simpson were not attending that meeting as Bart was getting married.

P	Helm	Crew	Nat	R1	R2	R3	R4	R5	R6	R7	R8	Pts
1	R Scheidt	B Prada	BRA	4	4	1	4	1	1	30	3	18
2	I Percy	A Simpson	GBR	2	1	6	2	4	3	10	4	22
3	F Loof	J Tillander	SWE	1	3	5	6	2	5	4	2	22
4	F Marazzi	E De Maria	SUI	7	11	9	5	13	15	13	5.5	63.5
5	J Babendererde	T Jacobs	GER	12	7	2	12	39	18	12	1	64
6	R Stanjek	M Koy	GER	5	6	19	8	7	14	31	7	66
7	M Mendelblatt	M Strube	USA	9	5	11	17	3	8	35	16	69
8	X Rohart	P Ponsot	FRA	19	20	20	1	5	BFD	1	12	78
9	H Pepper	C Monk	NZL	13	8	28	3	BFD	4	11	11	78
10	D Negri	G Stilo	ITA	BFD	14	17	23	11	2	5	13	85

2.4 Metre

Type	Keelboat
Crew	1
PN	1260
Length	4.1 – 4.35 m
Beam	0.75 – 0.9 m
Weight	225 – 260 kg
Sail area M & J	8 sq m
Spi type	None
Designer	Various
	www.24metre.org.uk

The 2.4 Metre is the most popular single-handed keelboat in the world. The UK association has a series of open meetings, aiming for one meeting per month during the summer. There are also European and World Championships. The nature of the boat means that crew weight and agility are of little matter, but the very tweakable rig makes for a technical boat, requiring good boat tuning skills to sail at its full potential. Whilst it is the present single-handed paralympic boat, the majority of 2.4 Metre sailors are able-bodied.

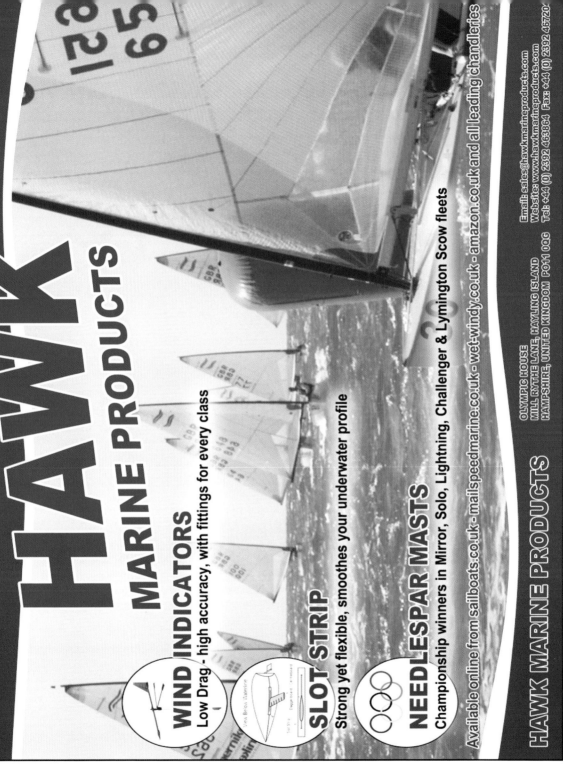

Youth Sailing

The Dinghy & Smallcraft Review
2009~2010

Volvo Youth Sailing ISAF Worlds

Buzios, Brazil   9 - 18 July 2009

Two hundred and two boats, spread across five different classes and representing some sixty countries, competed for the 2009 Volvo Youth Sailing Worlds in mid July, with the most popular fleets being the single handed Radial classes, particularly the boys with fifty three entries. During the event, one day's racing was lost to gales, whilst another was lost to insufficient breeze.

Photo courtesy of Dave Kneale/Volvo Ocean Race

Boys' One Person Dinghy

The fifty three boat Boys' Radial fleet was dominated by New Zealander Sam Meech. Discarding a sixth position, Meech finished thirty three points clear of second placed Tomás Pellejero from Argentina. Having won bronze last year, Meech has obviously put his additional experience to good use, and is certainly destined to do great things in the future. Third this year was Pascal Timshel from Denmark whilst young Oscar McVeigh from the UK finished in thirty fifth position, having been up against it since he was declared to be OCS in Race Three of the event.

Girls' One Person Dinghy

Hannah Tilley represented GB in the thirty eight boat Radial fleet for girls, finishing in twenty first position with the class win being taken by Elizabeth Yin of Singapore, who showed great consistency throughout the week to finish with a four point winning margin ahead of Denmark's Anne-Marie Rindom, with Mathilde De Kerangat of France in third position.

Hobie 16 Class

Seventeen boats contested the multihull division of the Championships, with the GB entry being Adam Butler and Nikki Boniface, who were selected following the Eurocat event at Carnac in France. They finished in a commendable fifth position overall, with the fleet trailer Australians, Jason Waterhouse and Lisa Darmanin who finished just one point clear of France's Romai and Valentin Bellet at the top of the standings, with the Italian representatives, Francesco Porro and Luca Marsaglia earning the Bronze medal.

RSX Boys

In a twenty four strong fleet, it was the fast finishing Frenchman, Joseph Gueguen who took overall victory and the Gold medal. Three wins in the final three races enabled Gueguen to overhaul Michalis Malekkides of Cyprus, and Jorge Renato do Amaral Silva of Brazil, who finally took the Bronze position. The UK sailor Alistair Masters finished in a commendable ninth position overall, including a race win during the week, obviously feeling increasingly comfortable in this type of company as the event progressed.

RSX Girls

There were fifteen entries in the RSX Girls' division of the racing and, whilst much of the racing was dominated by Hei Man Chan from Hong Kong, who had a clear run on first and second positions throughout the event, the increasingly experienced Izzy Hamilton took Silver medal with a consistent and impressive stream of results, ahead of the French girl, Leonore Bosch. This is the fifth Youth Worlds Chan has competed in, and this was her last opportunity. After spending some time in Europe training this spring/summer, her preparation was obviously adequate to at last take the medal that she had been striving for, especially after finishing fourth last year.

420 Boys

The thirty one strong Boys' 420 fleet was the cause of greatest pleasure for the UK sailors, with Philip Sparks and Ben Gratton stringing together an excellent set of results, with the exception of their discard (which was a DSQ). Otherwise the four race wins and three second places were enough to give them the Championship by twenty points ahead of France's Bernard Skoczek and Thibaut Soler with Chile's Benjamin Ahrens and Carlos Infante taking the third position.

420 Girls

In the Girls' 420 fleet, there was considerable local delight as the title was won by Martine Grael and Kahena Kunze for the home nation with a day in hand. Grael is the daughter of Brazilian Olympic/Round the World star, Torben Grael, and it is apparent that some of his abilities have rubbed off! Silver medallist at the end of the regatta was Camilla Marino, crewed by Slaudia Soricelli from Italy, and these two crews really dominated the racing, finishing more than thirty points clear of the third boat, sailed by Briselda Khng and Cecilia Low of Singapore. Itchenor's Rebecca Kalderon and Rosie Sibthorpe, sailing for GBR, put up a good display, particularly during the early part of the week, and finished in seventh position overall.

Team GB's World Champions Philip Sparks and Ben Gratton

VOLVO
YOUTH
SAILING
ISAF WORLD CHAMPIONSHIP 2009
BUZIOS BRAZIL

TEAM GB 2009

Ali Masters

Hannah Tilley

Oscar McVeigh

Philip Sparks and Ben Gratton

Photos courtesy of Dave Kneale/Volvo Ocean Rac

The Dinghy & Smallcraft Review
2009~2010

Rebecca Kalderon and Rosie Sibthorpe

VOLVO
YOUTH
SAILING
ISAF WORLD CHAMPIONSHIP 2009

TEAM GB 2009

Izzy Hamilton

Adam Butler and Nikki Boniface

Photos courtesy of Dave Kneale/Volvo Ocean Race

The Dinghy & Smallcraft Review
2009~2010

331

RYA Volvo Youth Nationals

Largs Sailing Club   13 - 17 April 2009

The Easter weekend saw the start of the 2009 Youth Nationals, which also served as a selection trial for the ISAF World Youth Championships, with one hundred and ninety six entries across the five classes. The conditions throughout the week varied from light to strong winds, with Thursday being completely lost for racing and the prospect of three races on the final day, after a change in the sailing instruction permitted the alteration of schedule.However, conditions continued to fight the competitors, and racing was called off on Friday, calling a halt to the Championships.

The Princess Royal again graced the event, visiting ashore and venturing out onto the water on Day Three of the Championships, when the wind dropped from forty two knots in the morning, to a baffling breeze coming from every direction, and exhibiting the full range of strengths, preventing much racing from taking place!

29er Fleet   **27 entries**

In the absence of the previous year's winners (James Peters and Ed Fitzgerald) and runners up (Frances Peters and Claire Lasko) who had both gone on to win their respective sectors at the Youth Worlds, all the running in the 29er Fleet was made by the eighteen year old pairing of Bleddyn Mon, crewed this year by Nick Redding. With two wins and a second place in the first three races, the fleet were always chasing the pair, but their consistency throughout the week ensured that they took the title, and with it, selection to the World Championships. The race for the minor pla-cings was far more intense, with Max Richardson and Alex Groves finally taking the Silver medal, ahead of Art Romano and Ed Romano, with Henry Lloyd Williams and Sam Batten in fourth, and Tom Durham and Rupert Jones-Warner if fifth.

The RYA Volvo Youth National Girls Championship in the 29er went to the seventeen year old pairing of Lilly Carlisle and Becky Wallbank, who finished third last year; turning the tables on the previous year's runners up Becky Diamond and Fiona Hampshire, with Phillipa Gray and Joanna Lucas in third spot.

P	Helm	Crew	R1	R2	R3	R4	R5	R6	Tot	Nett
1	Bleddyn Mon	Nick Redding	1	2	1	5	1	1	11	6
2	Max Richardson	Alex Groves	4	13	OCS	2	2	3	52	24
3	Art Romano	Ed Romano	10	12	2	1	6	6	37	25
4	Henry Lloyd Williams	Sam Bayyen	5	5	4	6	5	9	34	25
5	Tom Durham	Rupert Jones-Warner	2	15	7	8	9	2	43	28
6	James Briggs	George Hand	9	3	9	4	7	7	39	30
7	Alex Horlock	Tim Walton	8	7	3	3	10	12	43	31
8	Alex Mothersele	Hamish Ellis	20	1	5	7	17	5	55	35

420 Fleet   **27 entries**

Again in the absence of the top two boats from 2008, the 420s were also dominated by the previous year's Bronze medal winners, with sixteen year old Philip Sparks and Ben Gratton leading the way from the off, with three wins in the first three races and a final tally of four wins and two second places. In hot pursuit were a group of evenly matched boats, including Ben Palmer and Konrad Weaver who finally took the Silver medal, and Matt Rainback and Simon Foskett (who had finished ninth in 2008) earning the Bronze. Top girl crew at the end of the regatta was seventeen year old Rebecca Kalderon sailing with Rosie Sibthorp. Amy Seabright and Katrina Brewer finished in second, four points in arrears, while Imogen and Hermione Stanley finished third.

P	Helm	Crew	R1	R2	R3	R4	R5	R6	Tot	Nett
1	Philip Sparks	Ben Gratton	1	1	1	2	2	1	8	6
2	Ben Palmer	Konrad Weaver	3	2	2	17	6	2	32	15
3	Matt Rainback	Simon Foskett	2	12	3	15	1	3	36	21
4	Rebecca Kalderon	Rosie Sibthorp	5	4	12	4	8	5	38	26
5	Tim Gratton	Ed Riley	7	9	6	5	3	11	41	30
6	Amy Seabright	Katrina Brewer	4	5	8	8	5	9	39	30
7	Mike Wood	Hugh Brayshaw	OCS	7	7	1	13	4	59	32
8	Imogen Stanley	Hermione Stanley	OCS	3	4	7	12	13	66	39
9	Sam Robinson	Peter Alton	11	6	18	11	4	8	58	40
10	Joanna Freeman	Hannah Mitchell	6	10	10	13	7	12	58	45

Laser Standard Fleet   **23 entries**

Phillip Reynolds showed that experience is a huge benefit, by taking the Laser title, having finished in tenth position the previous year. He battled throughout the week with Martin Evans (2008 Worlds Silver medallist), and Alex Mills Barton, with all three boats going into what should have been the final day within one point of each other. In the absence of final-day racing, of course, the three boats finished in that order overall, with Reynolds taking the title on count-back.

P	Helm	R1	R2	R3	R4	R5	R6	Total	Nett
1	Phillip Reynolds	1	4	1	BFD	4	1	36	11
2	Martin Evans	4	2	3	1	1	4	15	11
3	Alex Mills Barton	2	3	2	BFD	2	3	37	12
4	James Spencer	6	1	6	2	6	5	26	20
5	David Carpenter	14	8	4	6	3	9	44	30
6	Robert Holmes	7	10	5	BFD	7	2	56	31
7	Peter McCoy	3	9	BFD	5	11	7	60	35
8	Shane Terry	10	5	10	4	9	8	46	36

Laser Radial Fleet   95 entries

The Laser Radial Fleet was divided into two equal-sized fleets after the initial qualifying races, which were raced in flights.

Gold Fleet

The top two boats in the Gold Fleet following the qualifying were fourteen year old David Grant (the 2008 Laser 4.7 Under 15 World Champion) and his brother, sixteen year old James (the defending RYA Youth National champion), ahead of the boats of Oscar McVeigh and Max Robinson. However, the Grants both had a disappointing Wednesday in the first of the final races which were held in very trying conditions, and left themselves with a lot to do on the final day. In the absence of this opportunity, the Grants were left back in the pack, and McVeigh took a well earned Gold medal, with Robinson gaining the Silver medal, and Jack Wetherell in a deserved Bronze medal position. The top girl in the event was Hannah Tilley, who was also scheduled to sail in the Laser 4.7 World Championships during the summer. Hannah took Gold on her first visit to the Youth Nationals, with Charlotte Greenhalgh in Silver and Sarah Butterfield making the podium for the second year running.

P	Helm	C/F	R1	Tot	Nett
1	Oscar McVeigh	23	2	25	25
2	Max Robinson	23	10	33	33
3	Jack Wetherell	25	11	36	36
4	Elliot Hanson	38	4	42	42
5	Phil McCoy	33	12	45	45
6	Freddie Connor	26	20	46	46
7	Duncan Keates	40	9	49	49
8	Andrew Brown	45	5	50	50

Silver Fleet

Cameron Scott led the fleet into the final section of racing after the competition was divided into two flights, just ahead of Harvey Davies, but with just one race in the finals completed, it was Davies who took the top position. Liam Gardner finished in second, and Josh McLynn in third, with Scott dropping to fifth position with a bad race on the testing Wednesday, which had to be included in his final tally.

P	Helm	C/F	R1	Tot	Nett
1	Harvey Davies	103	6	109	109
2	Liam Gardner	110	7	117	117
3	Josh McLynn	117	1	118	118
4	Ben Robinson	115	10	125	125

RSX Fleet   20 entries

Sixteen year old George Bowles (who has only been sailing the RSX for seven months) and the experienced seventeen year old Ali Masters led the sail-boarders for much of the week, with both sailors maintaining top three positions throughout the week prior to the final day, which they entered level on points. In the absence of further racing, the event went to tie break, and Bowles took the title as a result of beating Masters in what proved to be the heat. The chasing pack were led by Connor Bainbridge in third, with the previous year's Bronze medallist and top girl, Izzy Hamilton (still only sixteen years old) in fourth. With no chance to complete the race schedule, these remained as the final results, with Bainbridge finishing in Bronze medal position, and Hamilton successfully defending the Girls' title. Silver medal in the girls' fleet went to Sophie Bailey, whilst Claudia Carney finished in Bronze.

P	Helm	R1	R2	R3	R4	R5	Tot	Nett
1	George Bowles	3	1	2	2	1	9	9
2	Ali Masters	1	2	3	1	2	9	9
3	Connor Bainbridge	5	3	1	7	4	20	20
4	Izzy Hamilton	2	10	4	3	3	22	22
5	Callum Stewart	7	9	5	5	7	33	33
6	Tom Owen	6	5	7	10	6	34	34

At the conclusion of the Nationals, despite the event being somewhat fore-shortened, the squad was named for the dinghy classes at the 2009 Volvo Youth Sailing ISAF World Championships at Buzios in Brazil. The trials for the SL16 Cats were held a little later in the season at the Eurocat meeting in France.

420 Class   Boys: Philip Sparks/Ben Gratton
                     Girls: Rebecca Kalderon/Rosie Sibthorp

RSX   Boys: Ali Masters   Girls: Izzy Hamilton

Laser Radial   Boys: Oscar McVeigh   Girls: Hannah Tilley

Hobie 16   Adam Butler and Nikki Boniface (at the Eurocat event)

Cadet

Photo courtesy of Fotoboat

Type	Dinghy	Weight	54.48 kg
Crew	2; Sit out	Sail area M&J	5.16 sq m
PN	1432	Spi type	Symmetric
Length	3.22 m	Spi area	4.25 sq m
Beam	1.27 m	Designer	Jack Holt, 1947
			www.cadetclass.org.uk

The Cadet was designed in 1947 by Jack Holt, and continues to be used throughout the world by children under the age of eighteen, as a two man racing dinghy.

The class has a successful annual National Championships as well as World and European Championships, and there is an active squad training system to get the best out of the young sailors. This year the rules have again permitted the Cadet to be constructed in plywood as well as GRP, which is a facility that had not been available for a few years and reopens the class to home manufacture.

Cadet European Championships

Club De Mar de Almeria, Spain   18 - 24 July 2009

With one hundred and eleven entries from ten countries, the European Cadet Championships saw teams of boats from the UK, Spain, Belgium, Australia, the Czech Republic, Germany, Hungary, the Netherlands, Poland and the Ukraine.

The event was planned to run with an initial qualifying series of races, with a lay-day prior to the two final Silver and Gold fleet racing days. However, the first two days were both lost with no wind to permit any racing to take place, and the schedule began to become a bit more concentrated! All restructuring came to nothing after the third day, when yet again a windless race course prevented the meeting from getting underway, and it was decided that a minimum three race series would be necessary for the event to be considered valid.

At last a breeze arrived for Day Four, and the committee fitted four races into the schedule to ease the backlog. Early overall leaders were the UK's Chris Brewer and Ole Alcock with three wins, with Krzysztof Matecki and Mikolaj Mickiewicz from Poland in second and Brits Sophie Dingwall with Christopher Sycamore in third, ahead of a cluster of four Spanish crews.

Two more races followed on Day Five, with Brewer and Alcock still leading at the end of the day scoring a third and thirteenth, whilst Dingwall and Sycamore had a forty-third and seventh, to hold onto second by one point from Tom Alleman and Danis Tanguy of Belgium who had a second and a ninth to count. This was sufficient to decide the destination of the title after what was a terribly difficult start to the event, and the Committee must have been delighted to get the event completed despite the difficult conditions.

P	Nat	Helm	Crew	R1	R2	R3	R4	R5	R6	Pts
1	GBR	Christopher Brewer	Ole Alcock	1	15	1	1	3	13	19
2	GBR	Sophie Dingwall	Christopher Sycamore	12	4	4	10	43	7	37
3	BEL	Tom Alleman	Danis Tanguy	16	39	7	4	2	9	38
4	POL	Krzysztof Matecki	Mikolaj Mickiewicz	10	2	11	6	10	12	39
5	BEL	Toon De Munck	Eline Spittaels	45	28	8	2	7	1	46
6	POL	Szymon Wierzbicki	Wojciech Lewand	5	1	17	39	5	20	48
7	ESP	Roi Rogel	Juan Luis Millán	20	7	2	5	34	19	53
8	DEL	Sam Vynckier	Thijs Klumpers	75	11	9	9	27	3	59
9	UKR	Butenko Ivan	Moroz Ivan	3	5	33	32	13	8	61
10	GBR	William Kennedy	Rhos Hawes	106	14	19	12	6	11	62

Cadet National Championships

Pwllheli   22 - 28 August 2009

Ninety three Cadets travelled to north Wales for the 2009 National Championship, with ten races scheduled over the week, and discards coming into play after the fifth and tenth races. Apart from the home fleet, there was also a small European representation, including two leading Belgium crews. The event was being used as one of three selection meetings for the Cadet World Championships to be held over the new year in Argentina; so a pretty good prize was up for grabs!

On the first day, a prompt decision was made to cancel racing because of high winds, plenty of rain and poor visibility. Thus on Day Two they scheduled three races to try to get the schedule back on track. Sophie Dingwall and Christopher Sycamore ended the first day in the lead overall after winning two of the three races and scoring a fourth I the third heat. Chris Brewer and Ole Alcock won the third heat, and added two third places for second overall, whilst reigning National Champion Arthur Henderson, sailing with Matthew Currell, had a disappointing tenth to start the week, but then began to find his feet with two second positions. Dingwall and Sycamore added a ninth, third and win to their score-line on the second day of racing which left them tied on ten points with Chris Brewer and Ole Alcock, who added a first and second (together with a discard) to their score. This left these two crews fairly well clear of Henderson and Currell, who also collected a poor result to add to an eighth and a third in third position overall at the end of the day.

High winds caused racing on Day Four to be cancelled, and the rest obviously worked for Henderson and Currell, who added three race wins to their score, and took over at the top of the overall table. Three good results also lifted William Kennedy up to third overall, behind Dingwall and Sycamore who had a poor day by their standards (seventh, fifth and forty fourth), and ahead of Brewer and Alcock, who were similarly off the pace (thirteenth, sixth and twentieth). Sadly, the return of the gales prevented the final races taking place, and positions at the end of the penultimate day became the final results, leaving Henderson and Currell as National Champions, successfully defending the title that they won in 2008.

P	Helm	Crew	Club	R1	R2	R3	R4	R5	R6	R7	R8	R9	Pts
1	A Henderson	M Currell	SYC	10	2	2	8	23	3	1	1	1	28
2	S Dingwall	C Sycamore	FGSC	4	1	1	9	3	1	7	5	44	31
3	W Kennedy	R Hawes	FGSC	8	5	4	17	18	2	4	3	3	46
4	C Brewer	O Alcock	PYC	1	3	3	1	2	21	13	6	28	50
5	O Palierakis	W Palierakis	FGSC	7	4	23	5	16	9	8	2	13	64
6	A Frost	W McMahon	SCSC	5	29	6	7	5	38	3	8	4	67
7	A Croft	M Shorrock	FPSC	9	11	36	6	14	12	5	21	11	89
8	C Lauwers	R Hambrouck	WVD	6	10	DNF	2	6	11	19	24	18	96
9	J Quinlan	A Warrington	RCYC	11	6	8	15	13	17	35	12	17	99
10	T Alleman	J Van Craenenbroeck	VVW	3	13	46	12	15	4	36	10	10	103

Laser 4.7

Photo courtesy of Digigraphics

Type	Dinghy	Weight	59 kg
Crew	1; Sit out	Sail area M	4.7 sq m
PN	1175	Spi type	-
Length	4.23 m	Designer	Bruce Kirby
Beam	1.37 m		www.laser.org.uk

The Laser 4.7 is again based on the standard Laser hull and foils, but with a further reduced sail. It is a boat that is ideally suited as a stepping stone from the Optimist to racing the Radial and Standard Lasers, or of course any other larger dinghy. With the addition of a different sail and mast section, the 4.7 gives the scope for the Laser hull to suit anyone in the family, in all conditions. The boat has a Championship programme and open meeting circuit.

Laser 4.7 World Championships

Buzios, Brazil   24 - 31 July 2009

The Laser 4.7 World Championships were held in Buzios, Brazil, at the end of July. Ten boys competed from twenty four countries, including forty four boats in the Under Sixteen fleet, along with nine girls from twenty three countries, with thirteen Under Sixteen entries. A total of seven youngsters from the UK made the long journey to compete while their compatriots were battling for the UK National Championships title in Devon.

Several days of racing were lost due to torrential rain and no wind. After Day Three the Boys' Class was led by Jonathan Martinetti (ECU), whilst the girls saw Urska Kosir (SLO) at the top of the table. In the Boys' fleet, Hermann Tomasgaard from Norway took over the lead in close company with Ecuadorian Jonathan Martinetti after Day Four when the fleet was divided into Gold and Silver divisions. It was another day of light and fickle breezes and two more races were completed. Amongst the girls, Japanese sailor Tomoyo Wakabayashi won both races to pull herself up to third overall behind Kim Pleitkos and Urska Kosir from Slovenia. By the end of Day Five, Jonathan Martinetti had clambered back to lead overnight, with Tomasgaard Hermann in second. In the girl's fleet, it was Urska Kosir who led overall into the final day, ahead of Japan's Tomoyo Wakabayashi, with Hitomi Murayama, also from Japan in third. Racing on the last day was again denied because of the weather, leaving the previous evening's leader's positions, to decide the medals. This all left Tomasgaard Hermann as the Under 16 World Champion, with GB's David Grant in third position and Tom Britz in fifth. In the Girls' section, Japan's Hitomi Murayama won the Under Sixteen section ahead of Slovenia's Kim Pletikos.

P	Nat	Helm (Girls)	Born	Q1	Q2	Q3	Q4	F1	F2	F3	Total	Nett
1	SLO	Urska Kosir	1992	1	2	2	1	4	6	11	27	16
2	JPN	Tomoyo Wakabayashi	1993	15	1	22	8	1	1	2	50	28
3	JPN	Hitomi Murayama	1994	14	9	24	3	2	7	3	62	38
4	SLO	Kim Pletikos	1994	20	3	4	2	7	9	16	61	41
5	ESP	Leveque Patricia Coro	1992	4	16	11	5	15	8	1	60	44
6	PER	Daniela Zimmermann	1992	21	35	5	7	5	3	10	86	51

P	Nat	Helm (Boys)	Born	Q1	Q2	Q3	Q4	F1	F2	F3	Total	Nett
1	ECU	Jonathan Martinetti	1992	23	1	1	1	15	1	2	44	21
2	NOR	Hermann Tomasgaard	1994	7	1	12	1	2	7	9	39	27
3	CRO	Juraj Divjakinja	1992	11	3	2	2	10	10	6	44	33
4	PER	Guillermo Arce	1992	4	3	13	9	8	22	3	62	40
5	ESP	Tono Alcazar	1994	8	2	29	3	4	31	1	78	47
6	CRO	Bartul Plenkovic	1993	9	4	13	8	17	4	20	75	55
7	ARG	Agustin Vidal	1992	16	5	41	14	14	8	12	110	69
8	GBR	David Grant	1994	3	7	5	31	21	42	4	113	71

Laser 4.7 Nationals

Paignton Sailing Club   26 - 31 July 2009

With a thirty nine boat fleet, racing in the 4.7s was confined to a single fleet format, and after two days, there were three boats all on the same points, to underline the closeness of the class. Michael Molloy of East Down YC had a race win and a third to his credit, discarding a fifth position, whilst Will Harris of Queen Mary had the same results, but was discarding a fourth place from the second race. Grafham's Ross Williams had two second place finishes in the first three races, and was hoping to shed a tenth place finish.

Two more races on Tuesday saw Harris reinforce his position with two more race wins, leaving him eight points clear of second placed Molloy and a further point in front of Harvey Davies, who had added a second and third place to lift him into third place overall.

As the fleet came ashore at the end of Thursday, with just one day still to sail, Harris had reinforced his position at the top of the results table with five race wins, a third and a fourth to count for eight points; twelve ahead of Ross Williams and thirteen ahead of James Parker-Mowbray, whilst both Michael Molloy and Harvey Davies had been on the receiving end of poor results on two races on Thursday, opening a small gap back to fourth and fifth positions overall. Will Harris won his sixth race in the morning and couldn't be beaten overall, so he had the luxury of an early bath and packing his boat up before the mad rush. The final win went to Jamie Diamond, which helped him to third overall behind Parker-Mowbray, and one point clear of Ross Williams.

P	Helm	R1	R2	R3	R4	R5	R6	R7	R8	R9	R10	Pts
1	Will Harris	1	4	3	1	1	1	4	1	1	DNC	13
2	James Parker-Mowbray	7	5	4	4	4	5	1	3	9	4	30
3	Jamie Diamond	4	11	5	7	8	3	6	5	2	1	33
4	Ross Williams	10	2	2	BFD	5	6	3	2	4	17	34
5	Harvey Davies	3	7	7	2	3	4	12	12	3	6	35
6	Michael Molloy	5	3	1	5	9	2	10	11	8	5	38
7	Dan Bullock	14	1	8	11	11	9	2	6	7	20	55
8	Peter Cameron	8	15	20	12	7	7	8	4	5	7	58
9	Charlie Williams	9	22	9	3	6	10	24	8	6	10	61
10	William Nicholls	2	6	10	8	2	DSQ	16	7	17	BFD	68

Optimist

Type	Dinghy	Weight	35 kg
Crew	1; Sit out	Sail area M&J	3.59 sq m
PN	1646	Spi type	No
Length	2.3 m	Designer	Clark Mills
Beam	1.12 m		www.optimistsailing.org.uk

Photo courtesy of Paul Wyeth

The Optimist is the best way to start sailing, have loads of fun, get great training, make friends for life, and even become a Champion. The Optimist is the RYA's favoured singlehanded junior dinghy class for children aged 7 to 15, weighing 34 kg – 55 kg. Sail and rig adjustment allow boat set-ups for children of different sizes and weights, so that all can compete on equal terms. The Optimist class has exacting standards for hull construction, foils, sails and rigging that level the playing field and make boat tuning and handling, together with personal fitness and skills, the deciding factors in competition.

Optimist World Championships

Niteroi, Brazil   4 - 15 August 2009

Two hundred and eleven entries from forty seven countries competed in Brazil for the 2009 Optimist World Championships, including a five boat team from Great Britain made up of Scott Wallis, Craig Dibb, Sophie Hamilton, and Annabel Vose. It is unfortunate that the event ran at the same time as the UK Nationals, obviously preventing their attendance at the home event. However, with a maximum of fifteen races scheduled, the event was likely to be an exhaustive test of the new Champion.

The UK Team for the Opi Worlds 2009

The first day's sailing was lost due to lack of wind. However, the fleet lauched early on Day Two, and enjoyed a steady seven to nine knot breeze, with the fleet separated into six divisions to make starting and control less of a problem! Race Two was very shifty but it was still possible to get three races completed before the light started to go; which it does surprisingly early in Brazil. Despite the inevitable inconsistencies caused by the conditions, Mohamad Faizal Norizan from Malaysia shone at the end of the first day with two race wins and a fifth position, ahead of Ahmad Syukri Abdul Aziz, Mathias Robertson (Chile) and Antoine Lefort (France).

On Day Three the wind was again light and tricky, but Mohamad Faizal Norizan continued to show his form, pulling eleven points clear by the end of the day, ahead of Antoine Lefort of France, whilst Noppakao Poonipat (Thailand) had a good day and was then first girl in fourth overall.

After a three day gap for the Team Racing Championships, fleet racing recommenced with three more races planned. After the sixth race, an initial discard could be counted and this meant that Noppakao Poonpat was not only first girl but first overall, with a two point lead over the next three sailors, who were all tied on twenty eight points, Ahmad Latif Khan, Ali Subri Khan and Mohamad Faizal Norizan from Malaysia and Ignacio Rogala of Argentina.

The penultimate day's sailing provided perfect conditions, and saw former overall leader Mohamad Faizal Norizan back at the front of the leader board with eleven races completed. One more race would permit the second discard to come into play, which would obviously see a reorganization of the points order, but the final day looked to be a close run affair with everything to play for, with three Malaysian competitors in the top ten, and Noppakao Poonpat looking to set to become the Girls' World Champion as the only female in the top ten overall.

Whilst the final day started with no breeze, it gradually filled in and enabled Race Twelve to start, although a number picked up black flag penalties. The left hand side of the course was favoured, and the whole fleet headed left, keeping them all together. Mohamad Faizal Norizan had a poor score and was unable to improve on his overall tally, but his top pursuer, Sinclair Jones, finished in ninth position, and this gave him the title by a substantial eight points.

P	Nat	Helm	R1	R2	R3	R4	R5	R6	R7	R8	R9	R10	R11	R12	Tot	Nett
1	PER	S Jones	1	21	2	1	5	7	DPI	2	6	4	1	9	86	38
2	MAS	M F Norizan	1	1	5	8	3	7	13	3	13	2	3	30	89	46
3	ARG	I Rogala	5	37	1	2	3	12	3	2	21	12	5	6	109	51
4	THA	N Poonpat	4	13	11	3	2	4	1	1	23	15	1	37	115	55
5	BRA	R Aranhos	38	6	2	8	14	11	22	14	12	6	3	3	139	79
6	MAS	M F Hamid	10	15	2	9	14	16	4	5	4	3	17	14	113	80
7	FRA	A Lefort	3	4	7	7	8	9	11	32	6	11	15	30	143	81
8	CHN	Y Yang	7	27	13	49	6	2	6	8	9	2	OCS	3	205	83
9	MAS	A Khan	3	16	32	1	3	3	1	1	14	28	19	25	146	86
10	ESP	C Robles	21	11	1	4	4	17	DPI	31	5	4	7	OCS	199	95
11	SIN	R J H Lo	OCS	11	12	2	11	17	5	3	64	18	10	7	233	96
12	JPN	K Okada	9	1	42	18	9	4	7	17	1	32	48	13	201	111
13	SIN	A Tang	5	12	3	26	10	OCS	15	6	17	9	10	42	228	113
14	POL	E Szczesna	21	8	21	1	7	1	12	7	2	OCS	35	OCS	261	115
15	GRE	K Oikonomidis	4	3	38	11	5	6	45	28	41	4	12	6	203	117
62	GBR	S Wallis	14	26	OCS	6	27	37	36	39	22	28	16	15	338	226
141	GBR	C Dibb	35	32	25	19	46	55	62	51	49	53	23	32	482	365
157	GBR	S Hamilton	30	14	69	5	43	13	OCS	38	59	42	53	49	538	396
170	GBR	A Vose	26	32	OCS	53	71	55	35	57	46	3	56	3	570	426
188	GBR	J Sparks	31	OCS	65	17	58	59	50	OCS	53	29	45	OCS	626	480

Optimist European Championships

Piran, Slovenia   1 - 7 July 2009

A team of seven GBR boats ventured to Piran in Slovenia for the 2009 European Championships in early July. Racing started for the Optimist Europeans with a light six knot breeze and the sailors split into four fleets; two for girls and two for boys. After several recalls the fleets took off in a decreasing breeze with a large shift coming in on the final leg. Subsequently the wind continued to disappear and no further racing was possible for the day. On the second day, the breeze began to build more optimistically, with twelve knots across the course, and the first four races started on schedule. The Committee proceeded to start Race Three of the series as soon as possible after the completion of Race Two in the hope that they could gain some time back on the schedule, but the wind suddenly turned chilly and increased to twenty five knots; thus ending sailing for the day. After two races, Malcolm Lamphere (USA) was leading the boys with a fifth and a second and Jennifer Poret (France) was leading the girls with a first and a third – a significant achievement in these trying conditions. Paulina Rothlauf (Germany), the previous year's winner of the Girls' title, was in fourth place, only six points behind the leader.

As the new day dawned, everyone was hoping for much better conditions and their prayers were answered. Race Three started on time in about twelve knots of breeze, and continued to swing to the east to northeast and increase to the sixteen knots expected of the Bora, providing perfect conditions for the rest of the day, leaving the German team in good shape as they sailed for shore; Annika Matthiesen and Paulina Rothlauf were in first and second places in the Girls' fleet and Maximilian Hibler was leading the Boys'.

With the Bora continuing overnight, conditions looked ideal for Thursday, but the wind slowly began to drop, leaving large swells which had built up overnight. Attempts were made to start the first boys' race, eventually calling for the black flag, and this caught seventeen sailors on their first attempt. As the wind continued to shift, and drop, the first discard came into play, and the German team made its presence felt, with Paulina Rothlauf, ahead in the Girls' fleet by five points from her fellow team member Annika Matthiesen, and Maximilian Hibler leading the Boys' fleet by eleven points.

The winds for Race Eight were eighteen knots with half metre swells. The Race Committee brought the black flag in from the start of play, and the fleet got away at the first attempt with three races for each group. As the racing on the penultimate day ended, everything was still to play for in the results. Following another tense, and testing day afloat, the 2009 European Optimist Champions were soundly congratulated after a great, competitive week's sailing in a beautiful venue with competition of the highest order.

Final Results: Girls Open European Championship 2009 in Piran

P	Nat	Helm	R1	R2	R3	R4	R5	R6	R7	R8	R9	R10	R11	Pts
1	GER	Paulina Rothlauf	7	3	3	8	1	2	2	5	4	1	2	23
2	POl	Sara Piasecka	7	1	13	1	3	18	2	1	3	28	6	37
3	ITA	Francesca Russo	2	5	13	5	10	1	28	2	12	1	4	42
4	GER	Finja Cipra	23	15	3	1	3	7	4	3	4	16	OCS	56
5	GER	Annika Matthiesen	12	1	1	3	4	15	40	7	7	16	7	57
6	TUR	Zeynep Yentur	11	2	12	4	2	30	1	7	1	26	29	66
7	GRE	Maria Drosou	4	17	25	2	9	34	3	5	OCS	5	2	72
8	FRA	Jennifer Poret	1	3	27	6	8	3	22	24	OCS	7	1	75
9	SLO	Lea Janezic	21	18	23	3	6	8	1	2	6	23	13	78
10	GBR	Karianne Hammar	29	5	5	5	20	23	6	4	16	17	12	90
28	GBR	Georgie Mothersele	34	13	6	15	15	ocs	5	13	5	27	39	133
50	GBR	Melissa Hamilton	47	8	46	11	17	31	33	12	14	42	19	187
53	GBR	Zoe Parkinson	17	31	3	27	26	13	23	30	35	5	20	192

Final Results: Boys Open European Championship 2009 in Piran

P	Nat	Helm	R1	R2	R3	R4	R5	R6	R7	R8	R9	R10	R11	Pts
1	GER	Maximilian Hibler	8	3	5	2	7	3	BFD	1	5	19	18	52
2	HUN	Benjamin Vadnai	5	16	6	23	2	2	5	6	21	12	7	61
3	USA	Malcolm Lamphere	5	2	16	22	9	8	7	12	45	1	3	63
4	POL	Konrad Lipski	11	46	5	17	1	BFD	2	4	5	8	12	65
5	POL	Filip Florek	30	9	17	1	12	15	12	5	9	5	6	74.3
6	NED	Wouter Sonnema	15	6	18	1	2	35	9	2	8	29	23	84
7	ITA	Stefano Ferrighi	10	4	10	5	26	32	11	8	4	34	8	86
8	FRA	Arthur Fortune	OCS	11	27	12	20	1	11	2	9	19	2	87
9	TUR	Sergen Birincioglu	11	7	24	10	5	3	10	42	2	20	44	92
10	GRE	Alexandros Magouras	4	3	3	26	27	14	19	1	10	31	20	100
65	GBR	Sasha Bruml	49	43	15	4	20	BFD	43	28	20	61	48	270
75	GBR	Callum Airlie	62	60	7	4	31	18	6	38	RQF	70	64	290
79	GBR	Harry Derbyshire	54	41	31	28	56	36	30	23	18	48	37	292

Photo courtesy of the Int Optimist Assc.

Paulina Rothlauf and Maximilian Hibler, 2009 European Champions

Optimist National Championships

Largs, Scotland   7 - 14 August 2009

Some three hundred and fifty Optimists travelled to Largs in Scotland for the 2009 National Championships. The fleet was divided into four different racing "sections", the largest being the Junior Fleet with some one hundred and forty six entries in the eight to twelve year old age group. The Senior group had some one hundred and nine competitors, and was aimed at the thirteen to fifteen year olds. The other two groups, for the less experienced, saw some seventy eight entries in the Regatta fleet and twenty four in the Regatta Starter fleet.

Senior Group

In the Senior group going in to the final day, American Roger Dorr led overall with a two point margin from Josh Voller and Callum Airlie, both of whom had had two race wins during the week. Oliver Grogono was comfortably in fourth position with the first Spaniard, Oscar Pijoan, rounding off the top five. American Megan Grapengeter-Rudnick was favourite to win the overall girls' title, having broken into the overall top ten in the course of the penultimate day, whilst Guernsey YC's Johanna Asplund led the challenge for the National title as top "home" girl, with Megan Brickwood just six points behind. The final day was destined not to be a great day for the American, and in the end his three results of nineteenth, twenty sixth and twenty third were to drop him down to third in the title race after a great week's sailing. By contrast local boy Callum Airlie put together a dream ending with second, first and seventh to lift him well clear in the title race ahead of Josh Voller with twenty fourth, sixth and eleventh, leaving him in second position.

P	Helm	R1	R2	R3	R4	R5	R6	R7	R8	R9	R10	R11	R12	Pts
1	Callum Airlie	24	26	2	1	1	13	7	3	9	2	1	7	46
2	Josh Voller	19	2	14	4	2	1	11	19	1	24	6	11	71
3	Roger Dorr	2	6	4	6	10	6	15	7	2	19	26	23	77
4	Oscar Pijoan	1	20	21	30	3	5	17	5	10	13	4	1	79
5	Oliver Grogongo	25	5	5	3	53	8	8	6	12	4	16	17	84
6	Harry Gozzett	15	79	11	13	12	16	18	2	4	3	20	4	98
7	Toby Morsley	3	19	27	12	11	9	6	38	13	9	8	8	98
10	David Pain	70	18	10	28	24	20	2	40	16	6	2	5	131

Junior Group

The Regatta Fleet certainly had an "international" feel about it and, with one day to go, the top ten was made up of four American boats, four Irish boats, and two British boats. Leading by five points at this stage was Jack Johansson of the US, with fellow American Adele Whitmyer (the top girl). Ireland's Peter McCann, and Cian Byrne were in second and fourth positions respectively, with top Brit Matthew Whitfield in sixth position. Again, with a great final burst, Byrne pulled himself up to the top of the fleet to win by three points from Johansson and Freddie Grogongo did himself no harm by also scoring three results in the top five to take the third overall position.

P	Nat	Helm	R1	R2	R3	R4	R5	R6	R7	R8	R9	R10	R11	R12	Pts
1	IRL	C Byrne	5	4	2	8	2	4	9	1	9	3	3	3	35
2	USA	J Johansson	2	18	8	3	2	5	2	1	1	39	4	10	38
3	GBR	F Grogongo	3	17	3	1	4	1	6	13	38	5	2	2	40
4	IRL	P McCann	1	2	4	2	1	4	1	2	16	21	7	5	41
5	GBR	M Whitfield	9	15	6	3	9	3	3	3	11	1	1	13	49
6	USA	A Whitmyer	11	1	1	7	1	6	3	20	5	2	23	26	60
7	IRL	S Donnelly	28	8	2	4	8	7	4	4	15	10	25	1	63
8	USA	I MacDiamid	3	8	11	7	7	12	1	8	10	6	9	19	70
9	GBR	J Parkin	13	2	12	4	5	28	4	15	6	16	42	6	83
10	IRL	A Hyland	6	19	1	1	12	12	10	8	13	4	19	NYF7	86

Regatta Fleet

In the Regatta fleet, Alasdair Ireland sailed consistently to lead the fleet going into the final day by seventeen points from Oscar Lindley Smith of the United Arab Emirates. Tomek Bruml and William Bedford were tied together with just a one point margin in third and fourth positions. Whilst Ireland's lead was significant, it was not quite sufficient to assure him of victory on the final day, and there was still much to play for! However, his final day's performance was sufficient to leave him safe in first, whilst William Bedford added a first and a second to his score, to lift him to second overall ahead of Oscar Lindley Smith.

P	Nat	Helm	R1	R2	R3	R4	R5	R6	R7	R8	R9	R10	R11	Pts
1	GBR	A Ireland	1	15	6	9	3	6	3	1	5	4	15	38
2	GBR	W Bedford	19	7	2	4	13	24	4	5	2	20	1	57
3	UAE	O Lindley Smith	2	1	13	8	24	5	6	11	4	9	16	59
4	GBR	T Bruml	21	2	4	7	8	52	5	6	7	15	7	61
5	GBR	K Hutton-Penman	46	4	1	2	7	1	26	33	20	5	4	70
6	GBR	B Marstaller	10	13	3	25	14	9	2	14	12	6	2	71
7	GBR	J Smith	29	NYF	20	14	2	3	11	2	9	12	5	78
8	GBR	R King	17	3	29	27	1	12	21	4	14	7	10	89
9	GBR	M Viney	18	6	49	5	4	10	12	10	18	21	8	91
10	GBR	J Lee	3	5	19	13	12	4	10	13	22	33	17	96

Regatta Fleet Starter Group

The Regatta Starter Group enjoyed the most relaxing of schedules, and as they entered the final day with five races under their belts, there were three front-runners who were likely to share out the podium positions. William Heritage had three race wins, a third and fourth, whilst Daniel Thorne-Large sat just two points behind, level on points with James Grant. Heritage made the most of the end of the week, adding another two race wins and taking a comfortable win in the regatta, whilst two more seconds gave the runner-up position to Daniel Thorne-Large.

P	Nat	Helm	M/F	R1	R2	R3	R4	R5	R6	R7	R8	Pts
1	GBR	W Heritage	M	3	1	4	1	1	NYF	1	1	12
2	GBR	D Thorne-Large	M	1	3	2	3	2	5	2	2	15
3	GBR	J Grant	M	2	2	1	4	3	NYF	4	3	19
4	GBR	K Webb	F	4	8	8	6	8	4	5	5	40
5	GBR	E Elder	F	7	7	5	8	10	NYF	6	4	47
6	GBR	E Bishop	F	8	6	3	5	5	1	NYF	NYF	52

RS Tera

Type	Dinghy	Weight	33 kg
Crew	1; Sit out	Sail area M	4.8 sq m
Length	2.87 m	Spi type	None
Beam	1.23 m	Designer	Paul Handley
			www.terasailing.com

The RS Tera has been designed specifically to promote fun sailing; for young-sters or all of the family, and for beach fun, as an entry to club racing or as a junior boat for sailing clubs, schools and holiday company fleets. Manufactured in tough thermoplastics, the boat is rugged enough to withstand every-day usage, and is even offered with a rowing package so that it offers something for everyone. The boat has become a recognized class by ISAF, and is spreading quickly throughout the world, with a regular World Championships now being held.

RS Tera European Championships

Lake Garda, Italy   2 - 6 August 2009

Forty seven RS Teras attended their European Championships on Lake Garda, with the entry being split over the three different classifications of boat, with twenty five "Pro" class, twelve "Sport" Class and ten "Fun" Class.

In the Tera Pro European Championships Matteo Dall'agnola (ITA) became the first European Champion for the class, whilst in the Sport Europeans, Sweden's Kevin Olsson became the first European Champion. Dall'agnola dominated his division throughout the week, scoring three firsts and never finishing outside the top ten, but the overall result was still decided by discard, as runner-up, Italian Macopo Fanti had also put together a very good series of results. The Pro European Ladies Championships were won by Arianna Stradolini (ITA), whilst Britain's Matthew French, the UK Tera National Champion, switched to the more powerful Pro sail for the Championships, and won a specific Merit award as a result.

In the Tera Sport Europeans, the racing was dominated by the Swedes, with Kevin Olsson taking the victory from Julian Dellnas by a mere two points, and Kanicha Ekdahl one place further back.

P	Nat	Helm	R1	R2	R3	R4	R5	R6	Pts
1	ITA	Jacopo Fanti	14	10	1	2	3	3	19
2	ITA	Matteo Dall'agnola	9	7	7	4	1	1	20
3	ITA	Riccardo Vincenzi	5	11	5	1	7	2	20
4	ITA	Francesco Drago	7	17	3	3	6	6	25
5	ITA	Alvise Weber	6	3	6	5	9	13	29

RS Tera Pro European Championships

P	Nat	Helm	R1	R2	R3	R4	Pts
1	SWE	Kevin Olsson	4	2	1	2	9
2	SWE	Julia Dellnas	5	3	3	1	12
3	SWE	Kanicha Ekdahl	1	7	2	3	13
4	SWE	David Axen	2	1	DSQ	6	22
5	DEN	Kasper Jllobsen	7	4	4	11	26

RS Tera Sport European Championships

P	Nat	Helm	R1	R2	R3	Pts
1	ITA	Leonardo Stocchero	1	1	1	3
2	ITA	Margherita Porro	2	5	4	11
3	GBR	Greg Kelly	7	2	3	12
4	ITA	Jacopo Nulli	3	4	7	14

RS Tera Fun European Championships

RS Tera National Championship

Dabchicks Sailing Club   19 - 20 September 2009

The RS Tera National Championships were held over the weekend of 19 - 20 September with an entry of five boats for the Pro Fleet division, and thirty four youngsters competing in the Sport Fleet division.

With sunny weather for most of the weekend, despite a gloomier forecast, the entrants got enjoyable sailing at the meeting, which was held in conjunction with one of the RS Feva events. In the Pro Fleet, the eventual victory was taken by reigning champion, Matthew French. However, he was pressed for the second half of the meeting by Harry Gozzett who had not competed in the first two races, and could never close the gap as he had to count one of his six point results in his final score. Third place was taken by Hamish Echstein, giving the Dabchicks fleet a whitewash in this sector of the racing.

Pro Fleet (5 entries)

P	Helm	Club	R1	R2	R3	R4	R5	R6	Pts	Nett
1	Matthew French	Dabchicks SC	1	1	2	2	2	2	10	8
2	Harry Gozzett	Dabchicks SC	6	6	1	1	1	3	18	12
3	Hamish Echstein	Dabchicks SC	3	3	3	4	3	1	17	13
4	Jonny Watkins	Dabchicks SC	2	2	4	3	4	4	19	15
5	Oskar Bisset	Downs SC	4	4	5	5	5	5	28	23

The Sport Fleet was a more open affair, with thirty four boats entering, led by James Hutton-Penman with three race wins. He finished four points clear of Josh Aldridge, and a further five points in front of William Taylor, both of whom counted a race win in the event, as did fourth place Crispin Beaumont, an indication of the closeness of the racing.

Sport Fleet (34 entries)

P	Helm	Club	R1	R2	R3	R4	R5	R6	Pts	Nett
1	James Hutton-Penman	Corinthian Otters	1	1	6	1	4	4	17	11
2	Josh Aldridge	BSC	13	5	3	4	2	1	28	15
3	William Taylor	ASC	4	9	4	26	1	2	46	20
4	Crispin Beaumont	BGSC	7	16	1	5	6	8	43	27
5	Tristan Bracegirdle	CCSC	6	14	2	6	11	7	46	32
6	Flynn Davies	BSC	9	19	7	2	7	12	56	37
7	James Kelly	IofMYC	2	7	OCS	14	12	3	73	38
8	Greg Kelly	IofMYC	20	6	OCS	7	3	5	76	41
9	Guy Rivington	TSC	15	2	9	8	8	15	57	42
10	Rebecca Lewis	D WSC	11	3	12	3	13	18	60	42

Advertisers Index

**Please mention the *Dinghy and Smallcraft Review*
when you contact any of the advertisers.**